Walking For Our Lives

Donna Rankin Love

Park Place Publications
www.parkplacepublications.com

OTHER BOOKS BY DONNA RANKIN LOVE
Tell Me a Story

To Make the House Complete

Driving for Walking for Our Lives

— — —

Walking For Our Lives

Donna Rankin Love

Portions of this book previously have been published in
Tell Me a Story and *To Make the House Complete.*

www.donnarankinlove.vp.com
donnarankinlove.wordpress.com

Dedication

To Mildred Taylor Rankin
1902—2002

Thank you, Mother.

Acknowledgements

A memoir is as accurate as memory. This is my memory of events that took place in 1986, 1987 and 1988, about 25 years ago. Although I've made every effort to be exact, I'm as sure as I sit here that another participant on the Peace Walks would have a different recollection. I have compressed some events for clarity, expanded others for interest, jumbled the facts, but, from my perspective, have told the truth.

My sustained gratitude to Connie Fledderjohann, who first told me about The Great Peace March and became my first tent-mate. After The March, she, along with Franklin Folsom and Gerda Lawrence, wrote a fine resource book, *The Great Peace March;* Connie was generous in letting me use that information.

Thanks to Fred Segal for his book *The American Soviet Peace Walk*, to Sue Guist for her book *Peace Like a River*, and to Kathleen Hendrix, *Los Angeles Times* staff writer, whose feature articles of the Peace Walks greatly enhanced my memory of details.

Thank you to Jeff Share for use of his photographs that dramatically portray events and members of The Great Peace March and The Soviet-American Peace Walk. His big beautiful green photo is the basis for the front cover. Thank you also to Guy Colwell for his drawings, which animate several pages, and to Dan Coogan and Al Podgorski for their photos. I am grateful to Holly Near for permission to use her song as inspiration for the title, *Walking For Our Lives*.

To members of various writing groups for encouraging me to forge ahead, for several years, in the compilation of these episodes, I can hardly breathe without thanking you.

To publisher Patricia Hamilton, who has become my friend, for creative ideas and expertise. To Sandra Leader and Lisa Rothman, thank you for your professional editing. To Sarah Love, for her devotion and marketing skills. To John Love, for his practical suggestions, quiet encouragement and much more. To Derek Love, for help with the cover.

Like those of us on the Peace Walks, we are a diverse group. And I deeply appreciate your contributions to *Walking For Our Lives*.

Donna Rankin Love

Summer 2011

"I want nothing more than to speak simply,
To be granted this peace."

Giorgos Seferis
1900—1971

Introduction

"This child will never walk," the doctor told my mother the day in 1927 when I was born in Portland, Oregon. They both touched my poor little feet bent upward so the tiny toes almost touched the shinbones.

Mother met the doctor's gaze. "You wanta bet?" she retorted.

Life stories remind us that history is about events and about the making of ourselves. The world inside and the world outside are lived in tandem, like the present and the past. The woman in her 80s remembers the little girl, who, in turn, imagines herself grown up—up and away from her backyard swing set.

I celebrated my 59th birthday in Ohio en route from Los Angeles to Washington, DC. That year I would walk over 3,700 miles. The following year I walked and bused from Leningrad to Moscow. The next year, 1988, I participated in The American-Soviet Peace Walk from Washington, DC to San Francisco. The three peace walks totaled more than 5,000 miles.

If the delivering doctor had taken Mother up on her bet, he would have lost. She massaged my feet down until I stood, walked and ran like other children. Not until joining The Great Peace March had I walked for a cause. It changed me.

This is the story of how.

TABLE OF CONTENTS

SECTION TWO

SECTION THREE

EPILOGUE   271

THE GREAT PEACE MARCH
FOR GLOBAL NUCLEAR DISARMAMENT

February 15—November 15, 1986

Los Angeles, CA to Washington, DC
USA

Route of the Great Peace March for Glob
March 1 to November 15, 1986
Showing 104 of 191 campsite locations

Compiled and drawn by Guy Colwell

al Nuclear Disarmament

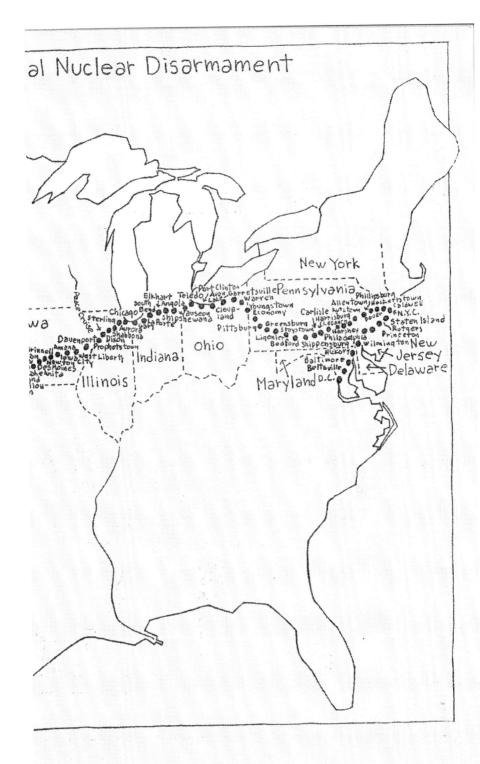

Donna Love and Connie Fledderjohann at the top of trail down to Itea, Greece, 1985

CHAPTER 1

Like to Walk?

I stood in a hot, steamy hole in the ground in Delphi. Awed, I was woozy from the glare of the surrounding white marble in the noonday sun. My arms stretched to touch the stones that lined the sides and I felt strangely connected to the Oracle who intoned in my head, "Be what you are."

In the spring of 1985, I was in Greece for the first time with world-renowned Jungian analyst and educator, Edith Sullwold, who was leading a group in the study of sacred sites and ancient myths. I was 58, healthy, curious, and beyond responsibilities of children and marriage.

We had been on and off buses for days and I needed to sit less and walk more. As I stood at the edge of the road and looked down at the expansive cobalt-blue sea and Itea, the fishing village we were going to visit by bus, I asked my roommate if she'd like to hike down the hill with me.

"No," she responded, "I'm going shopping, but ask that woman over there. I think she's a walker." I chuckled at her answer—she was such a city girl—and checked the trail again. If I couldn't find anyone to walk with me, I'd go alone. Little did I know that the trail to Itea would lead to changes in my life I never could have imagined.

I looked over at the woman my roommate had pointed out. She was standing alone, taking photos of the scenery. When I asked her, "Want to walk that path to Itea with me?" she peered down the slope and said, "Yes, I'd like to." Connie was about my age, with strong looking legs and a no-nonsense demeanor, pleasant in a quiet sort of way. We took off down a steep dusty path through an arid old grove of twisted olive trees and prickly weeds. Even the leaves were dusty and looked hot. Partway along the trail, we sat down on the ground to rest in the shade. Connie said, "I see you like to walk." Her tone was curious, as if she wanted me to confirm her impression.

"Yes, I walk whenever I can. Sometimes people ask me if I own a car."

She hardly waited for my reply. "Let me tell you about the walk I'm going to take next year."

I tilted back against an olive tree, picked burrs off my khakis, and listened. "Well," she said, leaning forward, "I have signed up to go on The Great Peace March. Five thousand of us will walk from Los Angeles to New York and then to Washington, DC." She had a *how-about-that!* expression on her face.

"That's a lot of people! And that's a long way! How many weeks will it take?"

"It'll take eight-and-a-half months from the time we leave Los Angeles, but we have to be there two weeks early for orientation meetings. So it's nine months altogether," she said. The March was being organized by PRO-Peace in Los Angeles, an international citizens' movement whose goal was to achieve bilateral nuclear disarmament.

Connie had met the director, David Mixner, and had confidence in his leadership. "He says he wants to raise the peace movement to the level of a presidential campaign," she explained. "There will be kitchen trucks, shower trucks, trucks to carry our gear. We get new dome tents from North Face. There will be plenty of support, and he says headliner entertainers will accompany us along the route to put on a variety of shows for local people who come out to our campsites." She reached for a long grass stem and waved it at a fly.

"Sounds very Hollywoodish, kind of glitzy. A plush walk. Is it expensive?" I asked.

"Each walker pays $3,200, but if that's too much, scholarships are available. And volunteer work."

My heart was beating hard; not from our hot, dusty walk, but from excitement. We got up to trudge down the hill to the seashore and in that moment I knew I'd go. I didn't know how, but I knew I would. What made me so certain? Maybe because I'd been learning to trust my intuition. Or perhaps because I'd always made quick decisions. Like the instant I saw Jim Love, the first moment on our first date. I came downstairs into the sorority house living room where he was playing *Satin Doll* on the piano. When he saw me, he smiled, stood up and walked across the carpeted distance between us. He was tall, slender and wore a delicious raspberry crewneck sweater. He had a vitality, an energy that caught me. My heart thudded, and I knew. That was in October. We were married the following August.

And now, 40 years later, The Peace Walk just felt right—for no particular reason that I could identify. It was like a puzzle piece when it clicks into place. I could afford the fee. I could make the time. Yes, I liked to walk, but across the United States? What a way to see the country! What a concept.

I was familiar with the fear of nuclear bombs. When our sons were in grade school in the 1950s, the students had been taught to hide under their desks and to persuade their parents to save gallons of water in their basements. But that was 50 years ago. Anyway, I'd never considered myself an activist or particularly political. I had voted as Jim did. Since our divorce, I had become only a bit more informed. I didn't support nuclear armaments, but I hadn't protested them, either. I didn't know what to do, so I didn't do anything. I had, however, become an enthusiastic walker. A trek across our nation seemed to be the ultimate hike.

For the remaining days in Greece, Connie answered most of my questions: Where will we stay? Do we have to carry a backpack? How will I get my haircutter to come every six weeks? What shall I do with my house?

"I have a thriving tutorial service for dyslexic students," I said. "What about them? This is not going to be easy, Connie. Well, we won't be leaving until March of 1986. That gives us seven months. Enough time."

Back home in San Mateo, California, I sat in a sunny corner at the kitchen table and began making a list:

- Tell the boys and their wives. Then my brothers, Mother and Pop.

- Get into shape.

- Who will pay the bills? Prepare and pay income taxes?

- My driver's license will need renewing.

- Rent the house?

- Arrange for an absentee ballot.

- What about the tutoring students? The tutors?

During the following months I walked up and down the hills of our neighborhood every morning. Anytime anyone asked me to go for a walk, I went. Anywhere. In an exercise class at the Y, I puffed through aerobics. In a friend's sauna, I panted and sweated. Before bedtime, I swam in the backyard pool. I bought weights to develop upper-body strength. It felt like I was training for the Olympics. By Christmas I felt fit and pretty in party clothes.

I told my family of my plans, and they paused in their busy young lives to clap and laugh aloud. "Way to go, Mom." One daughter-in-law hugged me and whispered, "You go for me, Sistah!" Another daughter-in-law immediately volunteered to pay my bills while I was away. "Have your mail forwarded to Matt and me. Put my name on your account and I'll take care of writing the checks. If you want us to, and when we know where you will be, we can forward your personal mail." Done.

Would she also get the tax information to the accountant? Yes. Together we could do some of the preparation before I left. She also would watch for the driver license renewal notice and pay it. Done.

Emily, a longtime friend who was a real estate agent and property manager, said she'd heard I'd be away for several months. She told me the pitcher for the San Francisco Giants, Mike Krukow, wanted to rent a house in a nice neighborhood for himself and his family. Mine, on

Occidental Avenue in San Mateo Park, qualified as nice. He'd pay for the entire baseball season and be away at out-of-town games half the time. Emily would find other renters after the baseball season. Done.

A friend asked if I'd like to sell my brown Mercury. He knew someone who wanted a car to leave in the garage of their vacation home. My sons said, "Get rid of that tank, Mom." Done.

Another friend, one whom I hadn't seen in over a year, greeted me in front of the lettuce section at the Safeway store and asked what I'd been up to lately. I told her about The Great Peace March. "The Peace March sounds like interesting news." she mused. She was now feature editor for the *San Mateo Times*, the local daily newspaper. "Come to my office next week and let's talk about it. I'd like you to write feature articles as you go along."

My son John offered to clip news articles about The March. Mostly he'd save the stories I'd write for the *San Mateo Times*, but also relevant articles in the *San Jose Mercury News* and the *Los Angeles Times*. I hadn't even thought of that.

All I had left to do was sort out the six tutors and the 40 or so students. In September, I let the tutors know we'd be closing in January. As we took new fall-quarter students, I told the parents that after the first of the new year, when my tutoring center would close, I'd make every effort to arrange for tutors for their children so their lessons could continue.

Everything was falling into place. It was as though the Universe approved of my decision to leave home for nine months and walk over 3,000 miles across our vast country. Is this what the Oracle had meant when I heard, "Be what you are."

Donna and Jim Love at Santa Barbara Biltmore Hotel, June 1969.

CHAPTER 2

A Look in the Rearview Mirror

In October, I drove for an entire day from San Mateo up to Coos Bay, Oregon, to tell Mother and Pop the details of The Peace March. Along I-5, I had time to daydream back over the epochs in my life. I remembered a serene day years earlier, in 1967, in our kitchen in Hillsborough, California, when two sisters-in-law sat at the old oval oak breakfast table in front of the large windows that looked out over the back garden. Gayle and her husband and four children were visiting from Eugene, Oregon. All the children were outside playing. Our husbands were off somewhere. She and I were making tea sandwiches; cream cheese and salmon on triangles, peanut butter and honey on tiny rounds, decorated with violets that the two girls brought in. We arranged the dainty sandwiches on doily-lined platters.

It was Mother's Day and the local charity, the Hillsborough Decorators' Show House, was having a silver tea to support the Junior Museum, where children learned about the environment, and could check out small animals: rabbits, guinea pigs, snakes -- to have as pets for a week or two. I was a dedicated volunteer.

Gayle asked, "Donna, Why do you do this?"

"You mean, why do I volunteer? Well, I believe children and animals belong together and the Junior Museum provides for that. I like working on the big old houses here in Hillsborough. Did you know that we were the first Decorators' Show House? Now they are fund-raisers all over the nation." I paused to open more cream cheese. "Most of what I know about interior design and women's organizations, I learned in my 14 years working on the Show House. And good friends, too. Many of my friendships came from the Junior Museum group."

"Maybe, Donna, but you'll never make it into Hillsborough Society." Gayle looked almost serious, just a hint of sparkle in her eye.

"Why do you say that?" I retorted. "I'm on the parents board at Crocker School, active at St. Matthew's Episcopal Church, secretary of the Hillsborough Family Service Auxiliary. I get my hair and nails done each Friday and shop at I. Magnin's. What do you mean, I'll never make it into Hillsborough Society?"

Gayle looked up from the cream cheese she was spreading and grinned, "Because you don't give a shit."

I laughed. Gayle was right, at least partially. I wasn't socially ambitious. At least I didn't think I was. But I was involved in the community. I cheerfully volunteered for all kinds of events and causes. I loved being a Cub Scout den mother for five consecutive years. Those little boys in their blue and gold uniforms, tucking in their shirttails, standing so straight to salute the flag. Georgie, usually late and skidding his bike to a halt, announcing himself with squeaky quail calls, dashing into the meeting. For St. Patrick's Day, instead of making cute little place cards with macaroni letters, we made Irish stew in coffee cans which the boys took home for dinner. Fifty years later, my son Sam would tell me he still had the recipe from that day.

Although I believed my husband Jim would have liked me to volunteer in socially prestigious causes and become friends with prominent San Francisco women, he also told me that a wife's place was in the home. I didn't know how to do both, so I chose home. I didn't volunteer for the San Francisco Opera Auxiliary nor the Symphony Auxiliary. I declined the invitation to join the San Francisco Junior League because our four boys, Matt, Sam, John, and Marty, were all under six years old. If I'd been in the City organizing a fund-raiser, I might have missed Matt's saying, "I like your dress, Mommy. It matches your toothbrush." Or Sam, who, having learned that seeds rattle in dried gourds and that babies come from something like seeds, patting my tummy while I was pregnant with Marty, and saying, "Jump up and down, Mommy. See if your seeds rattle." I loved my life with those little boys.

Maybe I enjoyed motherhood so much because for a while early in our marriage, we weren't sure we'd be able to have children. We'd been married four years. Jim had his diploma in Business Administration and had begun his career as a stockbroker. We owned an old rinky-dink house with more history than anything else, ripe for renovation, on Hobart Street in San Mateo, and one night he announced it was time for children. I agreed. Although I liked fixing up the house, I was 23 and definitely wanted to start our family. For months we monitored my temperature and he came home for "nooners." But I didn't conceive. In January of 1953 I wrote to my father, who was president of the Oregon Medical Association that year, saying, "If, in your travels around the state, you find a baby for us to adopt, we are ready."

I went to the doctor for tests -- to find out if I was barren or what else was wrong with me. I went until summer when, discouraged by the entire process, I stopped. I felt I was failing those tests, failing as a woman, and hid behind the garage to sob in frustration and disappointment. One Saturday morning in August, weary and despondent, I stepped into our St. Matthew's Episcopal Church. Only the altar guild lady was there, arranging flowers. I sat. The sun streamed through the stained glass windows. I noticed the dancing dust motes and heard distant outside sounds; traffic, birds, a thump or two, and spoke silently, "Okay, God, I always wanted to be a mother. I grew up preparing for motherhood. Even majored in psychology to help me understand family dynamics. But if you want me to do something else, just let me know and I'll do it. You decide and let me know, okay?"

I sighed, stood up, retreated back out into the sunshine, and walked on home.

The following Monday, Jim was home to lunch when Pop called. "Found one. What do you want to do?"

Tuna sandwiches forgotten, milk gulped, Jim and I, excited, agreed in moments. "This is what we've been waiting for!"

I returned Pop's call in about 10 minutes. "Yes! This is perfect! A boy? Oh, thank you! I'll fly up tomorrow. When was he born?"

"Saturday morning." Not knowing the significance of Saturday morning, that the baby had been born as I sat in the church and spoke to God, he said, "I'll have him here tomorrow afternoon."

I was dazed by such an immediate answer from God. I hardly slept Monday night and suddenly remembered the stone wall around the churchyard and the brass plaque with the name: Episcopal Church of St. Matthew. I slithered out of bed and felt my way downstairs to the bookshelves to find the old booklet of names and their meanings. Matthew. Gift from God.

When Matthew was almost two months old, I returned to my Ob/Gyn for a routine examination. Dr. Morrison looked up from behind the sheet and blurted out, "Oh my, you are pregnant! I'd say two months."

God had said, "Okay, you want children? You got 'em." How could I have even imagined cluttering up my life with volunteer work in San Francisco during those happy, fulfilling, exhausting years?

But sometimes the glory and recognition that society volunteers enjoyed was tempting. One day I asked my friend Elaine how she got to be president of San Francisco Museum of Modern Art Auxiliary. She drawled in her slow Texas accent, "Well, Aie drove up to the city twice a week and did anything they asked. Stuffed envelopes, helped arrange benefits, got on the board, and Aie jest scratched an' clawed m' way to the top." I admired Elaine for knowing so clearly what she wanted. I sometimes wondered if maybe I could do it all. Volunteer in the city and be a good mother. Others did. Elaine did. But, me? Was I more provincial, more comfortable in the suburbs? Was I really still just a small-town girl? I didn't know. I contented myself as a volunteer with groups who supported local families and children.

In 1960, when we had four sons, Jim and I were house hunting. I wanted a home where the six of us would have enough room to pursue any interests we chose, and also be within walking or biking distance to schools, and a bike ride to the orthodontist.

"All that's fine," said Jim, "but I want a house that I can be proud of and where we'll entertain." By then he had become a junior executive with a San Francisco brokerage house. Brisk, abrupt in action and in speech, always punctual, he'd look at his watch, pace in the front hall, and call out, "I'm ready. Where are the rest of you?" The rest of us would scamper down the hall and out into the car.

Jim seemed to live his life in a hurry, focused on success defined by the American corporate culture. That image was less important to me than it was to him, but I would not have been able to do what I liked without the financial success afforded by his ambition and drive. He provided well for us.

We found a graceful old Mediterranean-style home on an acre at 735 Brewer Drive in Hillsborough, fifteen miles south of San Francisco, two miles from the Burlingame train station. Jim enjoyed his walk to the commuter train. "I can get four miles a day just walking to and from work," At 6' 2" and slender, he often sucked in his midsection, smartly slapped his flat stomach, and grinned.

In the backyard of our new home was a flat, grassy space for touch football, a slab of concrete for half-court basketball, and enough trees for forts and tree houses. The gravel driveway was long and wide enough to park a dozen cars. As time passed, it gave our son Sam space for his collection of broken down Morris Minors. I liked to look out the kitchen window to see him lying under a car tinkering while the latest girlfriend handed him tools. Upstairs, I had a project room that was all mine. In the evenings, Jim took his cocktail and the paper into the living room and settled into his wing chair by a tall window. Sam, John and Marty had formed a teenage Dixieland Band and they practiced in the music room while I stirred dinner to the rhythm of "Sweet Georgia Brown" and Matt shot baskets in the backyard.

Our family liked to give parties. I kept a notebook of the dates, theme, and guests for each party including their food preferences and allergies, what we poured and served, and what I wore. Our sons learned to take coats, pass hors d'oeuvres and wait tables for the sit-down dinners to which Jim and I invited friends and business acquaintances. One night, while 40 guests milled around, I popped into the kitchen for something, and there at the table sat the piano player, taking a break. In the music room, our son John was playing Beatles songs for a group who surrounded him. I chuckled, found Jim, and pointed with pride to John. In the kitchen, I let the hired musician go. John became our party pianist.

As a family, we looked like a Maytag washing machine ad: all clean, shiny, smiling and happy. Our eldest, Matt, was accepted at Yale University. The following year, Sam would be going to college, then John. In four years, Marty would be gone. They'd all be away at school. Daily motherhood responsibilities would end, and I was staring at an empty nest in the near future.

Jim was not unusual in forbidding me to work for money. The place for a wife was at home, taking care of the family, sitting at the opening of the cave, tending the home fires. The man earned the money, fought off the lions and tigers, brought home the bacon. He sat at the head of the dining table, she at the foot. It was a man's world and women adapted. Jim adhered to these traditional principles and I followed, not always cheerfully, but I had been primarily an obedient daughter and now was, at least superficially, the obedient wife. My rebelliousness sometimes flared, but my duties were clear and mostly I did what was expected of me. That's the way wives behaved in the 1950s and '60s. Until the children left for college. In those days many marriages ended soon after the last child was launched. I wasn't looking to end the marriage, but knew I'd need something to fill the days.

Not looking for a paid job, I volunteered at nearby Burlingame High School. They didn't have a volunteer program, but they did want me as a teacher's aide. Would my family even notice that I was gone four hours a day? I didn't tell anyone what I was doing, that I was checking out teaching to see if that's what I'd like to do after the boys were gone. Nobody noticed. I opened a secret savings account and deposited my pay checks.

Six months later, in February, 1971, I was feeling really guilty about my deception. One calm Sunday afternoon while Jim was out in the side yard tidying up around the barbecue, I joined him and said, "I have something to tell you."

He didn't look up, "Yeah, okay, what is it?"

I told him, "I'm worried about what I'll do when all the boys are gone. I've done charity work and church work and PTA. I can't just go on doing the same things and filling in around the edges with tennis."

He kept on sweeping and said, "Go on."

I hurried, "So you remember how I liked teaching in San Francisco before the boys were born? I thought maybe I could see if I still do, so I went down to Burlingame High to volunteer and they don't have a volunteer program, but they wanted me to be a teacher's aide and so since September I have been going four hours a day. I know you don't want me to work, but there wasn't any other way I could find out what I want to do next. I didn't want to be sneaky, but I knew you'd get mad."

He didn't say much, just, "It looks like your choice," and I was relieved that he hadn't blown up. Instead, he began shoveling the ashes out of the barbecue. I watched him for a few moments and then went into the house to fix lunch. He had never looked up during the entire conversation.

March 10 dawned like any other spring day; damp, not wet. Jim, by then in his middle-40s, and looking as crisp as when we met in 1948 at the University of Oregon, commuted, as usual, before full daylight, to his office in San Francisco. The boys rode their bikes to school. Matt, Sam, and John to San Mateo High, and Marty to Crocker Middle School. They had their lunches—tuna sandwiches, apples, celery sticks, cookies. I went to the dentist to have a wisdom tooth pulled.

I had forgotten that the Izmarian Heating Company was coming to replace the wheezy old furnace. When I returned home, the men were in the basement dismantling it and tossing parts out the basement door. Hunks landed and sprayed gravel. Then I noticed that Jim's car was parked at the edge of the driveway. A director's chair that the boys and I had given him for Christmas leaned against the back bumper. That's odd, I thought to myself.

Upstairs, we met in the hall and I stretched up to hug my husband. "Everything okay?" I asked. "Have you seen the ice bag? I thought you were going to the meeting in New York tomorrow."

He corrected me, "I'm leaving today."

"Oh. Okay." I rummaged through the shelves in our bathroom. "You haven't seen the ice bag?" I asked again as I opened the door to the hall closet. Jim trailed along behind me, his hands full of socks. I headed for the boys' bathroom.

"I'm leaving today," he repeated.

I reached behind a stack of towels beneath the washbowl and found the ice bag. "Oh, I guess I just misunderstood."

"No," Jim looked down at his socks. "Tomorrow I'm going to New York. Today I'm moving out and going to live in a townhouse down at Woodlake." He paused and added, "There must be more to it than this."

Woodlake is where all the local separated husbands go, I thought. More to it than what? More to what than this? We had everything. We epitomized the American Dream Family. Stunned, I could only stare at him and utter, "Oh."

"Do you want to talk about it?" he asked.

"What? What did you say? No! I don't want to talk about it. I can't talk about it. At least not right now. My mouth hurts. Later, Jim. We'll talk later." I was shocked, confused, unable to absorb what I'd heard. All I could say was, "I'm going down to find some ice." When I climbed back upstairs, I shut the door to Marty and Sam's bedroom and lay down on a bed. I could hear Jim stamping up and down the stairs as he loaded his car and heard the car doors slam and the crunch of gravel as he drove away. The distant thumps of the furnace men in the basement continued until 4 o'clock. Then I was alone in the house. So very alone.

I moved across the hall and languished in our dim bedroom, jaw and mind both numb. Feeling shaky and fragile, my most profound decision was, in awhile I'll order pizza for the boys' dinner, but I did meander back over our marriage. Jim probably would have liked me to take an interest in his financial business. I had tried by taking a college course in Economics. I recalled holding infant Marty, stirring dinner, and cramming for a final, all at the same time. I got a D in the course.

I hadn't given him all the attention he wanted. Our sex was routine. We didn't talk about much except practical family matters. We had stopped laughing together. He'd told me I held back too much of myself. What did that mean? Protection? It was just too much to think about. It was too hard. I dozed off.

After a while, our sons infused life back into the house. They thundered up the stairs and flowed into our bedroom. Ringed around the foot of the bed, tall, slender, blond, eager; in many ways so like their father. We had had Matt's wisdom teeth pulled only last year. He bent to check the ice bag.

Sam, his tender heart in his eyes, touched my toes, looked

concerned, and asked, "How's the hole in your mouth, Mom?"

John said, "I'll get you more cold water," and took my glass down to the kitchen..

Marty, wide-open and bouncy, said, "I'll get you Dad's radio. You can listen to some of your favorite music." He disappeared into Jim's dressing room. We heard drawers and doors opening and shutting. He reappeared, empty-handed, his face pale beneath the freckles.

"What's happened to Dad?" he screamed.

"Well, I wasn't… I wasn't going to tell you until" I stammered and then rushed, "Dad loves you very much! It has nothing to do with you! He's overtired. He needs to be alone. He's moved to Woodlake."

"Oh," Marty sighed. "Is that all? I thought he was dead. Sam, go get Mom your radio."

They melted away into their rooms. I got up, wandered aimlessly around the house, sat at the kitchen table and stared out the windows without seeing the trees and shrubs of the back garden.

I hardly heard Elaine come in through the sunroom door. "Hiee!" she glided toward me. "Aie came to get the Auxiliary membership list?" Her voice tilted up. She paused. "Hey, what's going on here? What's happened to you?" Her amber eyes glowed with concern.

I told her. She reached over to tenderly touch my hand and in her slow Dallas drawl, summarized, "Well, my dear, it's been quite a day. You lost you' ol' fu'nace, you lost you' ol' tooth, and you lost you' ol' husband."

During the following months, the boys and I saw a therapist who taught us communication skills. I'd decided that our marriage had foundered for several reasons, but the main one was that we didn't talk about our feelings. One afternoon as I was delivering clean laundry to the boys' bedrooms, I found John sitting at his desk, gazing out the window. His long slender frame leaned back in his desk chair, relaxed.

"Hi, John, Where are you?" I paused to put my hand on his shoulder. He was a sophomore and growing up so quickly.

He snapped out of his reverie. "Oh, hi, Mom. I was just thinking."

I sat down on his other chair, the low blue one he'd had since grade school, and studied his lean serious face. "John, would you be embarrassed if your parents divorced?"

He looked directly at me and said, "Remember in fifth grade when I got braces? You asked me if I'd be embarrassed to go to school with wires on my teeth. And I told you no because almost everyone in class had braces. Well, now almost everyone's parents are getting divorced." He paused, shrugged. "We'll be okay, Mom."

He was too big to cuddle, but I stood behind him to give him a squeeze and to hide my tears. I admired his quiet determination, his apparent confidence.

But I didn't feel so sure about myself. After Jim left I was tormented with questions. Whatever would happen to the boys? To me? I had no marketable skills, hadn't even been in charge of the checkbook. Would I have enough money? Be able to deal with car repairs? I moped around confused and hurt and scared. I knew nothing! I bundled the bills and asked one of the boys to take them down to his father. He sent enough money for household needs and the boys' allowances. Not knowing how much money we had, I was hesitant even to go to the movies. Frightened into inaction, I sat. I huddled with the boys and watched what they watched on TV, sometimes, even on school nights, which we had never done before. I sat doing needlepoint, sat and wept, sat and felt lost. I managed to take care of the house and the boys and continue working at Burlingame High School. Those responsibilities helped to save my sanity.

Talking with my mother about Jim's sudden departure didn't help. She thought Jim was probably bored. She was sure it was my fault, I should have worn frilly underwear. I should have flattered him. I should have been more wifely. "But don't you worry, Donna, he'll act in a responsible way, I know he will." Married women friends weren't any help. They'd all thought we were the perfect American family and felt threatened by our collapse.

One friend, herself recently divorced, had some advice for me. "If you find yourself standing at the kitchen sink and having two martinis and a peanut butter sandwich for dinner, you know you're in trouble. I know. I did that a few times."

"Then what did you do?" I asked.

"I sat down." And we both laughed.

That September, I gave myself a new kind of birthday present: an hour with an astrologer. As we began, she swept her hand over my chart, referred to her text, and said, "I see you have three children. Sons."

"No," I corrected. "We have four sons."

She looked perplexed.

"Oh, wait a minute," I said. "I forgot. One is ours through adoption. I birthed three."

"That's right. And they were almost grown when your husband left?"

How did she know he had left?

"Yes, three were in high school, and one in junior high last spring. The eldest left a couple of weeks ago for college and the youngest now is a high school freshman. Why do you ask that?"

"Well," she answered. "According to his sign, your husband's job was to be a father to your sons. Once they were leaving the house, he no longer needed to be there. If you and I had met several years ago, we could have anticipated his leaving. It's that clear."

I wondered what I might have done differently if I'd known. Now, I'd just have to learn to manage. Somehow.

As I wandered through the days, I repeated to myself I am a child of God, I am a child of God. At least the boys loved me and I was a child of God.

I fumbled along and eventually realized I needed some basic information if I were going to manage what Jim had managed. I asked five of our men friends, a banker, a real estate broker, an insurance agent, an appraiser, and a stock broker, to come over. We met in the dining room and after I served coffee and home-made scones, I questioned them about fundamental finance. They explained the intricacies of money management and I appreciated what Jim had been doing for 23 years.

The real estate broker told me the value of our house, gave me his card, and said, "You call any time you have a question. I'm glad to help you."

One said, "You need a lawyer. Someone to represent you and your needs."

"Oh. I suppose you're right. I hadn't wanted to think about that."

He recommended one who lived nearby and was the father of one of Marty's classmates. I knew him and his family and gave him a call. So far Jim was sending money, but how long would he continue without some written agreement? I'd heard terrible tales about families being abandoned. I was sure Jim wouldn't be like that, but on the other hand, I'd not suspected that he would move out.

I called the attorney and told him, "I made a deal with Jim that if he would guarantee to support the boys through college, I'd agree to his wanting to stop paying alimony at the end of five years. I have that and the house." The attorney said he'd write up an agreement for Jim to sign.

One of the men must have thought he could "help" me in another way for as I, wrapped in nothing but a towel, stepped out of the bathroom one morning, there he lay sprawled on the unmade bed, his hands behind his head and his eyes bright. I jumped back into the bathroom, slammed the door, and cried, "How did you get in the house?"

"In through the sunroom door. I know it's always open."

"Please leave," I pleaded from behind the door.

"Aah," he sighed, "I thought you were going to be more fun than that."

I shouted, "Leave! Right now!"

I could never again look directly at him and his wife, even in church.

One day as I was sitting with other parents at a high school track meet, a woman said, "Donna, if you ever want to sell the Brewer Drive house, my husband and I would like to buy it. We wouldn't even need a real estate agent."

I didn't know if I should be grateful or suspect her of opportunism. "Thanks," I said, "but we're going to try to hold on to it for a while."

By the end of the 1971 school year when I was a teacher's assistant at Burlingame High School, I had decided that although I liked children and was excited about how they learned, I couldn't endure the bureaucracy of the school system. That summer a friend suggested I join her in attending a class about teaching dyslexic children. There, I was introduced to my next career, tutoring bright, struggling students. In the classic tradition of divorced women, I returned to school, to College of Notre Dame in Belmont and to any Bay Area university that taught what I needed to know. I was not working for an advanced degree, but for the information I needed.

One after the other, the boys left for universities around the country. When Matt left for Yale, I had taken up needlepoint and somewhere between the big gaping holes in my life and those small stitches, I stood, bit by bit learning to cope. I sat in the back of a classroom and occasionally did needlepoint as one professor, only a few years older than Matt, lectured on adolescent psychology. I knew four adolescents and got an A in the class. With my newly acquired knowledge in special education as well as two teaching credentials, I announced at the fall meetings of the San Mateo Junior Museum and Hillsborough Family Service Agency Auxiliaries in which I was involved that I wanted to help students whose needs were not being served in school.

In the early 1970s, women who found themselves alone and needing to work usually chose interior decorating, catering, retail fashion, teaching, or real estate. As suburban wives with commuting husbands, women had learned many of these career skills. I was fortunate to have found a field I liked... no, loved... well before the alimony payments ended. In the divorce, I received the house, half of Jim's financial worth, and three more years of alimony. A good friend who successfully handled his family's money recommended a financial manager in New York, one who has continued to provide income for me since 1974. It's a good thing, too! Tutoring didn't earn a living wage, but for 15 years, it kept me busy and out of the stores, so I didn't have time to spend very much. After the boys and I had spent the summer of 1972 in Eugene, Sam stayed to attend University of Oregon. The following Fall, John left for Northwestern in Evanston, Illinois.

Marty looked worried as he asked, "We're not going to sell the house, are we, Mom? We won't have to sell our home!"

I answered, "If you and I can do the Saturday chores that your dad, brothers and you have done, we can keep it."

He was thoughtful as he calculated all that work, and said, "Let's sell the house."

"Oooh, Marty," I reached up and hugged him. "So many changes these last few years." I wanted to weep, but then recalled something my mother had said a long time ago.

She was emotionally disciplined in an English sort of way and when I'd asked her if she ever got discouraged or depressed, she had answered, "I won't let myself get down in the dumps. My mother, your grandmother Taylor, was explosive. She blew up at her friends, her children, and my poor peace-loving dad. I watched her and long ago decided it's just too hard to recover from emotional upsets. I wanted to be more like my dad. He was quiet, considerate, polite. He was English, you know… came to America when he was three. I greatly admired him. I stay on an even keel. It's too hard to climb back up again from being down in the dumps." I must have learned from Mother or inherited some of Grandfather Taylor's reserve, for I took a big breath and didn't let Marty see my tears.

I wondered, though, why my most consistent response to deep feeling was tears. I cried when I was elated and fulfilled, when I was distraught and frustrated, when I was touched, or bewildered. I almost never shouted. Just teared up. However, I remembered one instant when Jim and I were in the upstairs hall and I shouted back at him. He stood not 10 feet from me and I grabbed a picture off the wall and hurled it at him. He ducked and it landed amid shattered glass on the floor.

"I'll not stand for that kind of behavior," he glowered and sailed down the stairs and out into the yard.

I was surprised at my flare-up, ashamed that I let the boys see our fight, and knelt down to clean up the shards. The picture was an ink drawing of our home.

Years later, Sam told me that watching his parents fight that day was the scariest thing he'd ever experienced.

Within a year of Jim's departure, a man I'd met casually called to ask if I'd like to go for a bike ride out to Coyote Point where we could have a glass of wine at the restaurant there and watch the birds over the bay. Or, if that didn't appeal to me, we could go out to dinner and a movie. I liked the choices he gave me. I liked his voice. We rode out to Coyote Point. When we came back, he went home to shower, and I went upstairs. An hour later, he was back and I met him at the door, all fresh and ready to go out to dinner. We talked so long we forgot about the movie. He had come at just the right time.

For over two years, he told me I was beautiful. He was warm and smart, liked the boys, loved me and loved music. He'd thump his fingers on the steering wheel in time to the radio, leer over at me, and say, "Ah, you're a woman, such a woman." Bill restored my sense of femininity and my sense of fun. I wanted to marry him, but he said, "You know I love you, but a marriage between us wouldn't work." He didn't tell me his reasons, so I asked a therapist and she said, "There are men who just can't make long term commitments. There are others who rescue damsels in distress and lose interest when the women regain their strength." That rang true. I was getting stronger. Before we moved from Brewer Drive, Bill moved away. I was saddened several years later to learn he had died. My son John took me to his memorial service in San Jose.

In spring of 1974, a friend called to say, "We were riding our bikes in San Mateo Park, and a new For Sale sign was going up. You should go look at that house. It'd be good for you." It was a well designed three bedroom/two bath house with a bonus room in the lower level and a pool in the back yard. I sold the Hillsborough house to the woman who wanted it. When Marty was an entering senior at San Mateo High School and his brothers were home from college for summer vacation, we had a giant yard sale in the gravel driveway. Someone paid $35 for my 1949 wedding dress. I gave her the veil and wished her happiness. The boys and I split the take, stacked the leftovers for Goodwill, and raked the gravel for the last time.

"Let's have one more party!" the boys shouted. We cleared out the house except for what we'd need to celebrate the "growing up home." They invited all their friends. We'd have an empty house party, dance in the living room as well as the front hall and dining room. The boys rigged up a sound system. I planned food and drinks and asked Ernie, our local policeman, to come, too, just in case. Bill came, mixed the Bloodless Sangria, and danced with me. The kids were boisterous and well-behaved. Ernie and I washed dishes.

The next night the boys and I slept six blocks away in the house on Occidental Avenue in San Mateo Park. For several weeks, we made improvements. Matt scraped up the kitchen linoleum, one of Marty's girlfriends dug up old flowers and put in new, my friend Carolyn came with her sewing machine to make bench covers. My parents arrived from Oregon and Pop helped the boys lay bricks in the new front patio. Until school started again, the house teemed with industrious crowds.

One afternoon Marty announced, "Mom, I've invited Lexie and Peter and Karen to dinner. Is that okay?" Lexie and Karen had transformed the front flower beds. Peter had helped lay bricks in the patio. I stood with one limp chicken in my hands and almost burst into tears. Carolyn passed by, trailing thread from a bench cushion. Mother looked up from unwrapping china. Pop made his way toward the refrigerator for a beer.

How was I going to feed 10 helpers with one chicken? Matt took the chicken, lay it in the sink, led me out to the back steps and sat me down. "You stay there, Mom. I'll be right back." He returned with a glass of wine for me, sat down, and said, "Okay, what shall I get when I go to the grocery store?"

By the time school started, the house was habitable. I had carpeted the garage, arranged books and supplies on shelves, stored stacks of writing paper in the unplugged freezer, and had begun the next phase of my life.

My first tutorial student was seventh-grader Julie, daughter of my friend Elaine, who had clawed her way to become president of the San Francisco Museum of Modern Art Auxiliary. Julie didn't enjoy reading. I asked her to bring a book she thought she might like. She chose Little House on the Prairie, and read aloud, "Laura and her family climbed into the covered wagon and drove into the ice."

I stopped her and asked, "Then what happened? Did they drown?"

She read that paragraph again and, with a surprised expression in her big blue eyes, looked up at me. "Oh," she said, "they drove onto the ice." History changed by one letter. By the end of the school year, Julie was reading two grades above her class level.

The day Marty left for the University of Washington, I helped him load his orange Toyota truck, laid a shoe box of lunch—tuna sandwiches, celery sticks, an apple, some cookies—on the front seat near him, and hugged my last chick goodbye. I stood on the curb, waved, dried my tears, and returned to his room to transform it into yet another teaching room. My years of active participation in the community were rewarded as friends trusted me with their children who needed academic help. One child brought her younger brother. Another convinced his mother to enroll to learn algebra. I hired Stanford graduate students with double majors and an enthusiasm for learning that they'd share with our students. Occasionally, someone, a friend, a referral, joined the staff. I asked the immediate neighbors if they would be bothered by parents dropping off and picking up their children, maybe even parking in the street for an hour. Several offered their driveways and two sent their children across the street for math tutoring. All around the house, in the laundry room, upstairs and down, in the bedrooms, at the dining table, as well as in the garage, seven tutors coached students aged five to 42. I'd give my student a 10-minute writing assignment and take that time to pass chamomile tea in Peter Rabbit cups. The students sipped their tea, responded to the respect the tutors had for them, and learned to succeed in school.

Then, in May of 1985, in Greece, 15 years after I'd started tutoring, I'd heard for the first time about The Great Peace March.

And here I was, six months later, driving alone through rain and memories, already almost to Coos Bay and wondering if I were making the right decision. It felt right, but was it? What would my parents say about my leaving home to wander with strangers across our country?

Pop, 88 and terminally ill with Parkinson's Disease, lay and listened to my plans. He was quiet and attentive, then mumbled, "That'sthegoddammestdummest thing I'veeverheardof."

Her father said, upon hearing about the Great Peace March, "TheGoddammest dummest thing I'veeverheardof."

CHAPTER 3

Goodbye, Pop, I'm Going

Pop had thought I would be walking alone! When I told him I'd be with many people, that it was to be well organized, and peaceful, he gripped my hand and using his term of endearment, said, "You be careful, Sis." Those were almost the last words I heard from him.

My father died in his sleep about a month later on November 9. I drove up I-5 again to be with Mother. She was her usual stoic self. "We both knew there was only one way out of that long illness," she said in her down-to-earth fashion. "The past few months have been hard, but at least we kept our sense of humor." She cocked her head in the way she often did when accepting the inevitable, gave a little shrug, and smiled. "One day not so long ago, he had to get up for the bathroom. I was helping him along the hallway when he lost control. He clutched the front of his pajama pants and said, 'Aaaawww, now look what I've done. I'm sorry, Ma.'

"But I told him, 'Oh, what the hell, Pop. Let it go; what difference does it make?' We both laughed so hard we had to lean up against the wall. I got him cleaned up and back to bed before the visiting nurse got here."

Several days after Pop's memorial service and the other members of the family had returned home, Mother and I sat at the dining table. She poured us a glass of wine while she helped me send notes to everyone we knew to ask them to support The March in any way they could. Many sent letters of encouragement to me; some sent money to The March itself; one sent me a sheet of stamps and admonished, "Remember to write to your mother." One wrote a long letter saying that there was no reason to worry about nuclear bombs, that our military would see to our security.

Connie, who had first told me about The March, sent me printed information. It said PRO-Peace (People Reaching Out for Peace) was "founded on the belief that each individual, joined with others, can make a difference and that great ideas put forth by honest people can alter history." David Mixner, the 38-year-old executive director, wrote, "We mean business. We believe there are moments in history when citizens can create a moral force to correct deep wrongs by deep sacrifice. We believe the time is now. We believe we can dramatically reduce, and maybe eliminate, nuclear weapons." I thought, "What an audacious, altruistic statement!" I wanted to meet David Mixner, a man who thought big.

Since its inception in early 1985, only about eight months ago, PRO-Peace had grown into a professional, well-financed, nonpartisan organization. At least that's what I read in their brochure. In the PRO-Peace office at 8150 Beverly Boulevard in Los Angeles, 80 volunteers attended to the details of moving marchers across the nation, 15 miles a day for 255 days. The staff of young people had interrupted careers in government, law, architecture and other fields to work at PRO-Peace for a year. Connie volunteered, too.

I invited her to San Mateo to speak to a group of my friends. "It'll be good publicity for The March. Just come and tell them what you told me that day when we walked down through the olive groves below Delphi."

About 30 people sat around my open living-dining room

and listened as she explained that 100,000 people would gather at a rock concert in the Los Angeles Coliseum for The March's send-off. Five thousand marchers would leave LA that day to "bring down the manufacture of nuclear weapons." That afternoon was almost volatile. While some agreed with Pop that it was "Thegoddammestdummestthing I ever heard of," most friends were at least politely interested. "Walking! You're going to walk all that way! Will you stay in motels? Eat out? Who will carry your luggage?"

Some admired my courage; others got up and walked out. Most of my friends had already responded to the notes Mother and I had mailed in November, and when Connie referred to the need for financial support, some thought they'd been asked again to contribute. I was embarrassed to hear her appeal for money. Not recognizing the change in the mood of her audience and fueled by her own enthusiasm, Connie explained the details to those friends who would listen. I sat to one side, scanning faces, anxious for acceptance of The Great Peace March plan and my part in it.

I was stunned when one couple stood up, glared at me, and made their way to the front door. I followed them, and, with my hand on the doorknob, asked, "Why are you leaving? Are you all right? What's happened?"

The gentle husband mumbled something about, "You know, Donna, we don't believe in this kind of disruptive demonstration. It's an insult to our government."

The wife pulled his arm. "Come on. I've had enough of this."

We had been friends for over 30 years. If I hadn't been so committed, so certain that going on The Peace March was exactly right for me, their behavior might have shaken my confidence. I shrugged and returned to the group in the living room.

A few weeks later some of those friends who had stayed to the end of Connie's presentation dressed up in camping clothes and gave me a going-away celebration -- a dinner party with fried chicken, potato salad and wine. We all thought this menu might be typical of what I'd be eating for the months on The March. I received humorous gifts, trail mix with a note, "fruit and nuts for fruits and nuts," a book on survival, a pedometer, a shiny bright red rain hat, socks, and a stack of postcards that each friend self-addressed so I'd write to them.

One Sunday late in January, just weeks before I left, my four sons, three with their wives, John with his fiancé, took me out to dinner at a nice restaurant in Menlo Park -- white tablecloths and fabric napkins, just what I like. I ordered baked salmon. Marty ordered grilled salmon. Someone wanted salmon teriyaki. Everyone ordered salmon. Matt said, "Here's to us, the Salmon Clan."

We talked about their childhood days, laughed and celebrated being together. I looked around the table at four handsome, healthy, independent sons, all 20-something, each with a woman who was smart and loving, friends to each other and to me. How could I have been so greatly blessed?

After dinner, they all gave me presents. A brass and tortoise-shell bracelet, a small album of family photos, a sketch book and colored pencils, a battery-operated headlamp so I could read "in bed" -- gifts that were small and light and reminders of their love. Marty gave me Birkenstocks.

John said, "That's because Mom's in her hippie period."

Sam advised, "Walk in the middle of the pack, Mom. It's safer there." I hadn't realized that any of them might be worried about me. I was the mom. Moms worried, not their children. I was touched by Sam's concern.

"Thanks, Sam. I'll remember."

Marty asked me, "Are you really going to walk every day! I know you like to walk, Mom, but every day?

I filled out application forms, had the required physical examination, including a stress test. When I told the doctor about The Peace March, he looked up, put down his pen, and said, "Where do I sign up? I'd like to go." He paused. "Well, I guess not. My wife and children would probably not like my being gone. You know, when it comes right down to it, I'm only an hourly wage-earner."

I checked with my insurance broker to be sure I had the necessary health coverage. He, a conservative, safe, perfect insurance man, said, "Are you sure you want to do this? We'll cover you, but it sounds risky to me. Out there. What more do you want? You have everything right now that money can buy."

I wrote a check for $3,200, a dollar for every anticipated mile, and mailed the papers and check to PRO-Peace headquarters.

By the end of January, I was saying goodbye to my students. One farewell was especially memorable. Karl and I had worked for over a year on his reading skills, and he was doing well. Karl's mother looked upset and wailed, "How could you go out to try to save the world when you could stay right here and save my boy?" Karl and I had just completed his final tutorial session, and he, his mother and I were saying goodbye at the front door. I would miss Karl and his cheerful second-grade industriousness.

He looked up, "But, Mom, if she doesn't save the world, none of us will be saved." I would think of Karl when The March days were long, and I was exhausted.

In early February, in the hills behind Redwood City, I attended a meeting of San Francisco Bay Area people who were signed up for The Great Peace March. I met Gene Gordon, a long-time activist, writer, and radio personality, who asked us to join him in a Sunday afternoon walk in downtown San Jose. He would lead us and have signs for us to carry. We would walk for about an hour. I said yes, and when the day dawned with a forecast of rain, I put on my new March clothes: cinnamon colored cords, a grey wool sweater with stylish cinnamon elbow patches, shiny yellow rain slicker and sturdy New Balance hiking boots. Driving from San Mateo down to San Jose, I chuckled and wondered just what I'd agreed to do. I wasn't used to calling attention to myself. Walk in the street? With a sign! But it was for the cause of peace. I took a big breath and told myself that all would be fine.

In the parking lot where we met, there was an assortment of about a dozen people standing around in the drizzle as they waggled hand-lettered signs—"No More Nuclear Weapons!," "Give Peace a Chance," and "Farms Not Arms"—and sang some song I'd never heard. Gene called us together. He would lead us along the downtown streets of San Jose, and we were to follow, waving the signs, giving drivers the peace sign and calling out greetings. I followed son Sam's advice and stayed in the middle of the small pack. I couldn't bring myself to lift my hand in the peace sign and call out to drivers. I felt ridiculous and was relieved there was so little traffic that day. What if someone I knew saw me! All the glory and purpose of demonstrating for nuclear disarmament eluded me.

Had Pop been right? In my mind, I heard all the arguments

against going. Was this demonstration an insult to our government? Was it risky? Was it dangerous? Was I abandoning the tutorial students? And to every question, my intuition, my heart replied, "I'm going! This will be great! What a grand opportunity to walk across our nation!" The gypsy in me chortled and said, "We're going to have an exciting adventure." The best part of that Sunday was the new boots. I loved those new walking boots. I drove back to San Mateo and thought, "You have a lot to learn, Donna, and you can do it."

At home, I called Connie and was comforted to hear her say she'd felt awkward the first time a similar group of peace marchers walked the streets of Santa Monica. "We'll be okay once we're all together. Enthusiasm here in Los Angeles is running high. See you in a couple of weeks!"

By February 14, I was packed and on the plane to Los Angeles. Connie met my flight and we—two grounded, sensible, mature women— were almost hysterical with excitement. We hugged each other and danced around like a couple of teenagers. I got my duffle bags off the carousel, and we were almost out the door when I heard my name over the loud speaker. "Donna Love, come to the information desk." The lady at the desk held up my brand new Brother word processor, purchased so I could write feature stories for the *San Mateo Times*. I'd inadvertently left it on a drinking fountain when Connie and I greeted each other. Whew!

Donna Love and Connie Fledderjohann in their tent.

CHAPTER 4

Ready, Set, GO!

"A totem?" I was puzzled. "What's a totem?"

Connie and I had read Lynn Andrews' book *Medicine Woman* and wanted to talk with her before we began The Peace March. She met us at the door of her home that Friday, a small youngish woman of quiet confidence and dignity, which was a relief since the dust jacket of her book showed a cute, fluffy, curly-haired Hollywood blond. The interior of the house was hung with Native American artifacts and smelled of candle wax and fireplace smoke. Lynn offered us mugs of fragrant tea as we settled into deep couches covered with Navajo rugs.

After a brief explanation about The Peace March, Connie asked, "What can we do when The March gets difficult?"

Lynn had answered, "Get a totem."

I had no idea what she meant. "A totem is a spirit animal," she explained. "Natives on both American continents celebrate rituals in which an animal appears as a guide. You can watch your dreams for an animal or you can just think of animals until one feels right. Make yourselves small red cotton bags to hang around your necks. Put in some sage, maybe a special small stone, and the fur of your totem animal. When you are exhausted, become that animal."

Connie knew immediately her totem was a female mountain lion. I first considered a bear. It's brown, earthy, motherly, the way I thought of myself. But bears are also awkward and round, close to the ground. I needed an animal whose motions I could emulate, with long legs, erect posture, good eyesight. How about a giraffe? It has a 25-pound heart, is a vegetarian and sees great distances. I was not a vegetarian, but otherwise, the giraffe felt right. Yes, I decided, my totem would be a giraffe.

Connie drove us to the home of a friend in Westwood where she had been staying because she already had let go of her apartment. She told me that Mordecai Roth had sold his dental practice in Northridge so he and his wife could go on The March, and Marjorie Celliti, 74, had sold her farm near Santa Rosa. Others used up their savings, left their jobs, even sold their homes in order to participate. My preparations seemed wimpy compared to changes others had made.

I'd enjoy sleeping on the floor in my brand new sleeping bag on my brand new self-inflating air mattress. I'd happily read with the battery-powered headlamp that my son Matt had given me.

Connie and I sorted through our clothes, winnowing down, down, until we could fit everything into four green plastic milk crates, two each, that Connie had picked up from the PRO-Peace headquarters. Support trucks were being outfitted with shelves to transport our crates of clothing and other vital personal belongings. Our tents, sleeping bags and air mattresses would be carried along in other trucks from one campsite to the next.

Every day we did 10-mile practice walks, usually along the beach in Santa Monica. Sometimes with other peace marchers, sometimes just out the door and down the blocks. We visited The Peace March campsite out at White Oak and Victory Boulevard on the National Guard property in Reseda near Van Nuys, in the San Fernando Valley. Victory Boulevard sounded good to me—and it seemed ironic that the property was owned by the National Guard. The brightly colored rainbow of The Peace March dome tents—red, yellow, green, blue—sat just east of the camouflaged trucks of the 144th Field Artillery Battalion. Heavy rain had made mud, lots of mud everywhere, and the tents, even though they sat in a soggy, grassy meadow, lent a mood of festivity to the site. It was pretty and pretty wet. I was glad we were still, for the time being, living at Connie's friend's house.

The rain subsided, and we loaded our gear into Connie's car and drove out to Victory Boulevard. A tall blond youth greeted us with a perfect smile and contagious enthusiasm, "Welcome to The Great Peace March! Glad you are here!" After we registered, he handed us identification tags. At the main reception desk, our files were found, we were checked in and directed to the medical center. The nurse reviewed our medical histories. The records were complete. Next, a bearded young man beamed from behind a card table and gave us an appointment with the tent set-up instructors.

Inside a red and white circus-type tent, new arrivals were being taught how to set up their two-person North Face tents. We got a red tent. Our instructor told us that we could set up our "home away from home" in about 15 minutes. We struggled with the bendy poles and tight lightweight fabric. I grunted and muttered, "This is too hard! Where are our sons when we need them?"

"We can do this," Connie answered me. "We just need to practice." Connie poked the end of a metal pole into a little pocket at the edge of the tent and stood up, a look of triumph on her face. "By Washington, we'll do it in the dark in six minutes!" We took it down, stuffed it back into the bag and went out to look for Red Tent Village, our color-coded Peace March neighborhood.

In spite of the makeshift appearance of The March headquarters, with its temporary buildings and flattened cardboard slabs for walkways through the mud from one "office" to another, I felt an underlying approval. I noticed muddy boots respectfully lined up outside doorways. Signs to facilitate the transition from home life to camp life were clearly, if crudely, written on cardboard. Above a crate of oranges, "Help Yourself.

Please add peels to compost can," and tacked to a wall, "This Way to Porta-Potties." Parents sat with their children, quietly talking with them, reading stories together, sharing an orange. People held open doors, helped carry bundles, shared apples and cheese with us. I was impressed with the courteous behavior because it was more than courteous. I felt the organizers had a real desire to make everything easy and pleasant. So, although the setting may have looked rough and grubby, it felt like a celebration—maybe even a sacrament.

Some of the eagerness we witnessed was based on youthful enthusiasm, but not all. Forty percent of the marchers were between 16 and 26, but we ranged in age from toddlers to those in their 70s. I had walked the Santa Monica beach with Suzanne Mendelson, 75, who had painted a canvas mural that she hoped would surround our campsites across the country. Her children mixed pride with concern for their mother who would walk such a long way.

On the other hand, May Spiegel, 71, was wringing her hands with worry as she prepared to bid farewell to her 43-year-old daughter, Shelah Notkoff. "What does she know about hiking and camping? She's a city girl!" Shelah was a dance therapist who would, on The March, instruct us in Tai Chi, Native American ceremonial dances and dance aerobics. I gave her my tape of dance aerobics routines I'd done at the San Mateo YMCA in preparation for the rigors of The Peace March.

In spite of her concern for her daughter, Shelah's mother invited a dozen marchers to brunch one Sunday. The lavish offering, made from scratch, was served to a group whose members she was sure were crazy. I showed Mrs. Spiegel my sweatshirt, the red one I'd had printed with Great Peace March across the front and my father's response, "Thegoddammestdummestthing I've ever heard of" across the back.

"I like your father," she said. "He knows you're all crazy!"

Maybe she was right. Sometimes I, too, wondered about our sanity. Connie, a psychotherapist, and I, an education specialist, were actually leaving our homes and professions to embark on an expedition that required setting up our tent almost daily for 255 days in places we'd mostly never heard of.

We had heard, though, that in addition to the trucks and trailers to carry our tents and green crates of personal possessions, there would be tents for meetings and sit-down meals, a mobile commercial kitchen and cold, as well as dry, food-storage trucks. Additionally there would be a mobile store, the laundry, a medical unit, a dentist with his dental chair, and a library/bookmobile. A shower truck, where each person could shower each day, was to be provided. That would be a total of 1,275,000 showers. There was even a school for children who would get home-study credit. Some independent-study courses were to be offered for college credit. The March would have its own radio broadcasting station. This adventure was going to be fancy and fun!

The third week in February, we marchers walked 18 miles from Van Nuys to Los Angeles' Griffith Park. Beneath sycamore trees, the green rolling meadows were soon dotted with our colorful tents arranged in color-coded neighborhoods. Connie and I were in Red Town, in our rosy red dome tent. Until March 1st, we attended lectures and demonstrations to learn about nuclear arms, about talking with folks along the way, and about obeying laws governing walking along public roads. In addition to these intensive educational meetings, we focused on physical conditioning—stretches, aerobics, yoga, Tai Chi.

Connie and I had not forgotten Lynn Andrews' advice to get totems. We found a fabric store, bought one-eighth of a yard of excellent red cotton, and stitched up our small bags at a friend's home. Now, to get the fur. Griffith Park was just around the corner from the Los Angeles Zoo. Connie and I strolled over to the giraffe enclosure. No way to reach even a tuft of airborne fur. Same with the mountain lion fur. We found the office of the zoo director. He was out, but his officious secretary assured us she would ask the director in the morning. I could tell by her manner that there was only a slim chance we'd get any mountain lion or giraffe fur.

The next morning, her closed face told us the answer. I tried, "I know this is an unusual request, but this is an unusual cause."

"Oh, no, you are quite wrong," she contradicted. "We have Native Americans in here all the time asking for hanks of hair and bits of fur. We can't accommodate them all." With an antiseptic grimace, she dashed our hopes, "Anyway, disease can be spread that way." Now what would we do? There had to be a solution.

The following day Connie and I were doing a few errands along Melrose Avenue. At an open door, a paunchy furrier lounged against the wall, smoking in the sunshine. I saw behind him, beneath a cutting table, scraps of fur.

I smiled and asked him, "Do you have any very small scraps we might have?"

He squinted and shook his head.

I pointed. "Just a handful from those beneath the table?"

"Oh, those! Sure! Take as much as you want!" He offered a shoebox. We filled it, thanked him, and took it to the nearest sidewalk bench.

"Sit down, Connie," I said. "I am going to find your piece of mountain lion fur." I pawed through the scraps and chose a pale one. "Here. This is it. This is mountain lion fur."

She looked skeptical. "How can you tell?"

"Trust me. This is it. And, now, you choose a piece of giraffe fur for me."

She rummaged a little while, picking up and discarding pieces. Finally she said, "Here. This is a piece of a dark spot from a Rothschild giraffe."

"Looks like mink to me," I countered, but put it into the red cotton bag I had hanging around my neck. She put her mountain lion fur into her bag. We left the box of scraps on the bench for someone to discover. Maybe a Native American on a totem-fur search.

A few days later, as we idled in our small, rosy tent, I dug the bit of fur from my totem bag. It still looked like mink.

"Come with me," Connie invited. "Let's go back to the zoo." I followed her through the gate and into the gift shop. She wandered away and then returned. Her face had the bright look of discovery. "Let me have your bag." From it, she took the bit of dark soft fur and attached a tiny enameled giraffe pin to it. "There! Now you can see this is most certainly giraffe hair."

I laughed and was satisfied.

On the first of March we wakened early, took down our tents, rolled our sleeping bags and pads, had oatmeal for breakfast, and were ready to be on the move. Our first day of real walking toward Washington! First, we were bused from Griffith Park to the Los Angeles Memorial Coliseum. We were not the expected 5,000. We were 1,200. That seemed fine to me, but I was not an administrator of PRO-Peace. I milled around in the parking lot with the rest of the marchers. We were beautiful in our diversity, or raggle-taggle, depending on one's frame of reference and perspective.

As we waited to assemble into our walking columns, a young man from New York produced several bags of balloons. We blew them up and tied knots in their necks. Immediately someone else contributed a ball of string. Within a few minutes a streamer of blue and white balloons over a block long was ready to be carried through the streets of Los Angeles to City Hall.

Along the five-mile route, policemen halted traffic at intersections, smiled at us and waved. The parade of marchers, walking four abreast with no gaps, was over one-quarter-mile long. Peace groups, church groups, school groups crowded on curbs to wave and cheer us on. Mothers with young children in their arms and tears in their eyes called, "Thank you!" Marchers dashed from the column to give a child a balloon. Several marchers had plastic grocery bags and were picking up trash along the gutter and scurrying to receptacles to empty them and start again. A Saturday *Los Angeles Times* was passed back among us, and we read about ourselves. We liked the photos of the campsite in Griffith Park and the printed statements that described us as "determined and courageous." Several young musicians strummed their guitars and sang *Give Peace a Chance*. Occasionally I heard chants and thought of those times in college when we had trooped along in a similar fashion to pre-game pep rallies. This march created the same kind of high excitement. Twelve hundred of us marching in downtown Los Angeles were much more powerful than on that drizzly Sunday in early February when a dozen of us, some novice peace activists, wandered through almost deserted downtown San Jose. This was Big!

The sidewalks at the entrance to the block where City Hall was located were jammed with masses of onlookers. We were greeted by cheers and were sung into our seats by Holly Near. Mayor Tom Bradley welcomed The Great Peace March and called us heroic. Singer-songwriter Melissa Manchester, the pop band Mr. Mister and movie actors Teri Garr and Robert Blake exhorted us to persevere in our commitments.

After three hours of rousing speeches and music, we exited back onto the streets for an evening walk through East Los Angeles. Neighbors called out, "Thank you!" Many mothers, holding their children, reached out to touch us. This definitely could become an ego trip!

As we passed a Mexican-American church, the doors swung open. Two marchers stood at the entrance listening to the music. They were invited in, and the congregation handed them the evening's collection of $275. "*Muchos suerte*," a man at the door called out to us.

By the time we reached that night's campsite on a California State University at Northridge parking lot, the sun had set and the streetlights were on. It was almost raining. "Only a dense fog," a nearby marcher said. The weather forecast was for 20 percent chance of rain that night. On went the rain flies over the tents.

As we lined up for dinner, I fingered the red totem bag that hung around my neck. Even though we were still within L.A. city limits, I had come a long way. Two weeks ago, on February 14, I had left San Mateo and arrived in Los Angeles, and since then I had slept on a floor or the ground. I had learned to accept porta-potties, to face the day without makeup. I had listened to political points of view I'd never known existed and, except for Connie, everyone on The March was new to me. I felt expanded, bigger than usual, capable. In every moment I was learning something new. And thriving, having a good time, enjoying the good humor and camaraderie of this large group called The Great Peace March. Was I ready?

Peace City.

CHAPTER 5

Early Days

Next morning, a gong sounded. I thought, a monastery on the parking lot campsite? and peeked out. No, it was a marcher weaving his way among the tents, beating slowly on a stainless steel salad bowl with a wooden spoon. "Get up, get up," he sang out. "It's a nice day for a walk." The difference between being in bed (sleeping bag) and being up was sitting up. I sat up. Connie handed me a baby-wipe. Clean the face; swipe the armpits; pull those clothes from the bottom of the sleeping bag, and, while they're still warm, get dressed. Kneel on the air mattress; roll up the bag and stuff it into its duffel. Deflate and roll the mattress. Toss sleeping bag and mattress outside. Crawl out; sit on the bag; put on shoes. Stuff the plastic shoe bags that had protected our shoes from the elements as they sat outside the tent overnight into the end of the duffel bag. Breathe the crisp air, and stand up. Face the moon. It's 5:30.

Someone asks, "Will it rain today? It didn't last night."

Out of the dark another voice responds, "They expected showers but couldn't get the water trucks." A good-humored reference to the lack of promised bathing facilities. Shower and water trucks were to have been available mid-February when we first arrived in Los Angeles. Only one arrived—16 showers and eight washbowls in a 42-foot trailer. It was not nearly enough for 1,200 people. We were promised more, as well as laundry facilities, "within the next few weeks." In Peace March vernacular, that was "almost now."

I didn't realize then the depth of the financial abyss The March was facing. Some of it would surface before Day Three, when we were supposed to camp in Claremont. The March needed liability insurance to camp on government land, city parks and school football fields, but there was no money for insurance coverage—half a million dollars. Claremont city officials revoked permission to camp. What were the options? Walk through the night? Lie down anywhere? Get arrested, sleep in jail? I whispered to Connie, "Motel rooms?" but she shushed me.

On Friday, Gaynl Trotter, the volunteer chairperson of the Claremont Welcoming Committee, heard about our predicament. She got on the phone and started calling churches in town. "We need to house The Great Peace March when it arrives tomorrow afternoon," she declared. The committee found homes for most of the 1,200 Marchers and allowed others to sleep inside church meeting halls or set up tents on church property. Connie and I set up our tent behind the Episcopal Church, washed our hair in the bathroom wash bowl, and walked down to a Chinese restaurant. Others were fed by church volunteers or in the homes where they stayed overnight.

Having no liability insurance turned out to be a blessing in disguise. In Claremont, MITH, Marcher in the Home, was born. Local families invited marchers into their homes to sit down at a table, eat warm meals and stay overnight. MITH continued across America and provided some of the best outreach opportunities. The Claremont crisis had led to one of those unexpected miracles that sustained The March. From then on, our rest days were most frequently on Saturdays to accommodate MITH. We took showers, washed our hair, did laundry, met neighbors, slept in beds, spoke to church congregations and civic groups. A rest day in camp provided time to speak to local groups as well as mend tents and seal seams, write letters, send out progress reports to those back home or along the way, and hold elections. It was a general catch-up day.

To keep our little village moving east an average of 15 miles a day, each person needed to do a job at least two days a week: food prep, dishwashing, vehicle maintenance, finding and mapping routes and sites, teaching the 40 school children, cleaning porta-potties, media. Of the 30 or so departments, I chose to work in media. That meant that on Tuesdays and Thursdays, when I worked, I did not walk. On those days I'd find Shelah Notkoff, whose mother in Los Angeles had thought us all crazy. Shelah was often in a clearing, surrounded by marchers whom she led in stretching exercises. She'd fling her arms skyward, sing out encouragement, and double over clapping and laughing when her followers imitated her. After a career in dance therapy and with her vivacious enthusiasm, she was easy to like. We often swung along the roadside together and sometimes, at rest stops, she demonstrated Tai Chi. On our work days, Shelah and I hitched a ride into town with a March vehicle and found phones to call in press releases to major newspapers in the country: *The Chicago Tribune*, the *Los Angeles Times, the Christian*

ments—responsible, as though I could

Science Monitor, the Denver Post, as well as smaller papers in towns along our proposed route. There were no cell phones then. We had phone charge cards and tried pay phones at gas stations, but they were too noisy. Motel hallways were quiet enough but the shelf beneath the phones was too narrow for taking notes. Eventually we found phones in offices, but that always took a while. When we were through our press release calls, we found a downtown restaurant and treated ourselves to hamburgers and chocolate milk shakes. Then we checked the laundromats until we found marchers who, as soon as their clothes were dry, were driving to the campsite.

We in media took turns stationing ourselves at the entrance of each new campsite to greet the local press and to direct the trucks bringing in the supplies from the previous campsite.

On March 4, it was my turn to be on the curb at the entrance to Chaffey College in Alta Loma, a few miles east of Claremont. The official media reception desk was a card table, a sign, and an upended milk crate. I sat on the crate and wondered how I had come to be there. What was I really doing? Was I saving the world for my tutorial student, Karl? Maybe I was just there for the adventure, the delight in living outdoors. The Walk was a great way to see the United States, in spite of the organized confusion. Someone said we were "shepherds in search of a flock." I wasn't even sure what that meant. Maybe it meant that here we were, 1,200 willing and able people committing our lives to an important social cause, but we were so focused on getting from one place to the next that we didn't have enough time to herd others into our point of view. Would we attract more attention as we went along? We would, but not in the way I had imagined.

I was having fun. More fun than I had had since taking my grade-school sons on a camping trip many years ago at Lake Almanor in northern California. I loved being outdoors, and I felt important at the card table on the edge of the field—responsible, as though I could answer any possible questions. In a ridiculous way, it reminded me of the Hillsborough Decorators' Show House front desk. That job had required the same cheerfulness, the same intelligent resourcefulness among staffers and posed similar logistical challenges. The Peace March and the Show House both had problems with tent-flaps, parking lots, and feeding large groups of people, if not the same visual aesthetics. The Peace March image hardly matched the tea party elegance of the Show House.

A reporter from the *San Jose Mercury News* Los Angeles Bureau pulled up, got out, and asked, "Where do I go to talk to a representative of The March? Someone I can interview." I saw Chris, a young marcher in media, and called him over. They walked off and in a few minutes I saw them sitting together on a couple of green plastic crates in the shade of a parked school bus, Chris talking and gesturing, and the reporter checking her tape recorder. A few days later, a copy of the *San Jose Mercury News* was passed back along The March column. On the front page, we read:

> *With not much more than a dream and sturdy shoes, 1,000 marchers set out Saturday to face an uncertain journey of heat and cold—and possible arrests—in a cross-country trek for nuclear disarmament.*
>
> *The overriding message is peace. But now, faced with near-empty coffers and insufficient liability insurance, the immediate message is help.*

I could almost hear Chris's voice when I read:

> *The unforeseen obstacles are all in keeping with the spirit of The March. It'll be a historic 3,500 mile journey to guarantee our future. We have the courage and determination to reach Washington, DC, in November. We will give all America hope."*

At 10 o'clock the trucks arrived with the advance staff and "campscape" directors. More than 100 volunteers had stayed behind to clean up the old site, fill in the ruts, remove the protective woven wire from small plants, pick up stuff for lost-and-found. They had driven ahead to set up the large Town Hall and dining tents, start dinner, and prepare for meetings. As the personal gear trucks lumbered around the corner, I referred to a penciled map of the campsite and pointed. They bumped off in that direction. The kitchen supply trucks shifted gears and headed across the dusty field.

The 40-foot-long dry-food trailer was as large as a moving van. At one time it carried 82,000 pounds of rice, beans, flour, salt and other staples. Thirty-five percent of our dry food was donated. For other food supplies, two of the kitchen team called ahead to churches for help in finding food banks. They came back to camp with a pickup loaded with cheese or loaves of bread. With donations and smart shopping, by Denver, the kitchen crew would feed 500 to 1,000 three times a day for about $1.70 each. The cold food storage trailer was also 40 feet long. They loomed huge as they thundered past my card table.

During the coming weeks of The March, logistics improved. Entrances to campsites were handled by receivers who walked ahead to the next site and decided where the kitchen trucks and gray-water bladder should be. The back of the dishwashing trailer needed to face the kitchen, as did the dry food tent, which was later replaced by a trailer. To create a sense of community, the main vehicles were placed in a circle. Receivers selected the areas for the Town Hall meeting tents and our color-coded clusters of gumdrop tents with the personal-gear trucks close by. Two sets of porta-potties were positioned, one nearer the tents and the other closer to the kitchen. Fisc & Disc (Finance and Computer) kept track of marchers, each day's budget, and eventually published a daily newspaper. They parked off to one side near a growling generator. The post office, Peace Academy, the Community Interaction Agency buses and the children's schoolroom buses parked where space permitted. All of this, like everything else on The March, slowly developed. Peace City was not in any atlas. No borders. No buildings. No phones or street lights. It was a city on the move. Eventually we in the media department were housed in a short blue bus routinely parked near the campsite entrance. The card table would be used for something else. But on March 4, after only three nights on the road, I sat behind it and waited for Connie to come trooping into camp with the rest of that day's marchers.

They would arrive by mid-afternoon. Only 11 miles that day, a short walk. As the walkers straggled "home," we who had been there all day gathered at the entrance to applaud and cheer. Connie, not changing her stride to accept the raisins I offered, smiled as we walked together to find our tent and bags in the stacks behind the gear trucks.

"How was it?" I asked. "Was it hot? Did many people come out to see The March? Did you find a shady place to have lunch?"

She answered, "It was hot, but not too hot. There was no shade. We did see quite a few people who gave us the peace sign or just stared at us. I'm glad it was a short walk today."

We chose a level spot to set up the tent and retrieved our green crates from their truck. I walked over to the kitchen area to get each of us an apple.

Connie asked, "Want to go to a meeting? I think we should."

"No," I said, "I've been sitting most of the day. Those meetings… they go on forever. You go and tell me what you find out. Do you think we might get a shower truck one of these days? I'm going for a walk."

Every step is a step for peace.

CHAPTER 6

Meetings and Misery

All of us, even marchers who had not worked in the PRO-Peace office in Los Angeles, could see difficulties cropping up. Where were the promised showers and laundry and medical services? Where was that $4 million dollars reportedly in the bank account? Every day new people wanted to join The March. And some already wanted to leave. Entrance and exit procedures needed to be formalized. The kitchen needed to be reorganized to meet sanitary health standards. Organizational meetings convened in the Town Hall Tents and in small circles in the field. I didn't attend many of these meetings. When I did, I was stunned by hour after hour of statements and counter-statements, the awkwardness and difficulty of making decisions through consensus. It was the first time I'd seen that attempted. I have since learned that in Boston's Faneuil Hall, from 1742 onward, our nation's founding fathers reached conclusions by consensus. Those, too, must have been long and noisy meetings.

Casey Kraft of Santa Rosa, California, growled, "Democracy is getting in the way of progress," left The March and hitched a ride to the nearest bus station. He went back to his lumberyard.

One day soon afterward, my son Sam, a contractor in Santa Rosa, stopped in to order some lumber, and Casey, noting Sam's last name, asked him, "Do you know Donna Love?"

"Yes, sure, she's my mom. Why?"

"I last saw her sitting in a dusty field east of Los Angeles, having a great time chattering with some women and scrubbing potatoes." He laughed, "She's not much for meetings, is she?"

"I think she gave up meetings soon after she gave up ironing," Sam answered. "Just didn't have much use for them anymore."

There were more meetings, many more. But because I didn't attend them, I was mostly oblivious to the serious problems that were threatening The March. All I really wanted to do was walk.

On March 8, before daylight, I heard a guitar and a melodic masculine voice crooning, "Get up, get up, it's a lovely day for a walk. At least right now, it's lovely; there may be strong winds later, so get up, get up. We're going for a wa-a-a-a-lk."

He was right. High winds blew right through our clothing, seemingly through our bodies. It was a long, tough day. At Hesperia, Joshua trees bent in the wind, and tents tumbled across the site. I wanted to write my report for the *San Mateo Times*, so I sat on my rolled-up sleeping bag in our tent, using a green crate for a table. As I typed, my weight held down the tent while Connie drove in the stakes to hold it in place. We lined up for dinner, and our salads blew off the plates, so we covered our food with bandanas and scurried back to the shelter of the tent. Dinner and bed, almost in one motion.

It rained that night. The next morning I pulled on long silk underwear, a turtle neck, the grey sweater, warm cords, yellow rain gear, two pairs of socks, bread wrappers over the socks, and the dependable New Balance trail boots. On to Victorville, a small town on the edge of the desert tucked into the San Gabriel Mountains. Cold wind, with 50-mile-an-hour gusts, blew drenching sheets of fierce, unrelenting rain sideways across the campsite just beyond the town. As Connie and I slogged along, I borrowed a tune, *Wouldn't it be Loverly*, from *My Fair Lady*, and made up a chant to sing:

Every step is a step for peace.
Every step and I release
My worry, fear and prejudeese,
Oh, isn't it so wonderful?

Connie was cold and coughing. I saw the inexpensive-looking Green Spot Motel and said, "Let's go in here and get warm. Let's not set up the tent in this storm."

She shook her head. "We joined The March. We're going to stay with it."

I answered, "We can catch up. Tomorrow's a rest day. Come on. There will be a shower with an unending supply of hot water. Look, you're shivering! Let's go."

I veered off toward the bright lime-green entrance, and Connie tagged along. The woman behind the desk said, "What are you girls doing out in this storm! Here's the key. You go on down the hall, and get out of those wet clothes." We did exactly that. I turned on the shower and without a word, Connie was in. I pulled the shades, turned up the wall furnace, draped our clothes around the room, and turned down the beds. It wasn't a fancy place, but it seemed luxurious to us. As Connie emerged, I stepped in. She dried off and leapt into her bed. Ah, the water was delicious. I could have stayed in a long, long time, but thought maybe other miserable marchers might be checking in. On my way to bed, I turned on the TV. As we lay watching the news, looking for ourselves on the screen, there was a knock on the door and the woman brought us two mugs of hot jasmine tea and a package of Ritz crackers. I loved her. On her way out, she picked up our pants and socks and the next morning brought them back, clean and dry.

At the campsite the next morning, we learned that seven marchers had developed hypothermia. A medical volunteer had wandered among the tents calling out, "If you are shivering, come to the Blue Town Hall Tent." There, doctors from Victorville treated stricken marchers. I gave a prayer of thanks out of gratitude for two fundamental blessings: warm water and dry socks.

The storm continued for the next two days. After a rest day, we walked across the desert to a Bureau of Land Management (BLM) site 10 miles west of Barstow, on Stoddard Wells Road in California's vast

Mojave. We were warned not to damage any creosote plants or drive over the berms along the roadside. Vehicles parked in a long string down the road, and we carried our gear, stepping carefully. Some young marchers protected small plants with corrals of sticks and string and fluttery little fabric prayer flags. Connie and I changed into dry clothes and drank warm water from the faucet on the side of the kitchen. Eventually the storm cleared, and the sun thawed us a little.

On the 11th day of The March, David Mixner, leader of PRO-Peace, flew out from his Los Angeles headquarters in a big red helicopter, climbed up onto a flatbed truck and said, "PRO-Peace is bankrupt. The March is over. Go home." He told us that commercial bus companies were offering discounted rides to those of us who needed them. He said the re-possessors were coming for the trucks. "Not the kitchen!" someone shouted. "Yes, that, too." was the answer. The young man in a hoody responsible for the kitchen truck keys wandered off among the tents. As he passed one that was open, not zippered shut, he tossed in the keys, and kept wandering. When questioned, he said he didn't know where the keys were. The repossessor had to wait a few days. He had to wait for the porta-potties, too. I marveled at the resourcefulness, the temerity, the determination of the young people with us. With their leadership, I felt we'd reach our destination, but it'd be a March different from the one we'd envisioned.

In the weak winter sunshine, the marchers, shaken and disappointed, joined hands, snaked around across the cold desert and sang The Great Peace March theme song that Holly Near had written for us.

> *We will have peace*
> *We will because we must.*
> *We must because we cherish life.*
> *And believe it or not,*
> *Daring as it may seem,*
> *It is not an empty dream*
> *To walk in a powerful path –*
> *Neither the first nor the last*
> *Great Peace March.*
> *Life is a great and mighty march*
> *Forever for love and for life*
> *On The Great Peace March.*

Dick Edelman said, "This is an amazing group. We have just heard that the rug's been pulled out from under us and what do we do? Join hands and sing a song."

I chuckled with Dick and could not imagine that The Peace March was over. "It *can't* be over. I've rented out my house!"

Connie pulled her wool hat down over her ears and said, "This is preposterous. We are too committed to quit."

Dick's wife, Ann, wiped her tears and said, "After all the work that has been done. After all the lives that have been interrupted. People have made great sacrifices to be here. Not like Dick, who got someone to take his patients this year, or me. I just took a leave of absence from the string quartet. Some people have gambled everything on this March. There has to be a way!"

We were standing in the dinner line discussing the immediate future of The March when I heard someone calling my name. From behind, a woman came forward, "Donna? Has anyone seen Donna Love?" When she reached me and had given me a big hug, she announced, "I'm Jacqueline Smith. Your friend Virginia Woodward is my sister-in-law. I'm with her brother Richard. I've been looking for you!"

What a surprise! Virginia and I were college sorority sisters, even our fathers had known each other at the University of Oregon. Virginia had told me about Jackie, about how artistic she was, that she was an activist, and had been voted Woman of the Year in Carmel. I was excited to meet her, and we walked back to her place in line. As we chatted nonstop about the chances of The Peace March reaching Washington, DC, the sunset became a solid vibrant vermillion. "A good omen," Jackie said.

Dinner was late that night, but it was there, and so were we. As we stood in line, I looked around at us and felt that we had become a tribe, a spiritual tribe whose primary purpose was to stay together to accomplish our collective goal—to demonstrate peaceful living in difficult circumstances. Together we could raise consciousness about global nuclear disarmament.

But not everyone shared my faith. Within the next 18 days, 800 marchers left; 400 stayed. A worried friend came to rescue me, but I had already decided I wasn't leaving. I'd rented my house, sold the car, closed down my life at home for nine months. I gave him my tent and asked him to save it for me. Connie and I could share hers.

Now the meetings really started, practically around the clock. Someone made up a song, "Let's have a meeting. We gotta have a meeting to meet to decide what to decide at the next meeting." Some Marchers left to solicit money in their hometowns. I thought of friends who had contributed on my behalf, some generously. A few had given over $1,000. How could they trust me or believe in The Peace March again?

The Press had something to write about. Papers across the nation blatted, "The Peace March is Dead." In a March 14 *Los Angeles Times* story, Kathleen Hendrix wrote, "Crippled by (lack of) Funding, The Long Thin Line Gets Thinner." I wrote in the margin, "Hi! This pretty much sums up the current state of affairs. A new group is being formed with a new checking account. If your office wants to support us, we could use it. I'm sticking with it. I don't know why, but I'm having fun. Love to ALL! Donna/Mom."

Then I walked the 10 miles into Barstow to mail the article to my son John. As long as I was in town near a phone, I called to let him know I'd mailed the article. "I'm fine, very fine, John. I didn't get the cough that so many have had since Victorville. The situation is not as bad as the newspapers say, but we are at a critical point." I told him I thought things would work out. "All we need is money and time. Would you call the others, John, to let them know I'm having a good time? There are so many interesting people here. Barstow is ugly, but the desert is lovely. Big sunsets."

He said, "Yea, Mom, I know. I was talking with Sam, and he said if you had to walk all by yourself, you'd finish. He said you're having a blast."

I urged him, "Keep on clipping news articles, John. And remember I love you." I found a ride back to camp.

The Hopi Indians viewed our March as the fulfillment of an ancient Native American prophecy. Marchers got involved with the issue of Big Mountain, where many Native Americans were to be relocated to make way for coal and uranium mines on their lands. This was one example of our Peace March becoming aligned with other causes. In Indiana and Ohio, out-of-work steel workers would try to convince us that we should join them in a collective demand for jobs.

One day, while we were still in Barstow, another marcher and I sat talking. I didn't know him, but he seemed bright and sensible. He told me he'd been in radio back home and had been looking forward to doing radio work for The March, but now there was no money, and we really needed to reach the world outside. I agreed with him and asked how much he'd need. He said, "To get it up and running would take $600." I thought about it for a while, found him in the dinner line that evening, and said I'd give him the money.

"I'll need it in cash. I'll give you a ride into Barstow so you can cash a check at the bank."

He gave me a grateful Peace March hug and said he'd have to go back home to San Diego to get supplies. No one ever saw him again. No one remembered him. No one had time to help me find him.

I felt abandoned by the marchers who I thought would know what to do and was bitter. No one seemed to care that I'd lost $600. More than that, I'd lost some of my faith and confidence in the goodness of people. I had been duped. Those in Fisc & Disc were more interested in found money than lost money. After a few weeks of anguish, I let it go and determined to be more careful in the future.

Day after day, for two weeks, re-organization meetings continued. A new provisional government was elected, then replaced by a new policy board, then changed again in a few days. Our camp location 10 miles outside Barstow was too isolated. People needed phones and stores. And showers. The Policy Board, the new Board of Directors, the various representatives from Red, Blue, Yellow and Green Towns needed to be in touch with people who could help us. Dan Chavez, one of The March's attorneys, was in Los Angeles. We needed incorporation and non-profit status. On Tuesday morning that week, another woman and I asked the Policy Board to change The Great Peace March to The Great Peace March for Global Nuclear Disarmament, a bulky title, but one that explained our mission.

Meanwhile, some of us went into Barstow to look for a more convenient campsite. Finally the manager of the BMX bicycle race track offered space. We took down our tents and walked into town. We were only 360 walking that day. On the way, we ate lunch at a dump. It rained. It blew. The glory had disappeared. But we were walking—10 miles closer to Washington, DC.

The first night in Barstow, not sure we could count on dinner, Connie and I went to the bowling alley, ordered BLTs and cokes to take out, crawled into our sleeping bags with our clothes on, giggled and ate and fell back, immediately asleep.

The pains of birthing a new Peace March were long and laborious. I didn't really care about the details of the new organization, just that it got together. I knew those young people, whose mean age was 27, would manage. I was 58 and didn't need to give my opinion. I gave them my vote of faith.

Waiting to see what would happen, some of us were restless. Seven joined demonstrators near Mercury, Nevada, at the southern edge of the Nuclear Test Site. Then four of them went camping in Death Valley, two returned to The March, and one went to jail. Suzanne Mendelson, 75, the Santa Monica artist with whom I'd walked on the beach early in February, deliberately stepped across the line at the Nuclear Test Site, knowing she would be arrested for trespassing. According to friends, she was jubilant. She grinned and waved from the police car. She didn't even have her cold medicine with her.

We had heard that the civil disobedience actions at the test site were led by a group of Benedictine monks, that the jail cells were not locked, that the food was edible, and there were showers. Maybe Suzanne had the right idea. One of us who had seen her reported, "A deputy took pity on her and saw to it that she visited a doctor to help get rid of her upper respiratory infection. The doctor told her, 'Your demonstration won't do you any good here. You need to go to Washington.'"

Suzanne had replied, "But, Doctor, we are!"

She probably had better medical care than many of us who were suffering from the cough picked up in Victorville. She showed her appreciation by drawing portraits of the police officers and washing their cars.

I couldn't imagine getting arrested. When I joined The March and first heard the acronym "CD," I thought of Certificates of Deposit. Someone told me it meant Cassette Disc. On The March, it meant Civil Disobedience. I couldn't have committed civil disobedience. It wasn't my style. Instead, four of us in the Over-50 group, Ann and Dick Edelman, Connie Fledderjohann, and I, climbed into Dick's car and went camping on the shores of Lake Mead. Near Hoover Dam, we found Kathy's Koffee Kup Kafé and the best Belgian waffles I'd ever eaten. They were light, crisp, tender, and had deep little craters to fill with butter and warm syrup. We walked, stretched, got back into shape, and agreed that if The March failed, we'd continue on to Washington, DC. If we had to, we'd buy a van to carry our gear and keep on walking. Then we drove back to Barstow.

But The Great Peace March for Global Nuclear Disarmament rallied! Some marchers who were experienced fund-raisers had managed to assemble $15,000 in cash, checks and pledges. We learned that across the country Peace March volunteer offices had opened. Contributions began to arrive. A woman drove out from Los Angeles to leave $500 on the contribution table. She didn't leave her name. Someone delivered a truckload of strawberries. Another person drove from Arizona with several hundred pounds of honey. The workers of the Santa Fe Railway collected money to buy us hundreds of pairs of socks. Three hundred people hiked across 16 miles of desert on March 28, our triumphant first day on the road in nearly three weeks. Many sang as we trooped behind The March flags.

An overnight in Yermo and five BLM sites along a dirt track near State Highway 15 consumed the next week. One late afternoon, I was particularly tired, and instead of finding Connie's tent and our gear, I lay down on the ground.

"Ohhhh," I groaned. "All day facing east. Where is that beautiful Pacific surf?" I was exhausted. "How can someone as old as I am feel homesick?" I dug a vial of California beach sand out of my day pack and passed it around to others who were lying down.

"This is great. Where did you get this?"

I answered, "From Half Moon Bay on the San Francisco Peninsula. Where are you from?"

"San Diego. Grew up there. Here, take a whiff of this." He pulled a tiny bottle out of his pocket. "Careful, though, it's ocean water. Might smell like low-tide." We talked about home and shared a few snacks. I didn't see Connie approaching until she stood over me.

"What are you doing?" she asked. "The tent has to be set up. Do I have to do it all by myself?" She was hot and tired and exasperated. She wasn't having much fun. Connie was disciplined, responsible, dutiful, serious. Maybe suffering. I wasn't. Tired, yes, sometimes cold, or hot, but never suffering. I irritated her when I didn't pay strict attention to duty. So I got up, retrieved my vial of beach sand, and followed her to help set up the tent and put our gear inside to weigh it down.

"Sorry, Connie. Here, let me have your water bottle. You rest here, and I'll be right back."

As I walked over to the kitchen area, I wondered at my desire to keep the peace with Connie. Sometimes I felt like a child trying to please my mother. I tried to please Connie—as I had tried to please Jim Love—and he'd left anyway. Was I afraid Connie would abandon me? What would I do if she booted me out of her tent! I was thrown right back into my old melodrama of, "No matter how hard I try, it's not good enough." I brought back her filled water bottle and two apples—the offering—and we sat on the ground together in companionable silence to write in our journals.

On April 4, 35 days since we had left Los Angeles, we camped so close to the California-Nevada border we could see Whiskey Pete's, a large, gaudy, turreted gambling casino on the horizon.

And our one truck-cab had broken down.

A cool, dry day—so far.

CHAPTER 7

Onward!

The walk across the desert from Barstow had been bleak. Highway 15 was too heavily trafficked for walkers, and the only remaining route was a dusty track under swags of high voltage power lines. With nobody to see our efforts, we felt isolated and ineffective. Did anyone even know The March had rallied and that we were still walking toward Washington?

Some worried about the effects of the power lines upon us. Scientific studies had linked exposure to electromagnetic fields of high-power lines with leukemia in children. Other possible illnesses could be brain cancer, breast cancer, and heart disease as well as fatigue, depression, hormonal imbalances, blood disorders and birth defects. Just to be sure mothers and children were not affected, they were bused ahead to Zion National Park where they would wait until The March reached Utah.

One particularly hot day, a group of us straggled along and talked about food.

Someone said, "I'd really like a frothy cold beer."

"Here, have some water," Connie said.

Dick Edelman declared, "I'd give my shoes right now for a big juicy orange."

A young marcher with dreadlocks dug into his backpack and handed an orange to Dick. "Here, man, but you can keep your shoes."

Dick carefully peeled the orange, put the peels in his pocket, and offered sections to those around him. The zingy fragrance alone was refreshing, but an orange section wasn't what I craved. "No thanks. I scream for ice cream! I'd like a jamoca almond fudge ice cream cone," I responded to his offer.

We rounded a curve in the trail and about one-quarter mile ahead was a blue pickup truck with three people, a man, woman and teenage daughter, standing alongside, ice cream scoops poised aloft. They had driven from Los Angeles with enough ice cream for all 350 of us. We were not forgotten, after all. We yelped, whistled and shouted our appreciation. With a little canteen water, I washed my hands, stepped up in turn, and said, "I'd like jamoca almond fudge, please."

"Sorry. We have vanilla, vanilla, and vanilla. Which'll you have?"

"Vanilla will be perfect. Thank you, thank you." I almost cried with relief and delight, but instead I licked that luscious sweet frozen treat before it melted down my arm.

For several miles, we talked about miracles. About MITH, and about the Mexican church congregation in poverty-stricken East Los Angeles that gave us the money from their evening's collection. And now, the ice cream. We may have felt lost in the desert, but, as one marcher said, "The Force must be with us."

By the time we came close to the border between California and Nevada, I noticed that in spite of hot, dusty, long days, I'd somehow reached a new level of awareness. I hadn't realized that I had merely been surviving until I began to notice, really notice, the beauty of the desert. The melon colors in the sky at dawn and dusk. The vast expanse of clear air, unobstructed to the horizon by nothing but gracefully swooping power lines, the great variety of rock formations and their deep purple shadows, the pungent whiff of creosote plants as we brushed by them, and, occasionally, the fluttering call of a bird.

Instead of standing in a bathroom staring at a rumpled face in the mirror, I brushed my teeth while scanning the scarlet hills in the crisp morning air. Twenty years later I would add a bathroom to my Capitola cottage, and instead of a mirror over the basin, I told the contractor to install a window facing east.

On The March, I learned how much I enjoyed living outside. I loved to sprawl over the breast of Mother Earth and listen to her heart. Or was it my own thudding so happily? But, even in my glee, I was constantly aware of the fragility of our earth, of life itself. I looked out at the mountains gleaming in the clean, sun-filled air and imagined how they would look scorched after a nuclear bombing. A devastating image.

Part of my deepening appreciation for the surrounding beauty stemmed from being more comfortable with The March routine. Both Connie and I were now quicker at waking, washing, dressing, stuffing our sleeping bags, rolling up the pads, collapsing and stacking the tent. On my way to the porta-potty in the morning, I dropped off the sleeping bags and pads in a designated area. In line I would read, or listen to someone read, the notices posted on the exterior of the porta-potty doors, which served as bulletin boards. There might be a poem, a joke, notices of more meetings, the arrival of a guest speaker, a petition, and a farewell letter. On the inside of one door:

> Porta-Potty Poets come here not to sit and think.
> (I bet you're sure I'm going to end this line with stink.)
> No. We sit for inspiration. For our goal, you see,
> Is to attain salvation, to emulate Gandhi.
> Mahatma was a lawyer, a statesman, and a seer.
> Yet the mean, lowest toilet-bowl cleaner was his peer.
> So be a great soul like Gandhi—hey, Tom, Sue and Gus!
> Join Porta-Potty Poets: come clean this john with us.

I'd return to the tent, pick up the stuff-bag of clothes and personal gear and push it into my labeled green plastic crate in the huge truck-trailer. Connie took our rosy dome domicile to the mound of Red Town tents so later it could be loaded into a trailer. Then we'd stand in the breakfast line.

First, we got a place, then turned to the person behind to ask, "Will you save my place? Want some fruit?" and walked over to a table for a banana, orange or apple, and later in the season, watermelon, grapes, sometimes very ripe figs or berries. Then we'd check back into the saved place, give away fruit, and proceed to the trash can to peel and eat the orange. We'd re-evaluate the line. Had it moved? Probably enough time to go to the hot-water spigot, fill my orange plastic cup, come back into line, drink half the warm water and use the rest to wash the sticky orange juice off my hands. By then it was time to reach up to the serving window to receive the warm oatmeal. I hadn't eaten oatmeal since my sons were small, or more likely, since I myself was small. The March oatmeal had raisins and cinnamon and sometimes other grains that gave it excellent texture. I added honey. With a cup of tea and some whole-wheat bread, it was a nourishing meal. We stood to eat or, if the ground was dry, we sat down. On rainy days, we ate quickly to avoid too much rainwater in our cereal bowls. After scraping our bowls, we dropped them into tubs of sudsy water, stuffed an orange into one pocket, and took our toothbrush out of another. All this among several hundred people who smiled, called out "Good Morning!" and hugged each other. There was no jostling or crowding. The same consideration and courtesy that Connie and I had observed at the very first campsite north of Los Angeles.

The day had begun at 6:30. The marchers assembled behind the flags—the American flag, the California state flag, the United Nations flag, and one, blue and white, connoting world unity, handmade by Dwarka Bonner, a leader of the kitchen crew. We loaded our daypacks with extra socks, fruit, sunscreen, lip salve, a compacted role of toilet paper, camera, windbreaker, and a quart of water. I carried a small notebook and pen to record events and thoughts that I'd later use for the articles I would write for the *San Mateo Times*. Laura Johnson strode through the campsite, looking much as she might have during her earlier career as a dude-ranch trail-ride leader. With her bull horn, she called out, "The March is leaving in 10 minutes. Meet at the flags. Nice day for a walk. Let's go!" She led the column of marchers as we headed out of camp and on down the road, facing the sun. I spread my arms wide to celebrate the clean, bright day.

Laura and three others took turns, not only leading the walk itself, but going over the route the day before and consulting in advance with the sheriff and police or state patrol. These conversations with the officials softened their initial caution and ultimately led to letters of recommendation that Laura could then present to other law officers as The March proceeded across the country.

We walked four miles in a little over an hour, then took a 20-minute break to use the porta-potties, eat some fruit, fill our water bottles from a tank tethered to the porta-potty trailer, and then we walked another four miles. Then another. Before 1 o'clock a truck came to deliver our lunches. I never would have thought I'd get so much pleasure out of the type of food we had for lunch: a section of cold cooked acorn squash, a chunk of jicama, a peanut-butter sandwich, a couple of carrots and a cold baked potato, followed by an assortment of granola, dates, prunes, dried papaya and peanuts in a baggie for dessert. All washed down with water, lots of water. We drank several quarts a day.

We ate in small groups sitting on the ground a little way off the road. Then I'd wad my daypack behind my head, tip backward and fall asleep. I felt contented and safe as I lay in the lap of Mother Earth and took a little nap. I'd hear the hum of voices around me, then oblivion, and in no time, felt a tap on my leg, "Come on, Donna, we're going. Only 10 miles left." I'd get a hand up and be off again. Our walks were long because we needed to make up time lost at Stoddard Wells Road and in Barstow. I didn't care. For me, the best days on The March were those when all I had to do was walk.

I had never lived among women. Girls, yes, at school, but not full-blown grown women. My mother was a private person. I had three brothers and four sons. On The March I learned a lot as we women walked and talked together. Some talked about their academic lives, scholarships that had made college possible. Some talked about their grandchildren, their own gentle childhoods. I was familiar with those kinds of stories. But others told stories of another type altogether: lost children, incest and molestation, rape, brutality, a brother in jail, an alcoholic father or mother. I'd only read such stories before, and they were about people I didn't know. On The March I was surrounded by new friends, many of whom had endured brutal childhoods. I ached for them and bristled at the unfairness of it all. Children should not have to suffer so. And I could see firsthand how the effects of abuse persist long after childhood ends.

Sometimes, if a woman wished, a group of us would meet in the afternoon, after the day's walk, to see if we could help, if only to be present and listen or stand together in a quiet group hug. Connie was part of the mental health team so she volunteered to listen and suggest. At night I wrote in my journal, stared up at the stars and wept with humility and gratitude for my good life.

On the BLM land at the California-Nevada border, we took three scheduled rest days, April 4-7. Lured by the opportunity to shower away accumulated dust and take advantage of inexpensive meals, several marchers took rooms at Whiskey Pete's. Others walked over to play the slot machines. I found a table in a cool, clean corner in the casino where I could type my bi-weekly article for my hometown paper. Earlier in The March, when we had camped in the desert near Yermo, I had sat in the tent to write, but a sandstorm came up. I weighted down our tent, as it violently vibrated. Some tents blew loose from their pegs and careened off across the desert. Dust and sand blew through the mesh skylight of our rosy dome threatening to ruin my word processor, so I'd closed it and waited for another more opportune time. Other days when rain came, grit turned to mud, and I couldn't find room in the crowded media bus to write. I was much happier typing away on my Brother word processor in Whiskey Pete's.

During our three rest days, the maintenance crew didn't rest. They repaired the truck-cab. These men were marchers who worked seven very long days every week to keep our support vehicles running. They had no rest days, no walk days, just work days. All major vehicles—the buses, vans, truck-cabs, recycled mail truck—were at least 12 years old. One was 57, only a year younger than I was! The maintenance bus was an old Los Angeles urban transit coach, donated by the Ford dealer in Barstow. Prior to The March, it had not run for two years; the crew took it apart, rebuilt the engine, and turned it into their workshop. It lasted for the entire March.

Six weeks had passed since I'd left home and my hair was getting shaggy. Before I left in early February, my hairdresser, Ted, had promised to meet The March in Las Vegas if I would pay his flight or line up several clients for him. Ted had cut my hair for 20 years, and during that time, I had never trusted anyone else. Even though on recent days we had walked 17 to 22 miles, The March was still three weeks behind schedule. I wasn't sure when we would arrive in Las Vegas, so I found a phone at Whiskey Pete's and dialed Ted's number.

"I'm really sorry, Ted, but I can't figure out exactly when we'll be in Las Vegas, so I can't invite you to come cut my hair." He expressed his disappointment, and I told him, "You can't be any more disappointed than I am. I don't know what I'll do."

Connie and I had learned to collect two cups of very hot water from a spigot in the side of the kitchen trailer. We found a small bucket and mixed the hot with cool water. With short hair, we could get a pretty good lather if we were careful. We rinsed with cold water. Connie fluffed her cap of curls with her hands. I'd take my hair brush and stand under the generator of the cold-food-storage trailer that exhaled warm air. Practically a real hair dryer!

One day I recognized a marcher from Southern California with whom I had previously walked. She was now standing up on a flat-bed truck, someone in front of her sitting on a folding chair holding a paper grocery bag. I recalled that she was a hair stylist and realized she was giving a haircut! To protect the campsite from wads of floating human hair, each snip was dropped into the bag. The woman had brought her scissors and was offering free haircuts. I stood in line. Other than Ted, she was the first person in a long time to cut my hair, and she did a good job. I realized there are capable hairdressers other than Ted. And I loved the vision of me sitting out on a flat-bed truck dropping snippets of hair into the brown paper bag. So different from the mirrors, glass and stainless steel tables, and slick black leather chairs in Ted's salon. I could hear the birds singing and watch shadows on the mountains.

During the year I had been preparing for The March, I stopped coloring my hair. No longer a brunette (Loving Care, Dark Warm Brown, No. 57), I quickly became salt and pepper, with more salt than pepper. I wondered if going grey would make me feel older. It didn't. And I didn't have to fuss with coloring it. My image changed, but no matter; with short hair, I felt natural and tidy.

There was no way our clothes could look sharp and crisp; our personal outlines had become softened. But getting a good haircut helped me feel presentable. Combine that with a "PTA," and I felt comfortable enough to accept invitations to give talks and presentations to any church or civic meeting.

PTA was a coarse March acronym that stood for pits, tits and ass that I learned from Ann Edelman. Not the phrase. Ann was a gentle woman who played the cello in a string quartet back home and wrote passionate March articles for the *LA Weekly*. No, Ann taught me that with a cup of water and a washcloth, I could stand in the privacy of a porta-potty, put down the lid so I wouldn't lose the soap down the hole, and wash myself. It worked pretty well. When I explained it to someone else, she said, "Oh, you mean a PTA!"

Special-interest groups were forming. One, a Shakespeare discussion group that met once a week, was inspired by Gene Gordon, who in January had led the small walking group on a drizzly Sunday in San Jose. Gene walked most days, rain or shine, pleasant or stormy, with Rhoda, a carpenter from Seattle. And as they walked together, they read Shakespeare to each other. On rainy days they protected their books with plastic baggies, on windy days, by clutching them tightly. During rest days, they found a tree and sat beneath it to read aloud. With others, they completed all 37 plays. That is about one for every 100 miles of The March.

Several groups of musicians wrote and performed Great Peace March songs. One group, comprised entirely of women, sang out, "We don't care how big your missile is."

Guest speakers, including Daniel Ellsberg, Joanna Macy, and survivors of the 1945 bombings of Nagasaki and Hiroshima occasionally spoke in the late afternoons. One of our Town Hall tents was packed the rainy night legendary folk singer Pete Seeger appeared. We sang along with him and his banjo and knew he believed in us and our mission.

Nonstop meetings continued. Decisions about entrance and exit standards and procedures were still needed. Elections were held almost daily. Changes in administration were endemic, and still The March held on. While the Peace City Council was in session about 11 o'clock one night, a man in a Stetson hat and fancy cowboy boots appeared, carrying rubber-banded bundles of money, each containing $18. As he walked through camp, he gave a packet to each marcher he saw. Someone brought a gallon-size mayonnaise jar from the kitchen and asked everyone to contribute from their windfall to benefit The March. When counted, the jar held $18,000, enough to buy a second truck-cab. The man explained he'd been lucky in gambling, had heard about our desperate need for funds, and had come to our camp. In Hebrew, the symbol 18 means new life. He had injected new life into The March.

Camp at California State Line near Whiskey Pete's.

CHAPTER 8

California! Nevada!

After three rest days on BLM land at the eastern edge of California, we prepared to cross into Nevada. With a stick, marchers drew a line in the dust where we imagined the border to be and lined up shoulder-to-shoulder or crowded close behind. We waited—silent, poised, weight on the forward foot. Led by Laura and her bullhorn, we shouted out in unison, "California! Nevada!" and stepped across. The kitchen crew brought out a huge carrot cake in the shape of California to give to the patrol officers who had been with The March all the way from Barstow. Several of us gave speeches of thanks for their help and support. This ceremony would be repeated 15 times as we crossed from one state into the next. On November 15, when we reached our final destination, we would shout, "California! Nevada! Utah! Colorado! Nebraska! Iowa! Illinois! Indiana! Ohio! Pennsylvania! New Jersey! New York! Maryland! Delaware! Washington, DC!"

Five days after crossing our first border, we would be in Las Vegas. Marchers looked forward to Las Vegas, some with the illusion that "big money will be there, and we'll get some major contributions." Big-talking promoters had promised rock concerts and other fund-raising events. These didn't materialize. Actor Robert Blake also fell short of his fund-raising promise, but he did garner media attention for us. The nation learned that The March was on the road to stay. That, in the vernacular, was a step forward.

In spite of financial worries, I felt buoyant that we had come this far, that we had surmounted obstacles and were still on our feet. I found a phone to call Mother. She sounded happy that I was fine and added, "Oh, Las Vegas. Your father and I liked that bright little town in the desert… but I suppose it has changed since we were there in the 1940s."

She was so right. My friends and I were drab compared to the miles of bright lights and clusters of glamorous people who populated The Strip. I couldn't help comparing the glitzy image of Las Vegas and the earnest passionate reality of The March. While Las Vegas seemed pretend, we marchers faced fundamental reality. Food didn't appear as if by magic, although I sometimes thought the kitchen crew were magicians to prepare so many meals for so many people. We had to deal with porta-potties. We were directly affected by the weather outside, not hidden from it by the turreted tops of glittering buildings with the clatter and clang of slot machines. We confronted our personal strengths and dependencies. Every day. We could not distract ourselves from our responsibilities, from possible nuclear annihilation. I thought this as Mother reminisced about her trip to Las Vegas.

On a local television station, a well-intentioned marcher asked locals to offer Marcher in the Home hospitality. People responded. There were more willing hosts than marchers. We went happily, looking forward to showers and hot meals in a home, as well as opportunities to talk about The March mission. Four of us women were invited by a pleasant middle-aged man and his immaculate wife, both in pristine polyester, who drove us to their home: a double-wide mobile-home complete with plastic flowers in plastic pots decorating the entryway. A short white plastic fence draped with plastic vines surrounded an Astroturf lawn. Plastic dwarves stood around on the turf. We had our choice of three Herculon hide-a-beds.

For dinner they served us Kentucky Fried Chicken and all the trimmings, mashed potatoes and quarts of gravy, biscuits and honey, coleslaw—served in the red-and-white paper tubs from the takeout place and eaten from plastic plates. Dessert was a frozen cherry pie. It all tasted wonderful. Our hosts were genial and kind. They had difficulty grasping our lifestyle or mission, but listened anyway. They couldn't imagine our diet of rice, vegetables and salads. I loved the homogenous quality, the consistency of their lifestyle. It was perfect Las Vegas. The house was immaculate, clear plastic sheeting on the sofa, and they offered us their best. I loved them and added their address to my little green book so I could send a postcard from Washington, DC.

Other marchers did not fare so well. One male host attempted to rape a woman marcher. Another, who turned out to be a dope dealer, threatened his male guests with a pistol. After this, Marcher in the Home planners were more cautious and made sure there were at least two of us in each home. Records were kept of who went where and with whom. From then on, we found our hosts through churches and other organizations that could vouch for people who offered overnight home stays. MITH was a way citizens could be a vital and intimate part of The March. They were involved, and that was exactly what The March was all about.

The media jobs also integrated locals with The March. Shelah Notkoff and I went together on Tuesday and Thursday mornings. At first we had hitched rides from other marchers who were driving into town on errands. When The March stalled in Barstow, Shelah went back to Los Angeles to get her car because she felt more secure knowing it was close by, and because she and I could use it to do our advance work. Others used her car, also. After the day's marchers left, sometimes a hundred people stayed behind to clean up the campsite and do the countless jobs that kept it all going. Many of these jobs required cars. Routes & Sites, for example, went ahead to scout the territory. Dick Edelman had his car because he was a doctor. During our days in the desert, there were few towns, so Shelah and I could only call in the press releases. Later, we'd find many small towns where we'd do our work, meet the folks, learn about their towns, and share perceptions of The Peace March.

Bad weather days didn't stop us.

CHAPTER 9

You Can't Come In

By now, I loved to walk through a town, raise my hand with the peace sign and shout, "Good Morning to you! Peace!" In Las Vegas, on April 12, 435 of us buoyantly paraded down the Las Vegas strip, and I thought about the many times in my life when I had stood on the curb, so to speak, and watched life flow by. I thought I was, by nature, not a strong leader, but an enthusiastic follower. I didn't carry the flags at the front of The March, but remembered my son Sam's advice and stayed in the middle. Feeling an integral part of something important, I raised both hands, looked up to the sky, and whispered, "Thank you, God. Thank you for sending Connie to tell me about this walk." I nearly stumbled over a rough patch in the street, came back down to earth and decided I'd better watch where I was going. In more ways than one. I didn't want to miss anything or stumble on this long journey to myself.

Local folks and marchers had time to meet each other. Hundreds came to our campsite just outside of town to share a potluck dinner, which raised $3,000 in donations. Actor Paul Newman contributed $25,000. Marcher in the Home offered additional opportunity for conversation between marchers and residents. Many of us spoke in churches to explain our mission.

Meanwhile, the Utah State Police announced we were not welcome. They told us, "The March will be barred at the border by the National Guard. You will be bused across the state because I-70, the proposed route, is narrow, without water, and parts of it are under reconstruction. It's too dangerous," the police said. "We'd just have to come rescue you, so you can't walk across Utah."

Marcher Bob Goss and several others from Salt Lake City drove to their home town to see church elders and government officials. Six more days we camped, mostly on BLM lands in the southern Nevada desert, fragrant with sage and sand. We continued to walk while we waited—that is all except the 40 children and their parents who didn't want to risk exposure to radiation from the power lines or from nuclear testing at the site north of Las Vegas. We had read the National Cancer Institute's report that "90 atmospheric tests at the Nevada Test Site deposited high levels of radioactive iodine-131 across a large portion of the contiguous United States, especially in the 1950s—doses large enough, they determined, to produce 10,000 to 75,000 cases of thyroid cancer." A significant excess of leukemia deaths occurred in children up to 14 years of age living in Utah between 1959 and 1967. That had been almost 20 years ago, but the Department of Energy was still testing. The March children and their mothers were hastily driven to Zion National Park to wait until they could rejoin the group when we were beyond the downwind threats. Past St. George. In Utah. If we were allowed to walk through Utah. Not bused.

April 20 brought The March to the Nevada-Arizona Border and our first time zone change. "California! Nevada! Arizona!" we sang out and shared another cake, this one with the Nevada Highway Patrol. This cake more square in shape than the elongated California cake we'd had weeks ago. We camped that night near Littlefield, our only night in Arizona.

The Salt Lake City marchers returned with exciting news. They had reached a compromise. We would be allowed to walk along the shoulder of a secondary road that paralleled I-70, except for that stretch in eastern Utah deemed too dangerous. The leaders in Utah had changed from a position of total distrust and had asked, "How exactly may we help you?"

We crossed the Arizona-Utah border, and no National Guard

troops stopped us. "California! Nevada! Arizona! Utah!"

Our first night in the Beehive State, the Shivwits Paiute Indians welcomed us onto their reservation and cooked dinner for us over an open fire. I watched a man dig ash-laden baked potatoes from the fire pit and salivated. I felt like Pavlov's dogs when the bell rang. Our kitchen staff prepared salad and a stew to share. Among the cottonwood trees we contentedly shared an evening of food, music and drumming. Peace March musicians brought out their instruments. Several marchers had guitars. Some had small drums. Others had primitive rhythm-band instruments made of gravel in soda pop cans, a hubcap and stick, rocks in bottles, or just two hand-held rocks to strike against each other. It was a musical experience we could all share. We lounged on the ground around the fire under the stars, hundreds of us, Paiute Indians and Peace Marchers and felt in harmony with each other. I felt a great affection for our hosts who, without much material wealth, but with hospitable hearts, shared what they had.

In the Sunday *Deseret News* of Salt Lake City, author and naturalist Terry Tempest Williams wrote:

> *Eudora Welty, one of America's most distinguished women of letters, when asked what causes she would support, replied, "Peace, education, conservation and quiet."*
>
> *The Great Peace March moving through Utah this week honors these concerns. I spent time with these marchers and was not prepared for what I found.*
>
> *Last weekend, my mother, my grandparents and I were in St. George. We sought peace of a different sort. Solitude. Tuesday morning we sat on the porch eating breakfast with gentle conversation. We knew The Peace March was to arrive that day and spoke of it. All at once, my mother stood and pointed, "There they are!" We turned to see what appeared as a slow-moving river; hundreds of people walking on behalf of nuclear disarmament.*
>
> *Up the hill toward the Green Valley Resort they walked, carrying their banner of peace. One by one they walked by us with dignity, with honor and purpose.*

These were familiar faces, not radical characters draped in dissidence, but common folks—mainstream Americans exercising their freedom. Never had I seen such an assemblage of compassionate intelligence and commitment. It was a generational gesture with children and grandparents marching on.

My mother, grandmother and I clapped as they went by. From the looks on their faces, you would have thought we were throngs of supporters. After the last marcher had disappeared, we held each other, knowing that they marched for all of us.

Later, Williams spoke with marchers, called them eloquent, brave, inspired, and wrote:

Seeds planted grow into trees. Ideals nurtured by courageous souls foster social change. It begins slowly. Someone has to believe in small beginnings. Peace in the name of gesture is hope. And hope flourishes in the reverence for life.

Can one small group proclaiming peace as they walk across America impact the conscience of a country?

As my mother and grandparents listened to these people sing, we were changed. We were changed because suddenly, peace was no longer an abstraction, but the right of all living things.

In the name of a world as delicate and strong as spider's silk, these people walk for all of us.

A day's walk brought us to a well-earned rest day in the Green Valley Resort near St. George. They invited us to enjoy the swimming pools, jacuzzis, tennis courts and showers, and served us a poolside breakfast of individually prepared omelets. The townspeople of St. George were friendly, too. Several dozen accepted our invitation to visit the camp, to meet us, and listen to March musicians perform original peace songs. At the same time, two representatives of the Environmental Protection Agency visited to try to explain away the effect of nuclear testing upon the residents of southern Utah.

Marchers were perplexed by contradictory evidence. The incidence of cancer in the St. George area was 70 percent higher than in other parts of the United States. A new wing for cancer patients was being built onto the hospital at St. George, yet the EPA representatives insisted, "There are no observable harmful effects from the underground nuclear testing." However, on days that the wind blew toward populated areas, testing was postponed. And why the new federally funded cancer wing on the hospital? I felt betrayed and insulted by our government. Did they think we were stupid? My anger was matched by everyone on The March. We knew that during the 1972-1986 Nuclear Test Ban, the USSR withdrew or dismantled 1,324 strategic nuclear missiles and 21 nuclear-missile-carrying submarines. The USA had dismantled 896 missiles and 11 submarines. The United States had continued to test. The disturbing news that the Nevada Nuclear Test Site had scheduled yet another detonation caused one of us to suggest that we, in protest, furl our American flag. Although we were sad and frustrated, the flag continued to wave at the entrance to our campsites and at the head of the column of walkers. The flag was the symbol of our country, The Great Peace March for Global Nuclear Disarmament was our protest.

Upon hearing the news of the compromise that the officials had offered about walking only part way in Utah, the purists among us countered that a march should be marched, not bused. They asked that a symbolic 10 people be allowed to preserve the integrity and spirit of The March by continuing the walk along I-70. Utah denied this request.

However, 50 marchers were granted permission to walk along an alternate route. They would walk 200 miles through Bryce Canyon, Dixieland National Forest, and Capitol Reef. With the sanction of The March and the support of the Utah State Police, they would walk as private citizens having, for insurance reasons, no official connection with The March. With support vehicles carrying food supplies and tents, this small group planned to average 25 miles a day and rejoin the main body of marchers in Grand Junction, Colorado, 19 days later. They became known as The Spirit Walkers.

Connie had volunteered to be one of them. "You'll need to find a new tent-mate for the next few weeks." She said. "I know the Spirit

Walk will be really hard. Cold. There's snow. But I'm going. You and the other marchers can bus to Salt Lake City and stay with local families. That should be a big chance for outreach." We hugged each other. "See you in Colorado!"

The rest of us were bused from the little town of Beaver to a rally on the capital grounds. Over a thousand people joined hands and sang, "We Are the World." Representatives of state government, the Mormon Church, and Utah peace groups welcomed us. During the next three days, marchers spoke in schools, churches, temples and civic groups. One-hundred-fifty were in the studio for the weekly radio broadcast of the Mormon Tabernacle Choir.

MITH arranged for Salt Lake City hosts to meet marchers. Noemi and Daniel Mattis, a couple whose children had grown and left a houseful of empty bedrooms, chose six of us: my friends from Los Angeles, Ann and Dick Edelman; Billy Leib, a Korean War veteran from Los Angeles, and Billy's partner, Jonnie Zheutlin, a psychotherapist; my media staff-mate Shelah Notkoff, and me. Noemi was a clinical psychologist and Daniel a physicist at the University of Utah; both were avid collectors of contemporary art. A rubber inflated version of Edvard Munch's "The Scream" stood like Bozo the Clown at the entrance to the dining room.

In preparation for hosting marchers in their home, Noemi had bought 30 kinds of dry breakfast cereal. I recall our first morning there—a row of cereal boxes, lined up like books, down the center of the table. There was milk, yogurt, bananas, strawberries, juice, coffee, everything! I had never seen such a variety of boxed cereals, not even during the days when my ravenous sons burst into the house for after-school snacks and reached for the dry cereals.

In Noemi and Daniel's breakfast room, we sat in mauve leather chairs at a chrome and beveled glass table, surrounded by art, and ate cereal and fruit from Dansk bowls. I recalled weekend visits we high school students took to each other's homes when we were boarders at St. Helen's Hall in Portland, Oregon. We girls often said that the best thing we learned while attending St. Helen's Hall was how to be a houseguest and about the small towns we escaped to on weekends. "It's sort of like that here, now, with MITH," I said. "We're learning about the towns and families when we are houseguests. A nice way to travel." We weathered marchers were showered, fed, bedded and protected. We were treated to an aesthetic experience, too, one which fed our art-deprived souls. It's hard to hang art on the sides of a domed tent. I hadn't realized how I missed doorknobs and walls—and pictures. Although major Peace March art was painted across the sky in sunrises, sunsets and in nighttime sparkles, sometimes I longed for the familiar confines of home and hearth.

That day Billy Leib and I were scheduled to speak about The Peace March to a class of fourth graders at St. Vincent Grammar School. The moment I entered the room, I was intoxicated by the fragrance of paper, of chalk dust, of warm nine-year-old bodies. Although I had been working with children in one capacity or another for more than 40 years, I had not been in a classroom since 1974, more than 12 years earlier. Billy gave his presentation. Then I stood in the front of the room, and, chalk in hand, surveyed those bright faces. "What do you think you could do to promote peace?" Hands shot up.

"We can pray," one said. I saw Sister Cabrini smile as I wrote it on the board.

"I could be nicer to my little brother."

"Right," I said and wrote it on the board.

"I offer to help my grandmother."

"I told Mom I would feed Shadow every Saturday, and she doesn't need to remind me."

Others suggested making posters, encouraging their parents to vote for peace-makers, giving money to The Great Peace March, having pen pals around the world.

"Those are good ideas," I said. "What would happen to you if there were a Nuclear War?"

They had answers. One serious little boy said, "If we are blasted, I will die and when I do, I will miss myself."

What was I doing? I was asking nine-year-olds to save the world, and I was out there taking a stroll across America. I had joined The March because it was a fine opportunity to see our country. I had thought it would be my own Outward Bound. An adventure. A unique walk. I wanted to have my picture on the front of *Time* magazine, to set up my tent in Central Park. That's how superficial I had been about The Peace March.

I didn't have to plan meals. People offered showers and others took my laundry with theirs to the laundromat. I didn't even have my own tent. I looked at those shiny trusting faces in the classroom and vowed I'd do all in my power to join them in saving the world from Nuclear War. I had walked into that class room a happy walker; I walked out a dedicated Peace Marcher.

Ann Edelman was on the Education and Outreach Task Force, so when we met at the end of the afternoon back at Noemi and Daniel Mattis' house, I told her, "Put me on your list. I'll speak whenever you need anyone: civic groups, church groups, school groups. I'm available."

She told me about the speaker training meetings held each afternoon at 4 o'clock in an old bus that housed the Peace Academy. "It's the heart of our outreach efforts," Ann explained. "In the training sessions, we give Beyond War lectures, show film documentaries, and share printed information." It was a place where we made day-to-day speaking engagement plans.

"I don't know how I can learn all that new information," I said.

Ann replied, "Just remember what Peace Pilgrim said. 'It's not more knowledge we need, it's just the practice of it.' You'll do fine. We'll prepare you to sell our dream."

I hugged her and promised, "When we get back on The March, I'll be there whenever I can."

That evening our hosts invited the six of us to a musical performance, a string quartet, at the University of Utah. We were introduced to the audience as special guests. At the reception for the musicians afterward, I was standing at the refreshment table, trying to decide which cookie to take, when a man's voice at my shoulder asked, "Well, do you think it'll do any good, your Great Peace March?"

I chose a chocolate chip with walnuts and turned to him. He looked exactly like a professor: tweedy, at ease, glasses on top of his head. "Yes. Don't you?" I asked.

"No, not really, but I admire your dedication."

"Well, I *have* to believe or I couldn't be doing all that we're doing." I almost chuckled at my own statement. I recognized in myself the zeal of a new convert. "One thing I know that I am learning on this March is to not take things for granted." I said. "I no longer take for granted warm water, dry socks, shampoo, menu variety, prompt mail delivery and conveniently located telephones. People must work diligently to provide those. And that's true for our earth, too."

I was on my soapbox now. "When we no longer take our earth for granted, and when we each assume responsibility for its health, then we will all be involved. We all must work, in any way we can, to preserve life on this earth." I took a bite of cookie and chewed. "If our March will touch you to do for peace just two percent more next week than you did last week, we will have succeeded."

His expression shifted subtly. "I rather wish I could go with you. It sounds like fun. Important, and fun, too." I looked at him a moment. Did my heart lurch a little? He seemed such a nice man. Intelligent. Well-spoken. He'd be great... on The Peace March. "I wish you could come. But if you can't, there are things you can do in your daily life here that will help."

"Yes, like what?"

I explained how he could write to his congressman, telephone the White House, join a local peace group, become a more informed voter. I mentioned some of the many small ways people could foster peace in their daily lives, for instance, being nicer to the checkout person in the grocery line. "You could be aware that each of us, in our daily behavior, can contribute to world peace. A lot of it is attitude." I told him about the fourth graders I'd met that morning.

"Alright. You've touched me," he said. "I can do that. And I'll tell my students. But how do I call the White House?"

"The phone number is 202-456-7639. You can call any time. A real person will answer and tally your comments and concerns." Not hesitating, I asked, "You say you have students? How many students do you have?"

"In the philosophy classes, I have 300. More in the seminars."

There! A woman. A man. A cookie. And more than 300 people to be affected by The Peace March. As we returned to the Mattis' home, stars fell out of the sky and sparkled across the basin of Salt Lake City. Angels laughing.

Back at the house, I told Shelah. She listened, smiled, and then asked, "Would you like to tent with me while Connie is gone?" Of course I would. I didn't know what prompted her to ask me, but I didn't care. I liked working with Shelah, and I was certain we'd be good tent-mates.

The March wasn't through Utah quite yet. Joe Broido, a middle-aged Harvard economics graduate who lived in Los Angeles, had long dreamed of celebrating a wilderness Passover Seder in the desert north of St. George. On April 24, his dream came true. The Los Angeles Jewish community contributed money for the food, which was prepared in Las Vegas and then transported to us in the desert. The ceremonial matzo was made by the children of The March. Rabbi Mel Hecht of Temple Beth Am in Las Vegas conducted the service at sunset. We who attended were inspired by Rabbi Hecht's comments as he drew comparisons between the ancient Jews in the desert to us in the desert. I felt as though for the first time, I understood a little of the life that had endured for centuries at the far end of the Mediterranean. Life in dust, living in tents on the ground, close to the earth and its rhythms. A nomadic existence unburdened by material excess. I was a long way from my home, with its Wallace sterling "Rose Point" place settings on a walnut table in a dining room with pale flocked wallpaper and oil paintings.

A bright-faced youngster looked at the Wasatch Range and said, "I like Utah. The have painted their mountains to match our tents."

One day in eastern Utah, Dave Miller, a big, red-haired man from Pismo Beach, California, and I walked together. We already knew each other because the two of us were always trying to find a dry warm place to write feature stories for our hometown papers. I told him of my conversion from casual tourist-walker to passionate Peace Marcher. He told me, as Ann had, about the Peace Academy office.

"It's in a good second-hand bus I found in Las Vegas. Its price had been $4,500, which was way more than I could afford. The owner invited me to 'make an offer I can't refuse.' He listened to me explain about The March and how the vehicle would be used."

"How about $1,500?" Dave had asked.

"It's yours."

By the time we reached the Utah-Colorado border, we had made up for 12 of the days lost on Stoddard Wells Road and in Barstow. If we continued at this rate, if we walked long days, we should arrive in Denver right on schedule.

Shelah Notkoff in Colorado.

CHAPTER 10

I Can See the Rockies From Here

Trees and Keys grew into an important facet of the Peace March. In Cedar City, Utah, Mayor Robert Linford gave us the key to his city during a rally in a local park. Our Peace City mayor, Diane Clark, accepted it on behalf of the marchers. She wanted to create a ceremonial exchange, so at the next town, she reciprocated and gave the mayor a key to Peace City, a 10-inch key carved by one of the men in the Maintenance Department from a slab of redwood he happened to have. Imka Bonner, with her bright earnestness and charming German accent, found a nursery that contributed a small tree to plant in a park. Shelah and I helped with the ceremony.

On Tuesdays and Thursdays, the days we didn't walk because we worked, Shelah and I wakened a little later than usual to the symphony of zippers zipping and Velcro ripping. As others were preparing to walk, we picked up our notepads and found Mayor Diane to see what she needed us to do. Diane had the exuberance of the nursery school teacher she had once been. She had won the mayor's position after she started the trash patrol along the routes we walked. She had set the example by collecting metal cans and glass bottles to recycle, as well as stuffing roadside garbage into plastic bags to be taken to a dump. Dubbed the Litter Lady, she was organized and colorful, animated and always recognizable by her perky red hat. Often she asked Shelah and me to find the mayors of the next three towns, set up Keys and Trees Ceremonies, and let the Chamber of Commerce know about The Peace March's arrival.

Shelah and I also checked with director of March media, Chris Ball, to collect the press releases that we were to telephone to several national newspapers, as well as to local radio and TV stations along our route. Before we left camp, we stopped by the Routes and Sites office to pick up a map of the area. Anyone who needed to go to the laundromat that day might hitch a ride with us, and usually they would do our laundry as well as theirs. At a table in the clean, dry laundromat, they also wrote invitations to groups to visit upcoming March campsites.

We'd drive to the next town, drop off our passengers at the laundromat, then cruise the main street until we recognized the coffee shop where the locals hung out. We did some of our best outreach in cafes. I was conducting my personal Belgian waffle survey, so I often ordered that along with bacon and hash browns. People at the next table, perhaps downtown business men lingering over coffee, would lean over toward us. "You some of them Peace Marchers we heard were comin' through town?" And we had our opening.

"Yes, we are. What a nice town you have here. Is one of you, by any chance, the mayor?"

"Ah, no. That'd be Charlie down the street. At the Ford Motor Sales. He's the man you want to see."

Shelah and I chatted for a while, gave them some printed materials, and asked them to greet the marchers when we all arrived tomorrow or the next day or, better yet, come on out to the campsite to see us. As we walked down the street, we stopped in the bakeries, the pie shops, the Dairy Queens to alert the owners. "Peace March will be here this week. Better make extra pies, get more magic powder, (the powder Dairy Queens used to make their soft ice cream), stock up on everything. We are a hungry lot." We'd find the Chamber of Commerce, announce our impending arrival and ask for printed literature about the local area so we could pass it along the column. Marchers could read it as we walked. That way we'd learn about each new area we were trying to save from nuclear destruction.

Eventually we'd find Charlie the Mayor sitting at his desk. Maybe reading the newspaper. Maybe a little bit bored. He'd stand up as we entered, shake our hands and invite us to be seated. Everywhere we went, Shelah and I were treated with kindness and respect. We explained that several hundred marchers would be coming to town, told him where we would be camped, invited him and all townspeople to come out to visit the campsite and hear what we were about. Then we explained the Keys and Trees Ceremony.

In each town where we stayed, we planted a peace tree, contributed by someone local. Imka usually found a tree at a local nursery, a grocery store or a college botanical garden. If she had not, we asked the mayor. "Where would you like the tree planted?" we'd ask. "Is there a park or school ground that would be appropriate?"

Charlie the Mayor always liked this idea. The tree planted in his town would be one of a linear forest of peace trees planted 15 to 20 miles apart across the nation. He'd offer to call his brother-in-law who worked in the local nursery. "Hey, Ned. I got a couple a Peace March ladies here who need a tree and want you to meet us for the peace-tree planting and keys-to-the-cities exchange."

Then he would turn to us and nod. "All set."

"Now," he asked, "what else can I do for you?"

Shelah and I explained that we needed phones to call in the press releases and that we had phone cards. He said, "Hell, use ours! We're going out to lunch in a little while, you can use our phones while we're out. Make yourself at home."

He might pause a moment, shift in his chair, and lean a little forward. "You know, ladies," he sometimes said, "my wife would sure like to meet you. Would you have time to come up to the house for a little while? She'd love to talk with you. Her sister's visiting today. They'd both enjoy meeting you."

Of course, we'd go. We'd follow him home. There, we'd meet his wife, sometimes the neighbors, or her sister, and talk about the importance of global nuclear disarmament and the experiences of walking, walking, walking. "How far each day? How many blisters? Where does the money come from? What could we do for you?"

We'd answer the questions and then ask, "Do you think we could use your shower? We have our towels and shampoo in the car."

"Why, of course! I'm sorry I didn't think to offer. You just help yourself."

After an hour, we'd be sure to get their address so we could send postcards as we progressed toward Washington. We'd exchange hugs and follow Charlie back to his office. We'd make phone calls while he and his staff went to lunch, probably at the coffee shop where we'd visited, then we'd collect the marchers in the laundromat, stop by the Dairy Queen for a soft ice cream cone—with sprinkles, and drive 15 miles to the next town. By dinnertime, we had met dozens of people, lined up several ceremonies, exchanged literature and felt we'd created some trust between small-town residents and marchers. Some of our best outreach was done not only in cafes and diners, but also at kitchen tables, in Dairy Queens and laundromats. At the end of the day, Shelah and I drove to the new campsite, found our Mayor Diane and gave her the details of the next few Keys and Trees ceremonies.

In the media bus, we'd file away our press releases we had called in that day. We often sat down with marchers who were clipping and photocopying local news articles about The March to make up press kits for reporters who came to our campsites looking for a story.

California! Nevada! Arizona! Utah! And on into Colorado. Three days' walk from the border we arrived in Grand Junction at the foot of the Rockies. I spoke with Ann Gibson, one of the members of a local peace group, Citizens' Action for Peace. With tears in her eyes, she told us, "I am thrilled that The Great Peace March is here. We are now part of something bigger, and I no longer feel isolated. The Peace March has the potential to really make a difference." I thought of the philosophy professor at the cookie table in Salt Lake City, who said, "I'll tell my classes."

We had enjoyed a home full of two- and three-dimensional art in culturally rich Salt Lake City. In Grand Junction, we again signed up for Marcher in the Home. Four of us women stayed with Jean and Joe Bisko. We walked across their porch and into their home. It was perfect Western Slope style: wide plank floors, comfortable rugged furniture, plaid blankets over the backs of chairs, wood fire in the stove. Dinner was real chicken with fresh mushrooms, asparagus grown along the creek out back and homegrown potatoes, mashed and served with Jean's own gravy. Jean was the ultimate homemaker. She quilted, canned apricots, baked bread, and planted the garden. She had left a glamorous life in Hollywood for the good life in Colorado. And Joe? He, of course, was a country and western singer. He had made most of his recordings in the 1950s and gave each of us an autographed tape of his most popular songs.

Five days later, in Glenwood Springs, we took a rest day. We soothed our aching muscles in the "world's largest hot springs pool." The pool was longer than a football field, and, for once, we 550 marchers were not overrunning a luxurious facility. Across the street from the pool was the grand 1893 Hotel Colorado. Shelah and I nipped in for a pot of tea. We asked if we could order any small tea treats—little sandwiches? A scone?

"Popcorn," said the friendly waitress.

Over tea, we learned that the teddy bear had been invented in this hotel. Teddy Roosevelt had returned from a bear hunt, discouraged that he hadn't shot one. The maids, in sympathy, sewed scraps of fabric together to shape a stuffed bear. The press heard of the charming gesture and dubbed the toy "Teddy Bear."

Not yet ready to pick up our laundry, Shelah and I searched for an ice cream shop. The Kellogg Family Ice Cream Parlor made gourmet ice cream. I enjoyed a triple chocolate and peppermint stick while we talked with the server about The Peace March. He invited the two of us home to meet his family and to stay to dinner. We had to get back to camp, but since that conversation, I have always appreciated natural, spontaneous hospitality and generosity.

Ever since Connie had gone on the Spirit Walk, I'd tented with Shelah, and we had fun, every day. One day she'd wakened, and before sitting up, exclaimed in an excited voice, "I really sleep so well here—on the ground, sometimes on a hillside, in this sleeping bag that needs to be washed. I grew up in Manhattan, you know. Never went camping. Hardly went walking in Central Park. My idea of outdoor activity was window shopping. Look at me now!" She'd often slip into her shoes and pull a jacket on over her pajamas, take our mugs and go to the kitchen trailer to fill them, hers with coffee, mine with hot water for tea. She'd be back almost before I was fully awake. Snuggled in our bags, cozy in our tent, we'd chatter and giggle before starting the day. Like girls playing house.

I asked her if she'd consider sharing her tent for the rest of The March. She approved that idea. "But what about Connie?" We both liked Connie and didn't want to hurt her feelings. She was serious and dedicated, but I often felt a little guilty around Connie, like I wasn't doing enough, not suffering enough. I laughed a lot more with Shelah. I had to think about this before deciding.

When the cold, exhausted, grumpy Spirit Walkers rejoined the main body of marchers in Glenwood Springs, I took big breaths to settle myself. I never have been good at confrontation. At the far edge of the campsite, I found Connie. She was sprawled spread-eagle, like the Da Vinci drawing of the man in the circle, across the floor of the tent looking tired and a little pale, but contented.

I asked, "Hi, how was the Spirit Walk?"

"It was exhausting, 20 to 30 miles a day."

"Yikes! That sounds really tough. Do you feel OK?"

"I have a cold." She paused. "I found out one thing, though. I liked tenting by myself. Could you and Shelah continue to share her tent?"

We could.

As we walked through the grand scenery of western Colorado, the dusty, dry, windy bleakness of the desert seemed a long way behind us. I loved the names of towns: Rabbit Valley, Grand Junction, Parachute, Rifle, New Castle, Eagle, Vail, Copper Mountain, Keystone. I dreamed of times a hundred years ago when eager, tired, resourceful families, just like those of us on The March, crossed these slopes.

Along the Colorado River, two days east of Grand Junction, is a town, immaculate and proud, with the quaint name of Rifle. It had a population of 3,500, which was about half of what it had been six years earlier. Exxon had come in to extract oil from shale; a building boom had ensued, but the price of oil dropped, and Exxon closed down. Union Carbide, employer of 250, producer of uranium and vanadium, used to harden steel, had also closed. At the counter in Audrey's Bakery and Café, Shelah and I enjoyed good chocolate donuts and coffee, and I turned to the man on my left to ask about Rifle. Walter Squires had worked for Union Carbide for 25 years. He told us how Rifle got its name.

"In the early days, more'n a hundred years ago, all the cricks had to be named, and sometimes it was hard to think of a name. A party of trappers or hunters were camped down nearby where you Peace Marchers are camped. They got up on the morning they were to go upstream, and one of them left his rifle leaning up against a tree. So they named the crick Rifle. Now we have East Rifle, West Rifle and North Rifle, all three cricks."

Shelah asked Walter what he thought of the nuclear arms race.

"We got enough," he answered. "No need for more. Russia and other countries, too. We all should stop now."

A World War II veteran, Walter had served in the Pacific and was among the troops ready to enter Japan at the time of the atomic bomb drop on Hiroshima and Nagasaki. "I'll tell you one thing. I think we would have lost a lot more of our boys had that bomb not been dropped. It was an awful thing but it had to be done. I'd hate to see any more have to be dropped."

Then he said, "You girls oughta go on up to the historical museum. It'll give a good idea what this area was and is."

We found the museum housed in the former city hall building and met the director who, with pride and grace, led the two of us on a tour of the exhibits. From dinosaurs through the evolution of barbed wire, up to World War II, the exhibits recalled the history of Rifle. The sense of individuality, freedom, enterprise and determination was strong in Rifle, more solid than just a romantic view of the Spirit of the West.

We'd heard the name Silver Plume. Such a pretty name for a town of 125 souls. We drove to see it and found a classic little town with a creek and a narrow gauge railroad running through it. The grocery store was for sale, and we almost bought it, the tiny town was so charming. We had turned off Highway 6 and entered 1886.

Not so Vail. It was established in 1966, too young to be romanticized. Vail is a new town full of condos and ski slopes, although both were pretty empty when we walked into town in the middle of May. There was no level space to set up camp and no place for our big trucks and trailers and old school buses cum offices. Instead, the Vail Resort Association opened their condos to all 550 of us for two nights. With a dozen or so other women, I swam in the pools and sat on high wooden decks to drink good wine and watch the sun set behind the mountains. We lounged in hot tubs and slept in beds with smooth sheets. This was The March I had signed up for!

Peace City near downtown Denver, Colorado.

CHAPTER 11

Crippled Daughter, Marching Mother

"This child will never walk," the delivering doctor told my mother on the day in 1927 when I was born in Portland, Oregon. They looked at my tiny feet bent up, with toes almost touching my shinbones. Mother raised her gaze to the doctor and retorted, "You wanna bet?"

She took me home, held me on her lap, and for 15 months, massaged my feet down. I walked late, but I walked. Early photos show me as active and normal with brother John, born in 1929. Our family moved to Coos County, and we shopped at The Hub Department Store. There were no corrective shoes in the 1930s. In the shoe department at The Hub, the salesman fitted me with sturdy, brown, lace-up Girl Scout oxfords. Then he had me stand up on the platform of a mysterious machine and stick my feet into the openings. Imagine my delight when I could peer down through a viewing cone on the top and see my feet within my shoes. The salesman explained, "See that space around your foot, between your foot and the inside of the toe box?"

"Toe box? What's that?" I asked.

"Never mind. I can see that these fit you. Step down, please."

While Mother was distracted, John and I took turns looking at our bones and wiggling our toes. I had to wear clunky ugly Girl Scout shoes until I was 12.

In high school, college and beyond, I wore Spalding saddle shoes just like everyone else and no longer felt like the Ugly Duckling. Sometimes, for dress-up occasions in high school, I wore black pretend-suede platform sling pumps, just like everyone else. I danced, ran and walked just like everyone else. And now, 40 years later, I was not only walking, I was walking across America for peace.

On Mothers Day of 1986, Laura, The March column leader, invited any of us marchers who were mothers to walk at the front of the column, and, if we wished, to carry one of the four flags. For a while that day, I led The March and carried the American flag for four miles, one mile for each of my sons. It wasn't easy on a breezy day. But, like so many things on The March, I just did it, and as the crippled daughter, I gave special thanks to my mother for her determination. At the side of the road, farm families cheered us on. One young mother with children clustered about her knees, murmured, "God bless you," and handed each of us marching mothers a pansy, Mother's favorite flower.

When I occasionally heard, "Walking to Washington? You'll never make it," I remembered what Mother had said to the doctor and replied, "You wanna bet?"

Lawson, Colorado, was four days west of Denver. We'd come almost 1,000 miles, one-third of the way. Denver was the largest city on our route since Los Angeles. As we had in Las Vegas, we held high hopes for recognition and contributions. Colorado organizers proclaimed that Denver would provide The March's greatest welcome. A notice on the porta-potty doors listed activities already scheduled that included numerous benefit concerts, house parties, rallies and speaking engagements. The culmination of these events would be a parade in Denver on Friday, May 30; a rally at the capitol on May 31, and a Marcher for the Day program on Monday, June 1, in which local residents could pay $15 to walk with us for a day. They could walk and talk with us, share our lunch and our porta-potties, and at the end of the day someone would drive them back to their cars.

The prospects were very exciting. But, before Denver, there was Loveland Pass. At 11,992 feet above sea level, it was the highest point on the cross-country route. That would be a hike. Through snow.

Before I could do all that, Shelah would *drive* me from Lawson over Loveland Pass to the airport in Denver. I was flying to Providence, Rhode Island, to meet members of my family and to attend the wedding of my son John and his fiancé, Holly Harper. I would transform from Peace Marcher to Mother of the Groom. I found a shower, climbed into my cleanest marcher clothes, packed my toothbrush, hairbrush, Chapstick and book into my backpack. At the airport, I hugged Shelah and boarded the plane. She would pick me up in a few days. The March would still be west of Denver, so I wouldn't miss any of the planned events.

On the plane, I slept and thought about my adventures on the road, how I was taking my cause to the streets like the hippies of the '60s, and how much I had learned about our country and about myself. I had changed since I'd last seen my family. I wondered if anyone would recognize me. I was deeply tanned, slender, fit, and my hair was just there, growing and being natural. I hadn't worn makeup in three months. I had lived in sweat socks and camp clothes. I had been living outside except for the occasional sleepover through Marcher in the Home. Holly's family was conservative, proper New England. I wondered if John would be worried about the image I might project. *I* worried about the image I might project. Would I be perceived as a wild and radical Californian? Would my sons and their wives look at me and wonder if I'd become weird? Would Holly's family and friends be cautious and severely judgmental?

I needn't have been concerned. As I walked off the plane in Providence and was navigating the exit signs, I heard "Hi, Mom! Come on! Walk with us." There was my son Sam! And Marty and Matt and their wives. John's brothers and sisters-in-law, all together, trailing through the airport. Sam put his arm around my shoulder. I was with my kin. I swallowed my happy tears amid the flurry of hugs. We all talked at once.

"Mom, You look great!" Matt said.

Sam's wife gave me a big hug, "You're so tanned! I want to come with you."

"How *are* you?"

"How was the flight?" Marty asked.

"What's the plan?"

"I am so glad to see you!," Marty's wife took my hand.

"Did you bring my MOG [Mother of the Groom] clothes?" I asked.

In January, when Holly and John were planning their wedding and I was planning to leave for The Peace March, one of my daughters-in-law had offered to bring my MOG clothes with her to the wedding. She had made life so easy for me!

Matt and his wife and I were staying with friends of Holly's family. I had my own room. Even my own bathroom! With no time to think about it, I changed into my soft cream-colored wool challis skirt, a silk blouse, my good pearls, stockings and moderate heels. Lipstick. Eye makeup. Lots of hair-brushing. Good thing Holly had made an appointment for me with her hairdresser in the morning! We were driven to a dinner party and mercifully, I fit right in. I had to fight the inclination to sit on the floor, though. Young men rose from their chairs so I could be properly seated. I realized that recently I had been living a life with few chairs.

In the morning I kept the hair and makeup appointment, buttoned up my mustard-colored jacquard dress, and was escorted down the aisle to witness a lovely classic wedding in the 18th century stone Episcopal church where Holly and her siblings had attended Sunday School. Holly, on her dignified father's arm, glided down the aisle, graceful as the dancer she once was, and glowing. John, the tall, handsome groom, grinned the entire time, except when they exchanged vows. They were 30 years old, mature and confident. The mother of the bride wore a jacquard dress of deep marine blue. We both wore our pearls. At the reception, Jim Love, father of the groom, asked me to dance. Although it had been 15 years since we had been divorced, and more years than that since we'd danced, I remembered how well we fit together. I also danced with our sons and the father of the bride and others. Chuckling to myself about my good life and happiness, I thought, my dance card is full, so to speak. I couldn't help but slip in a silent prayer that our world would be safe enough for John and Holly's children to have weddings such as this.

The next day, Holly's parents graciously entertained all the relatives at an outdoor brunch. I found Holly's sister Penny sitting alone on the little wooden dock down by the pond at the edge of the lawn that surrounded the Harper family grey shingle "cottage." Penny was almost

40, tall, and slender as a reed. She had an intense look about her and a soothing cadence to her speech.

"Please join me," she invited. "Tell me about The Peace March you left to come to the wedding. The group is in Denver, isn't it?"

I summarized quickly because I wanted to ask about her reputed abilities as a medium. I had never met a medium.

Penny lost some of her reserve and, brushing her glossy auburn hair aside, eagerly explained the spirit who comes through her. "Want to have a session?" she proposed "Yes! Do you think anyone would mind? How about now?"

We walked indoors to the library, a quiet room at the end of the hall. I watched Penny draw the draperies, set a lighted candle on the floor, and pull a multi-colored afghan about herself. "Just sit comfortably on the sofa," she suggested, "and I'll sit here on the floor near the candle. My spirit person is a gentleman from India. You might be surprised at the high pitch of his voice."

I was surprised at myself for even doing this! Especially surprised when I heard the fathers of the bride and groom approaching along the hallway. The library door opened a crack, and Jim Love's head intruded halfway past the edge. "Oh, excuse me." was his startled response.

The next day he told me, "That Penny is weird! Talbot was showing me the house, and I looked into the library and there was Penny sitting on the floor, wrapped in a blanket, staring at a candle and chanting something foreign. Right in the middle of the party, too."

Luckily for me, the door had shielded me from his view.

Penny had been correct when explaining that her spirit's voice would be different from hers. Instead of Penny's calm, cool melodious tones, I heard the high, singsong cadences of India.

"Ah," he said. "I see above and behind you the doves of peace. They are hovering."

I commented to myself, of course they are hovering. I'm just taking a weekend off from The Peace March. Penny knows that.

"And there are snakes of earth wisdom twining about your ankles," he continued. "That is very fortunate. Ah, I see you are going to St. Louis."

"No," I answered. "I have no plans to go to St. Louis and neither does the Peace March."

"But you must. I see the Arch of St. Louis and you are beneath it.

Wait! This is most unusual. It is not the Arch. It is a giraffe. You are sitting between the spraddled front legs of a giraffe that is curving her neck in an attempt to bring her face down close to yours. You are protected and guided by a giraffe."

"Amazing!" I leaned forward. "Penny, come back! Are you back yet?"

For a moment she was still. Then she opened her eyes, took a deep breath and spoke in her normal voice. She sounded like clear water over smooth stones when she said, "Tell me what happened. I think there was some confusion."

She didn't appear surprised as I related the story of Lynn Andrews' suggestion to "Get a totem," and that I had chosen a giraffe.

"Yes," she smiled. "that seems right. I am happy this has meant something to you and that we have had this time together. Now, perhaps we should join the others?"

As we walked along the hallway, I took her hand and said, "Thank you, Penny. I am so glad you and I are family now. We'll see each other again. And, here's a card with the White House phone number. Do you have anything you'd like to tell our government? Maybe to halt nuclear testing? You can call them any time and a real person will answer and tally your comments. If you try it, you'll find it's a pretty powerful experience, calling the White House."

That afternoon John and Holly flew to London for their wedding trip. His brothers and their wives returned to the San Francisco Bay Area, and I was back in my March clothes, on the plane to Denver.

I had time to think about the various lifestyles in America. Holly's family was gracious New England traditional with a hint of Southern charm left from their early life in Virginia. Ours was similar but instead of the hint of Southern charm, a dose of West Coast vigor. And a mother who walked with all sorts of people across the nation to protest nuclear weapons.

I dozed a little while and drifted in and out of thoughts about the staggering diversity of marchers: all religions, from several orders of Roman Catholic nuns to Quakers, Jews, Mennonites, Buddhist monks, agnostics and atheists. We had New Agers, numerologists, astrologers, Native American animists, Jungian and Freudian analysts, mystics, skeptics, computer analysts, Democrats, Anarchists, Republicans and several Communist sympathizers. Also, auto mechanics, metalworkers, professors, carpenters, members of AA, lesbians, gays, Vietnam veterans, teachers, Blacks and Hispanics, students, musicians, one clown on a unicycle, several lawyers, and a professional gambler. Marchers came from all 50 states and 10 foreign countries. I realized I felt comfortable with the wide variety of colorful folks, "rich diversity" it was called on The Peace March, yet still I felt comfortable among the more traditional and conservative friends who attended John and Holly's wedding. Years ago a gentleman friend and I had discussed the definition of "sophisticated." He had concluded "a sophisticated person is one who is comfortable with any person in any situation." I'd never thought of myself as sophisticated, more like a friendly small-town girl. My father long ago had said, "Be friendly with everyone and choose your friends carefully." If we could learn to respect social differences, to feel friendly toward everyone, we'd begin to live in peace. The March had become my crucible for this experiment.

I sat staring out the window at billowy clumps of clouds as my thoughts wandered. I remembered a young woman on The March who in Barstow complained that she was being stalked by a man who had recently joined us. Some members of the Security Department watched and observed that indeed, she was right. About a dozen marchers surrounded the "stalker," but instead of confronting him, they circled around and sang a sweet song to him. Others joined, and after a short while, he huddled on the ground crying and apologizing. The young woman emerged from the crowd, crouched down, and hugged him. He stood up. One hug grew to a group hug. His behavior changed. He changed. I was awestruck at the effectiveness of unconditional love.

I mused about Holly's father, a retired admiral in the United States Navy submarine corps. My son Matt, who had also been a nuclear submariner, was now a nuclear engineer with General Electric. "I'm not opposed to the peaceful use of nuclear energy, but am worried about nuclear weapons and the disposal of nuclear waste," I had said to my son.

Matt had said he was concerned with the ramifications of human error. He showed me a newspaper photo of a control panel in a nuclear energy plant. A dozen men sat staring at the lights. One had turned to look at the camera. Matt pointed to him, "There. That one. He's not paying attention. If you take your eyes off the panel for one second, a disaster could happen." He and I respected each other's choices and agreed that we lived under the threat of nuclear annihilation.

On the plane, I wondered if I had lost an opportunity to talk seriously with Holly's father about the dangers of nuclear armament. I realized I'd need more education about nuclear weaponry and training in political speaking before I could be an effective anti-nuclear advocate. I resolved to attend more of Ann Edelman's Speaker Training sessions in the Peace Academy bus once I returned to The March.

Monday afternoon Shelah picked me up at the airport and suddenly I was back into my other reality. The March was still in Lawson, as it had been when I left. The weekend had been spent mending and waterproofing tents, airing sleeping bags, doing laundry, preparing handouts for Denver, and more meetings. And rest. For me, it was as though the world had stopped, and I had stepped off for a few hours. The next day we walked through cool canyons to Golden, still two days west of Denver.

The hike over Loveland Pass was dramatic. I know I would remember it if I'd been among those walking. The day must have been Tuesday, maybe Thursday, one of my work days, so I didn't walk that day. I know it was bright and clear.

On Friday, May 30, Congresswoman Pat Schroeder came out to our muddy campsite at 7:30 in the morning to speak to us. Then The Great Peace March filed into downtown Denver and brought traffic to a standstill. As we paraded along 17th Street to the Colorado State Capitol, pedestrians and drivers cheered and clapped. Some merely watched. A woman stood by her idling car. "I think it's beautiful," she said. "If I didn't have to work, I'd be out there with them."

A man on the curb called out, "Get a job." I waved at him and called back, "This *is* my job."

Another block down the street, a marcher called, "Thanks for coming out!" and the onlooker replied, "I'm not coming out. I'm just here waiting for the light to turn green."

People stepped from the sidewalk to join the parade. Five thousand arrived at the Capitol steps. Representatives from farm, labor and ethnic communities joined members of local peace groups to hear speakers, music and a children's program. We staged a pep rally for peace: "One, two, three, four. We don't want a nuclear war," we chanted. "Five, six, seven, eight. We don't want to radiate."

Holly Near joined The March's musicians, "Collective Vision," to entertain the audience. She applauded and shouted, "Thank you all for being here!" The crowd stood, shouted, and clapped back to her. After the songs and chants, everyone joined in a circle on the Capitol lawn, ceremoniously planted a Peace Tree and exchanged keys to the city. The fragrance of the fund-raising barbecue lured marchers and residents to stand in line, and while there, talk among themselves about what everyone could do to address our problems. A local doctor, Y. S. Wang, was so moved he stepped up to the microphone and handed a representative of The March a check for $25,000.

Many people asked us to define our reasons for walking. We gave them copies of our statement of purpose, originally drawn by Pro-Peace back in the days in Los Angeles while The Peace March was formulating.

A Statement of Purpose:

The Great Peace March for Global Nuclear Disarmament, Inc. is an abolitionist movement. We believe that great social change comes about when the will of the people becomes focused on a moral imperative.

By marching for nine months across the United States, we will create a nonviolent focus for positive change; the imperative being that nuclear weapons are politically, socially, economically and morally unjustifiable and that, in any number, they are unacceptable.

It is the responsibility of a democratic government to implement the will of its people, and it is the will of the people of the world to end the nuclear arms race.

Specific objectives are:

1. A verifiable, comprehensive Test Ban Treaty.

2. No militarization of space.

3. To support a global freeze on testing, production and deployment of nuclear weapons and missiles and their delivery systems.

4. A "no-first-use" pledge by all nuclear nations of the world.

5. A nuclear-weapons-free Europe and Pacific.

6. Reductions leading to elimination of nuclear weapon stockpiles.

7. The redirection of resources from nuclear weapons manufacturers to socially useful projects leading to full employment.

8. Continuous, intense negotiations between the United States and the USSR leading to agreements on nuclear weapons control.

9. To encourage the governments of the world to enforce the non-proliferation treaty.

Several of us relaxed on the Capitol lawn and stretched our leg muscles in the spring sunshine. Leanne was first to notice a serious looking young woman draped in tape-recording gear. Followed by the ubiquitous TV cameraman, she walked toward us. Another interview!

She introduced herself as a reporter for a local TV station and hunkered down. Sure enough, she asked the usual question, "Why are you on The Great Peace March?"

As we were sometimes wont to do, we responded flippantly. Katea replied, "For thin thighs."

Ted bragged, "Gonna camp in Central Park."

Leanne occasionally complained, "This is *not* The March I signed up for. Sometimes I wonder just why I am here."

The young woman looked from one to the other of us, apparently perplexed by our cocky answers. So, since she seemed sincere, we gave her real answers. I told her I was walking to create a more peaceful world for all the grandchildren in the world, particularly mine. I showed her the button I wore, the photo of preschoolers Derek and Caitlin, and said, "Not just my own two grandchildren, but every child. When I was tutoring, I spoke with children who didn't do well in school because they thought 'What's the use? We're just going to get nuked anyway.' Others have told me they will never get a driver's license because they will be bombed. I want these sad, dispirited children to grow up. Maybe they, too, will walk for their convictions."

Katea listed political reasons, and Leanne told of her own fears of nuclear bombs.

The reporter lowered her microphone and said, "I've heard of

March miracles. Can you tell me about those?" We liked her question and encouraged her to tape our answers.

"Yes!" Katea responded. "My favorite is the one in the desert when we were hot and lonely and fantasizing about food. A family had driven from LA to bring us 15 gallons of ice cream, enough for 350 of us, and reminded us we'd not been forgotten. I don't even know how they found us. It was a double miracle."

Leanne liked the miracle of the man with $18,000 that infused new life into The March.

"I have a small one," I began. "We were camped in a parched stubble field behind a dam in western Colorado. It was an especially hot day. Some walkers dashed up the embankment to go swimming. I wandered over toward the mail bus with Jonnie. She asked for a drink of water from my canteen, and as I held it out to her, said, 'I wish we had some ice!' At that precise moment, a truck wheeled in through the gate and headed toward us. The window was down, an arm extended out. Swinging from the hand was a bag of ice! Without a word, the driver slowed down so we could grab it, and he headed on toward the kitchen. Jonnie and I sighed with delight and ran ice up and down our faces, arms, and legs. We gave away the rest to others standing in the mail line."

"Want another?" Ted offered.

"I think I've got it," the reporter retrieved her microphone and pocketed it.

The cameraman coiled his lines, stood a moment gazing at us, and then blurted, "You guys are the greatest!"

The reporter extended her hand, smiled, and thanked us. Suddenly, she lost her professionalism, clutched Leanne in a hug, and cried, "I wish I could go with you! I want a miracle!"

"Well then," said Ted. "Come on. You could walk a day for only $15. You can interview us and write a whole bunch of articles." I wondered if she would.

Kitchen crew in the flooded camp in Lincoln, Nebraska.

CHAPTER 12

Making Change

We are a gentle angry people
And we are singing, singing for our lives

We are a land of many colors
We are an anti-nuclear people
We are young and old together
We are gay and straight together
We are a gentle loving people

We are a gentle loving people
And we are walking, walking for our lives.
—**Holly Near**

When people met us along the way, they often were surprised to
see that we were in fact, peaceful, polite and gentle. People whom Shelah
and I met told us that we seemed "nice," but they were puzzled by some

of us. Especially the young unwashed ones dressed in shabby black, with dreadlocks and bare feet. They called themselves the Anarchists and set up their tents around a black flag decorated with a large white peace sign. They looked like the fringes of society, and were, in fact, the fringes of The March. We "Over-50s," who wanted the image of The March to be palatable, especially among Midwest conservatives, were disgusted with those "couch potatoes" who slept in instead of walking. When the media came to record The Great Peace March, we needed everyone who wasn't working to walk. Camp-scape, the marchers who stayed behind to clean up the site, had to urge those lazy bums to get up and out. "Come on. Get up. We gotta go! Come on. It's all downhill now from Denver to Pittsburgh. And we've saved some breakfast for you." That usually worked. The Anarchists would change from "potatoes" to "turnips" --"turn up" for a free meal any time. Accept the breakfast, toss their gear and tents and black flag into their psychedelic bus and drive off. They'd turn up at the next site, camp off to one side a little way. Their friends stood in line among the hard-working walking marchers to get enough food for all of them.

One morning the slackers still lazing around in their tents were startled by a column of several hundred of us snaking among the tents, calling by name those still not up. They were invited to join in the pleasure of a stroll on such a lovely day. It worked! The March column swelled.

The Over-50s held meetings to discuss the importance of shared responsibilities and acceptable appearance. We thought that if a person did not participate responsibly in The March, he/she should not eat March food. Standards must be maintained! And we felt it important to look presentable! To be tidy. We needed a dress code. Notices were posted on porta-potty doors, and announcements were called out over the bullhorn. Crowded meetings in the large town-hall tents droned on and on.

Ultimately, the Over-50s decided to invite the young Anarchists to walk, one-on-one, with us. The age-span between the eldest and the youngest on The March was 77 years. Some of us worried that there was, indeed, a generation gap. I chose a tall, handsome, scruffy teenage boy as my walking companion.. He had clear skin, straight teeth and a winning smile. He wore shreddy clothes, dreadlocks, and no shoes. No observable body piercings. I found him standing in the dinner line and asked, "Would it be okay if I walked with you tomorrow?" Although it's now been 25 years since that evening, I'll never forget his response.

"Me? You want to walk with me? Why would you want to do that?!"

I looked up at him and saw behind the disreputable appearance, a nice boy, one who could have been in our family, one who probably had a respectable family of his own and was striking out to establish his identity. I thought his mother was probably worried about him. "I think we have lots to talk about. I could learn something from you." I hoped he recognized my sincerity.

"Yeah, sure. I'll meet you at the flags tomorrow. If I wake up in time."

"Good enough. I'll watch for you, but we leave about 6:30. It's going to be a hot day. See you then." And I went off to find Shelah to tell her. I was surprisingly excited that he had accepted my invitation.

The next morning I dressed and got ready and looked all around the flags area. He didn't show up. After a while, I shrugged and walked on into the bright fresh morning. At the first rest stop, the handsome young man found me.

"I was late this morning. I had to help some friends."

"That's all right. We can walk now." His name was Oliver. He was 18. We strode out along the side of the road, and I asked him if the gravel didn't hurt his bare feet. No, it didn't, he said. "What will you do when the weather gets cold? Will you have shoes then?"

He kept looking straight ahead. "I dunno. Something will work out. It always does."

He told me that he didn't work for money. He just worked or made things and sometimes people gave him money. Oliver grinned. Maybe what I could learn from Oliver was to look beyond the surface. Giving up my judgments had always been hard for me. Maybe Oliver had a good philosophy; he appeared to be at peace. But he was very young.

I spoke to Oliver as I would have spoken to my own sons. I had learned from them that it's what's *in* the head that's important rather than what's *on* the head. But I didn't know anything about dreadlocks. His hair looked like a mass of fur balls on an angora cat. "How do you get your hair to do that?"

"Do what?" he answered.

"How do you get it twisted?" He just shrugged his shoulders, so I asked, "Does it itch? How do you wash it?"

"Oh, it's easy," he smiled. "I suds it up in the shower and wash out the soap, and it dries. It doesn't itch. If it does, I scratch it with a stick. It's no problem. I lost my hairbrush about six months ago, but now I don't need it."

We talked about the mission of The March, to raise awareness about the overwhelming need to work for peace, an issue we agreed was important. I told him, "Until The March, I had felt so helpless to do anything. I had students who thought they'd never grow up so they quit trying in school."

Oliver told me he had dropped out of school, but that he might go back. He didn't think his parents were worried about him; they probably were glad he was out of the house. After I told him what the Over-50s thought about making a good impression on those who watched us, he said, "Okay, I'll think about how I can clean up... a little. I don't know about the others, though."

At the end of the day, several of us Over-50s gathered at a picnic table at the campsite to talk about our experiences with the Anarchists. We all had learned that behind their yucky appearance hovered kids who were confused, hurt, searching, experimenting—in short, growing up. We decided it was wisest to accept them as is—and hope for the best.

Dick, a droll man in his '60s, said, "If I can't get along with the Anarchists, I can't get along with the Russians, and where does that leave world peace?"

In response to our pressure to impose a dress code, about 20 young men visited a thrift store, made their purchases and on Monday showed up dressed up. In dresses and hats. They pranced along in The March column, swinging their purses. Some wore wigs. Some were still barefoot. At camp that evening, they gave a Dress Code fashion show! After the laughter, several stood to say, "Let's remember why we are here. It's for peace, right? Let's be peaceful and accepting and show the world we can exist together. Tell ya what, though, some of us will help clean up the campsites and other stuff." Some of the townspeople who were visiting the campsite were uncomfortable with young men in dresses, no matter how witty, but I felt a great surge of relief that this dispute, even though not really resolved, was at an end. I laughed about it and gratefully let it go.

I thought I would never know what happened to Oliver after The

March, just as I'd never know how to answer people who asked, "How do you ever stay organized enough to walk across the whole country?" I was there, and I didn't and still don't know. I do know that those of us who plowed through the issues, who endured interminable meetings, who got up at two in the morning to bake bread and start breakfast, who kept track of routes and sites, of food, money, or broken buses, each one made The March possible.

That included the musicians who awakened us before dawn, walking among the tents with their flutes or guitars or salad bowl gongs or boom boxes playing Tchaikovsky. Except on Fridays. On Fridays Aloha Jack wore flowery Hawaiian shirts and wandered among the tents giving the Honolulu surf report. "Surf's up! Get up!" while someone strummed a ukulele.

That's how we started our days. We sat up, crawled out of the tent, stood up among hundreds of marcher friends who stretched and called out to each other. And we put on our shoes one more time. Then we put one foot ahead of the other, one day at a time. One person, in community with others, dedicated to making a change. As my young Anarchist said, things worked out.

Like the Anarchists, Gus was a young man, I think on the verge of 20. Unlike them, he walked and worked and was definitely presentable. He was from Pacific Palisades, one of five children in a family with a stay-at-home mother and an engineer father. One day Gus and I walked along together, and he told me his parents were coming to visit The March. They needed reassurance that he was all right. "They worry that The March might be full of weirdos," he said. "Could I bring them to meet you?"

I was complimented and said, "Of course, Gus. I'd like to meet your parents." A few days later, Gus introduced them. They looked like I might have imagined: fit, clean, bright, pleasant. We walked together and I answered their questions as best I could.

They first asked, "How about the food? Do you think Gus is getting enough?" and I reassured them that the food was plentiful and nourishing.

"And his friends?" his mother wanted to know.

"Well, I don't know who his friends are, but I do know that Gus is a dependable young man who does his share of walking and working. I doubt if he has time to get into trouble." I suggested, "You could talk with Shelah or Connie or Franklin and others. And go to the Peace Academy or our Bookmobile—we have 4,000 books—for more information." The March must have passed their scrutiny for Gus's father returned several times to walk for a few days. Both his parents walked with him into Washington, DC, on November 15.

Lisa was a young woman I talked with as we peeled potatoes one day. She was 19, with blond hair drooping long over one eye and almost shaved above her ear on the other side. She apparently didn't wear underclothes and walked most of the way barefoot. "I don't like the feel of shoes," she said. She was pregnant and due to deliver shortly after the end of The March. I didn't see her often during The March, but I did in Washington, and by then she was wearing a tattered ski jacket and shoes—no socks, but at least shoes. I asked her if she would be alright.

"Oh, yes. The baby's father is with me, and we'll find a good place to live as a family. You don't have to worry about us." Her confidence reminded me of Oliver's.

Several years later, I was in Oregon, driving with my brother John from Eugene out to Florence, on the coast. We stopped for coffee at a little store, Alpha Bit Café, in Mapleton operated by a community who lived an "intentional life." On a picnic bench on the wooden front porch of the store, a young woman, barefoot, sat cross-legged, reading *The New York Times*. She looked up as we approached and said, "Oh, I'm sorry. We're closed for inventory. But we have coffee. Just go on in and help yourself."

As we stood with our mugs, I said, "Excuse me, John. I need to go talk with that young woman on the porch."

Outside, I said, "I think we know each other, but I don't recall how or where."

She said, "Yes, I have the same feeling. Why do I have you associated with potatoes?"

And then we both knew. "Lisa! It's you! How's your baby? How are *you*? Are you married?" All my questions tumbled out.

She folded her paper and stood up and gave me a big hug. "Oh, Donna, I am so glad to see you. I have wanted to tell you that everything worked out just as I told you it would. Our son is fine. He's in grade school now. My husband helps manage this store. We live up the road in the hills." About 20 people in their self-sufficient community grew organic produce, made goat cheese and lived in harmony with the earth.

Back in the car, I babbled about Lisa for another 30 minutes; I was so happy to have found her.

I give our Peace Academy credit for fostering an important change in me. As a high school student, I had joined the debate team. I lasted exactly one debate. I knew the subject matter but didn't contribute a single word. I was totally mute and felt what I had to say was not important. Why would anyone listen to me? The English teacher replaced me with someone who would speak up. In my San Francisco Peninsula life, as president of the Coyote Point Junior Museum Auxiliary, I'd clutched my clipboard protectively to my chest and spoke barely enough to get through the meetings. Later, divorced and working toward teaching credentials, I still felt uncomfortable standing at the front of a classroom of 30 eighth graders. Instead I opened a tutoring center for dyslexic students and worked comfortably one-on-one.

But *now*, on The Peace March, I became a speaker. One day somewhere in the Midwest, when Shelah and I were doing our advance work, a man we met in a coffee shop asked if anyone on The March would agree to be interviewed for local radio. Shelah and I looked at each other. "How about us!" We followed him to his tiny broadcasting studio and talked for 30 minutes. On a Sunday in a large Presbyterian church, four of us sat in a pew near the front. The minister asked if one of us would come up to explain The March. I quickly glanced over the program, found the lesson for the day, took the program with me and started by reading those lines. I was astonished when, for 20 minutes, words flowed out of my mouth. After I sat down, I asked my friend next to me, "What'd I say? Was it all right?"

"Yes," she said. "It was inspired. Right on. How'd you learn to speak like that?"

"I don't know! I felt like God was speaking through me." I learned that day that when I am passionate about something, the words just come. As Joseph Campbell said, "Follow your bliss. When you do, doors will open and guides will appear." I reported back to Ann Edelman in the Peace Academy, and she signed me up for a local TV interview.

In talks with groups along The March route, I encouraged listeners to act both as individuals and within organizations. A single person could write a postcard to a government official, make phone calls, write letters to the editor, be an informed voter. He could encourage his classes to become involved activists, as the professor at University of Utah had done. High school students could form Peace Clubs. We marchers believed fervently that nuclear weapons were unjustifiable. We believed that to "bring down the bombs," everyone needed to become an activist!

The feature articles I wrote for the *San Mateo Times* informed readers about the adventures of seeing our country on foot and encouraged them to become more involved as citizens. On the 104th morning of The Peace March, I sat, word processor in my lap, in the middle of a field of wild wheat and listened to a meadowlark, Nebraska's state bird, that teetered on a wire fence. The sun was warm even before 8 o'clock. The sun had risen before we were wakened by melodic wind chimes. The Wake-Up Marcher had meandered among the tents and chanted, "It's 5 o'clock on a clear bright day. Only 19 miles to Ogallala." After breakfast, I sat in the field writing my next story for the paper. Then I hitched a ride to a post office to mail the story, and caught up with The March column about noon.

I wrote:

> We are in Nebraska! Our sixth state! Almost halfway to Washington, DC, and I am still, every day, surprised at the conditions, contrasts, and experiences on *The Great Peace March.*
>
> In Vail, Colorado, more than 500 marchers were housed in resort condominiums. Last week, in Wiggins, Colorado, it rained one-and-a-half inches in 12 hours while we walked and talked about the weather. We trooped through torrential rains, flooding, spectacular lightning storms and tornado warnings.

Laura had walked up and down The March column with her bullhorn calling, "If a tornado comes our way, we will lie down in the ditch along the side of the road. Keep your heads down and hold onto someone." The tornado veered off to the north of us, and I was relieved that we didn't have to lie down in that ditch full of murky water, tall weeds, trash, and probably frogs and snakes.

I wrote:

> *Our campsite looked like a rice paddy. Most of the marchers slept that night in the local community building. "Reminds me of a Red Cross flood victim scene—without the cots," quipped a dripping marcher. Our evening was lightened by a storyteller from Boulder who kept us entranced for over an hour. We snuggled down into our sleeping bags and turned out the lights while he told a horror story.*
>
> *"Ooooh," I said to the marcher next to me. "This is scary."*
>
> *"Shhhh," she hissed. "Just listen. I don't want to miss a single word!"*
>
> *Our pace increased to over 20 miles a day; 25 last Wednesday, and we don't have time to get sick. After walking so far, we were grateful when a farmer near Proctor, Colorado, offered us shelter in a scrubbed out former fertilizer factory.*

The former fertilizer factory was a large grey building, bigger than a barn, with a concrete floor and not many windows. I remember observing Franklin Folsom of Boulder, Colorado, a Rhodes Scholar and author of 46 books, at 79 the eldest on The March. He served on the Policy Board, the City Council and the Board of Directors. For a few minutes that afternoon in the fertilizer factory, I watched him on his folding camp stool in a relatively quiet corner near an open door where the daylight was best. He leaned forward over his portable typewriter that balanced on a green plastic crate. He could have been in his office back home. He was our elder statesman and lent dignity to our efforts by his very presence.

Marcher Tom Atlee wrote about that evening in the fertilizer factory:

> *As we stood there dripping and jostling, joking and complaining about our lives, we noticed a couple of marchers setting up a microphone and portable speakers.*

When the makeshift sound system was ready, they suggested we use this time to speak from our hearts about the issue that currently divided us—whether to walk together or strung out along the road.

Taking two minutes each, we shared passion and perspective with each other for more than two hours—weeping, cajoling, steaming and sweating in the muggy fetid air. Quite unexpectedly, as we talked and listened with great intensity, the answer to our problem began to emerge. We knew we had fully heard each other when the answer became as obvious as the rain on the sheet-metal roof.

All of us realized what we'd do for the next few months: we'd walk together through the cities, 'city mode,' (where there were rushing crowds, traffic, and media) and strung out in the countryside, 'country mode,' (where townspeople had time to talk and nature had time to be beautiful). It was so simple, and it handled all our concerns.

On cue, the storm subsided. We dispersed into the glistening dusk, a healed community ready to continue on our path together.

Six years later, in 1992, I read about Onondaga Iroquois tribal councils. It said, "We meet and just keep talking until there's nothing left but the obvious truth." I recognized that we'd stumbled upon something the Iroquois had known for hundreds of years.

In the fertilizer factory, I was dry and cheerful as we chose places on the concrete floor to "camp" for the night and listened to spontaneous music of guitars and rhythm band instruments: hub caps, sticks and pebbles in soda cans. Some of the marchers danced. Suzanne Mendelson, the 75-year-old artist from Santa Monica, the one who recovered from bronchitis in a jail cell, cordoned off a corner by stacking sleeping bags and set up an art show. She had invited several March artists to display their work along the top of the 3-foot-high sleeping-bag wall. We had our water, and each brought a snack to share, whatever we had in our pockets or backpacks for a festive Pretend Art Gallery Preview in the fertilizer factory. Eventually dinner was called: hardy chunky bean and rice soup and an assortment of breads. The rain pelted the roof as I ate while sitting on my sleeping bag. Then I unrolled it out on the floor, asked dancers not to step on me, and in my clothes fell sound asleep. Even the frequent night trains that thundered along the Union Pacific tracks behind the buildings didn't waken me.

I continued to write as I sat in the sun in the wild wheat field:

> *A new addition to our traveling village is a yurt. With a rainbow of stripes, reminiscent of stained-glass windows, and pure white vertical walls, it is a place consecrated by the burning of cedar and the lighting of candles—a place of quiet, meditation, and contemplation. Episcopal deacon Judith Ain, from Menlo Park, California, led ecumenical services in the yurt on Sunday while we camped outside Sterling, Colorado.*

The yurt traveled on a two-wheel cart pulled along by its owner.

Julesburg was our final town in Colorado. We had the traditional tree-planting ceremony, and about 350 marchers and guests walked the few miles to the Colorado-Nebraska border. The Colorado Highway Patrol liked their cake. We chanted the names of six states we had already crossed and stepped into Nebraska. A peace activist gave a marcher a giant banner, FARMS NOT ARMS, to carry across Nebraska. We would now watch for Nebraska's state flower, goldenrod, instead of Colorado's columbine, for cottonwood trees instead of aspen.

For more than a week in mid-June, The March route paralleled the Platte River. Ever since I'd read James Michener's *Centennial*, I'd dreamed of seeing the wide, shallow, braided river that drained the eastern Rockies into the Missouri River. The Nebraska hills are a rest stop for migrating whooping and sandhill cranes. The Platte River was the basis for the Oregon Trail, Mormon Trail, Pony Express, and Highway 80. I loved its name, Platte, from the French *plate/plat* and that it ran through Nebraska, also from the French, meaning "flat water." We stopped at Fort Kearney Park and saw wagon-wheel ruts on the old Oregon Trail that had been carved in the mid 1800s. My Grandmother Taylor's people had come west on that trail! The Great Peace March was the largest migration of people on foot in 100 years. The first major group headed west, and we traveled east. They were searching for a better life, and so were we. Both groups were pioneers—on foot. I looked out across the distances and knew my ancestors had seen the same hills that I was seeing. Ann Edelman browsed around in the Fort Kearney Park gift store and bought a sun bonnet like those the Western migrant women wore. Did my Great-Grandmother Thompson wear such a bonnet?

On June 21, a scorching Nebraska summer day, Gene Gordon and his group of Shakespeare enthusiasts performed *A Midsummer Night's Dream*. That afternoon Gene told me that he and Rhoda had walked 20 miles "through a furnace" as they forged the play, condensing and revising it to relate to The March. In camp, after a supper of salads and muffins, they rehearsed.

The performance was just what we weary marchers needed. In every scene, with every character, we saw ourselves reflected on stage. Every allusion and joke referred to life on The March. Even in the chaos of camp, in the heat and exhaustion, every member of the cast showed up. The children were the fairies. The production kept all of us in the audience laughing, laughing at ourselves. I loved the energy Gene and his cast still had after walking 20 hot miles that day.

In Lincoln, the rains came. The campsite was drenched. The kitchen crew had to use green plastic crates as stepping stones to get from the food storage to food prep to food cooking trailers. Shelah and I accepted a Marcher in the Home invitation from a young rabbi and his wife, Ian and Surry Jacknis. We enjoyed a home-cooked meal, and I offered to clear the table. I was stacking the dishes in the sink when our hostess dashed into the kitchen and threw up her hands. "Oh," she gasped, "not there!" I didn't know what I'd done wrong until she told me they were a kosher family and certain things could go only in certain places. She firmly led me back to the table where I sat chagrined. I felt embarrassed and absurd at not knowing. As Ian and Shelah chatted, Surry smiled at me, reached to touch my arm, and said, "It's alright."

The rain stopped, the sun came out from beneath clouds, and a giant rainbow appeared across the sky. The young father lifted their napping baby from his crib, took him out on the deck, jiggled him awake, and cooed into his ear, "Look, my son, it's your first rainbow. A blessing."

His father patted him, said something, a prayer I thought, in Hebrew, and lowered him back into his crib. I asked Ian what he had said while he showed his son the rainbow. He said, "God made a covenant of grace with Noah, who represents mankind, and with all the animals, to never again destroy all life with a worldwide flood. The rainbow shows us again his promise, and we are grateful."

Surry had to treat the kitchen some way so it would be kosher again. Years later, in Santa Barbara, I was a guest at a Seder, and offered to help clear the table. Recalling my ignorance in Lincoln, I followed the lead of our hostess in stacking the dishes.

In Omaha, I talked with Don Priester who devoted months of preparation for The Peace March in Nebraska and also walked. Many of the rallies and activities in Nebraska were a credit to Don. When I asked him his thoughts on marchers, he stressed that marchers appreciated their freedom to march and to demonstrate. He added, "This is a powerful experience in inner peace. Marchers live a simple life, in harmony with nature and, while we appreciate the material comforts, they don't control us. Instead, The March has led the participants to deepen the spiritual side of their lives." He added, "The challenges of the long walk strengthen our resolve. We are sending the message that we are committed. We go forward." Don reminded me of Leon Trotsky's quote, "Our best task is to move forward."

The March reached Papillion, Nebraska, a suburb of Omaha, on July 2. Papillion is the county seat of Sarpy County, whose total area is 4.2 square miles, all of it land. It has no lakes but lots of baseball diamonds. It was Tuesday, and Shelah and I were going into town to do our advance work. Peace City's mayor, Diane, asked if I'd like to be adopted by the city of Papillion.

"What is that?" I asked. "What would I have to do?"

"Oh, I guess you haven't heard. We have another new tradition now. Towns along our route are adopting marchers who will write back to keep in touch until we reach Washington. Just send pretty postcards." Diane held her pen, ready to add my name to the list.

"Yes, I'd love to do that." I said. "I'm already writing to some families who hosted us in Marcher in the Home."

"Okay, good. Today when you find the mayor in Papillion, just tell him you're their adopted marcher and that you'll write to him. At the Trees and Keys ceremony, I'll introduce you and you can say a few words."

When I asked the mayor about adopting me, he thought it was a great idea and gave me a small lapel pin, a butterfly inscribed, "Papillion." I'd felt for some time that a part of my inner self, symbolized by a butterfly, was cracking out of its chrysalis, emerging. So it was perfect. I copied his name, Bob Wallace, and address into my little green book and promised to report March progress once a week until we reached our final destination.

Next, Shelah and I found the Dairy Queen for our afternoon snack. "Better stock up on magic powder," we told them. "The Peace March is coming to town. You have no idea how we love Dairy Queen!"

Small businesses in towns from Utah to Nebraska liked us to spend money. They were having a tough time. We saw the effects of the farm crisis. Businesses were closing, and homes were for sale. The clerk at the Dairy Queen told us, "It's predicted that 10 percent of the farms in this state will be foreclosed this year, and, of course, that means that a lot of businesses will fail." I wondered if small-town rural America would soon be history.

"Such a sadness." I said to Shelah. "Such nonsense for our government to be spending on more nuclear tests when our farmers, families whose forefathers homesteaded, are losing their farms."

We sat on a bench outside, and, as we licked our ice cream, I thought, "Who can be sad while eating ice cream?" I said, "When we get home, let's start a spa for peace and weight loss."

"Yes," Shelah agreed. "We'll have it in a Dairy Queen and let everyone know they can eat anything they want—malted milk shakes, hamburgers, strawberry pie, ice cream—and not gain weight. All you have to do is walk about 15 or 20 miles a day. Easy!"

I told her how I'd felt when I rejoined the marchers after that solitary morning when I wrote in the field in western Nebraska: "I realized that I am proud to be among them. Truly proud to know people who run on courage, hope, faith, resilience, resourcefulness, good humor, and hard work. The March is not glamorous; it is… too complex to define in one word."

Neither of us could. But we agreed that the product of The Great Peace March was hope. Was there anything more profound than hope?

One purpose of The March was to dispel the sense of hopelessness surrounding global nuclear weapons.

Shelah slurped her ice cream, stood up, and said, "Well, we're making changes, but we have a long way to go. Come on."

A warm walk in Nebraska.

CHAPTER 13

When You Pray, Move Your Feet
(an old African proverb)

In January, when I was making arrangements to leave San Mateo to join The Peace March, one of my sons teased me by turning to his wife and saying, "Gee, Honey, what shall we do today? Wanna go for walk? Let's do that today, and tomorrow, and the next day; let's do it every day for nine months!" He grinned at me, "Mom! That's gotta be really boring."

The Great Peace March was a scramble, a jumble, sometimes worth a grumble, but it was never, ever boring. It was a series of daily miracles—even in Nebraska in July. A prayer in motion.

It was a 90-degree, high-humidity day, and even before noon, I was staggering. That morning I just followed the person in front of me, focused on putting one foot in front of the other, careful not to stumble, almost blinded by the sweat pouring into my eyes. I had a cold, too. Felt like I was drowning, barely treading water just under the surface. Luckily, the Blister Bus came by, and Madonna Newberg leaned over, opened the passenger door and said, "Donna, get in."

"Oh, gladly. Thanks! You're an angel." I rested my head on the dashboard, held a wad of tissues beneath my nose and let it run. I drank my canteen dry and leaned back in what my grandmother would have called a swoon. When we arrived at the campsite, Madonna let me out and said, "Go find water and some shade. Lie down and sleep until someone wakens you."

At Aqua II, the mobile water tank, I filled my canteen, drank, filled it again and looked around. There were no trees or buildings at this site, nothing to make shade. It was a huge parking lot; some of our trailers were clustered near the center, so I crawled beneath one and found space among other panting marchers who lay there dribbling water onto their bandanas. I lay on my back and for a few seconds inspected the underside of the trailer.

When someone jiggled my arm and said, "Donna, wake up. They have to move this trailer," I couldn't roll over. I was stuck, literally stuck. The asphalt had melted onto my shirt and glued me in place. "Pull, Donna. You can do it." I lurched up, heard a wrenching sound, and reached around to feel the back of my shirt, gummed with globs of melted asphalt. We crawled out and stood to admire our shadows. We were upright! The sun was setting. Someone passed by, smiled, and handed me an orange. It was a typical Peace March gift, small, given with sincerity, love and compassion. An orange was exactly what I needed right then. A not-so-small miracle.

Dinner that evening seemed especially good: fresh corn and several cold salads. Townspeople had brought out lemonade as well as 45 gallons of ice cream.

With the heat, humidity, flies, mosquitoes, grasshoppers, ants, ticks and chiggers, I sweated and scratched. There were no showers, of course. But children splashed in buckets of water, and people squirted each other with hoses from the tank truck. I ran out to be squirted by a hose and felt like a child running through the sprinkler. Ah, blessed relief.

For the next few days, I limited my walks to five hours a day. On the days I did walk, I fingered the little red bag that hung around my neck and remembered Lynn Andrew's advice: "Become your totem."

At a morning rest stop, Sue Guist came over and said, "I was walking behind you today. You were just plodding along and then I saw you straighten and stride out. What happened?"

I told her, "I became a giraffe."

One early evening, still in Nebraska, Shelah and I crossed a courthouse lawn shadowed by gigantic maple trees. Lightning bugs flashed and sparkled. A young man on a bicycle called, "Hi, do you know a marcher named Shawn? She's from Spokane."

"No," I answered, "but I probably could find her."

"I don't know her last name, but I have this booklet for her, so if you could deliver it, I'd really appreciate it."

How could I find someone named Shawn in our milling group of 600? But I took the pamphlet back to the tent with me. The next morning I was on truck-loading duty, and while we passed the bags along, I heard someone call out, "Hi, Shawn, I'll pick up your lunch for you."

"Are you from Spokane?" I asked the bright-eyed young woman next to me. "Oh, good! I have a message for you."

"Thanks," she pocketed the booklet without breaking the rhythm of passing the sleeping bags along to the truck. I shrugged and said to myself, nice little miracle you had there.

In her book *The Great Peace March*, Connie wrote:

> *Diversity in the way we walked, as in almost every other phase of March life, was obvious. Some of us read (aloud or silently). Others talked, chanted, drummed, sang, pulled a wagon (with a child or the yurt), pushed a bicycle, back-packed a baby, or picked up trash. Alternatives to walking were roller skating, running, race walking, skateboarding, bicycling, and one man, our clown Hinton Harrison, rode a unicycle.*

Those who walked ahead scrambled down embankments, collected aluminum cans, and tossed them up on the roadway. Others, as they came along, set the cans upright. Still others who followed stepped on them to smash them flat. Finally, marchers with big plastic garbage bags picked up the cans. These were taken to a recycling center, and with the money, the kitchen crew bought a huge popcorn popper. The fragrance of popping corn drew us to the kitchen area where we scooped with our mugs, sat on the ground and had a feast.

One of my favorite dinners was, and still is, popcorn and apples. And we were in corn country. In Colorado, the corn had been young, green, short. In Nebraska it was knee-high. In Iowa it would be head-high, growing across the landscape from one horizon to the other. The vast fields of windswept leaves, sun glinting on the broken surfaces, birds skimming just above the waves, reminded me of the precious Pacific to which our backs had been turned for many weeks. The corn rustled and grew so fast we listened to its crackling and were mesmerized.

Occasionally we passed a family who had set up a card table with paper cups and cold water or lemonade. One afternoon, I stopped to accept a refreshing drink and sat down on the lawn in the shade of a big overhanging maple tree. Several others stopped, too. Members of the family joined us, telling about farm foreclosures, the threat of losing a home that had been farmed by four generations. In their own words, they gave voice to the sign we'd been given at the Colorado-Nebraska border: FARMS NOT ARMS.

Near 114th Street and Cornhusker Road, west of Papillion, we had walked by a rather elegant, beautifully proportioned white frame farm house, and a big red barn, both desperately in need of paint. That sad farm told the whole story of the farmers' current plight. We listened to them, and they listened to us. The farmers informed others of our presence, "These people are not radicals. Some of 'em might look like hippies, but they're okay. Even worth talkin' with. Let's invite some of 'em to the barbecue tonight."

A few days later, while we camped in a farmer's field, I found Gene Gordon of San Jose, leader of the "Shakespeare on The March" group, looking discouraged. I asked him, "Why so glum?"

"We have been planning for a week to do *Twelfth Night* and now some guest speaker has preempted our evening."

No sooner had he spoken than an announcement sounded over the bullhorn: "This evening in about 20 minutes, Baba Ram Dass will be speaking to us over on the other side of the barn."

Gene muttered, "Sounds like something we had for dinner last night."

I had never heard nor read Ram Dass, but I slathered on insect repellent, took paper and pen for notes, my inflated sleeping pad to sit on and stepped carefully through the mud below the pigpen beyond the barn.

An attractive, slender, long-legged, bald man with trimmed moustache sat in lotus position on the broad metal steps of a porta-potty trailer. For three hours renowned spiritual teacher Ram Dass, formerly Harvard professor Richard Alpert, sat without stretching his legs and spoke to us—his rapt audience—directly, clearly, lightly with serious good humor. He said, "The Peace March will not be stopped. Your very walking will definitely make a marked difference. Your commitment is impressing people, touching and moving people to become aware and actively involved in creating peace. We are reminded to create peace within and among ourselves."

He scanned us, making me feel as though he really saw me, and continued, "To live in a world that is perfect in its imperfection is difficult, but maybe I can show you. Instead of getting upset by a person who doesn't measure up to your personal standards, look at him in his uniqueness and appreciate his individuality. When seeing one of your young members dressed in what you judge to be a sloppy manner, instead of getting upset, just exclaim to yourself, 'Look at that wonderfully weird outfit! Could anyone other than that one think up such a fantasy? Is he/she celebrating by going through life in costume?' "

I felt as though he were talking directly to me, reminding me to resist judging others by appearance. Not easy, but timely. Here was a world-acclaimed spiritual leader sitting cross legged on the porta-potty steps a few feet away from a pen of squealing pigs. Indeed, do not judge by appearances.

Walking. Walking. The days I had no responsibilities other than walking were still the best. I walked with friends or alone. And when I walked alone, I could observe our world in detail and feel a connection to other living things. Sleeping and walking across the breast of Mother Earth changed me. I wept with renewed gratitude. I had time to pause and watch the horses.

As we walked along their road, a large herd of horses cantered over to the fence to watch us. There must have been 30 of them. They got as close as they could to us, then whirled and thundered back along the fence, only to turn again, and race to catch up. They whinnied and snickered and strained against the fence. A few marchers crossed the road to pet them. Then the horses turned like a flock of birds in flight to run back and forth yet again. What were they thinking? Were they a mirror of us? Running along within our enclosure, excited but not making much difference? I imagined the horses ran with us to emphasize the importance of The March, that Ram Dass was right. My tears welled up at the magnificence of those creatures.

In Colorado, a Buddhist monk, the Rev. Katsuzo Sawada, joined The March. He walked along while beating a drum and chanting until some marchers, irritated by the constant day-long thumping, took him to mediation. He agreed to walk in the back of The March column where I liked walking along with him. In rhythm to his drum, I recalled the little ditty I'd made up in the rainstorm in Victorville, to a tune from *My Fair Lady*:

> *Every step is a step for Peace*
> *Every step and I release*
> *My anger, fear and prejudeese.*
> *Oh, isn't that so wonderful?*

Along our route, which paralleled the railroad, small towns called whistle-stops, had been established every 10 miles so steam engines could take on water. The engineer blew the whistle to alert the stationmaster.

In one of these whistle-stop towns, Elm Creek, population 800, residents closed their businesses and peeked out their windows because they feared our presence. Shelah and I, doing our usual advance work, peered in the windows of the laundromat, but no one was there. It was dark and empty. We walked around to the back, found the door unlocked, went inside and put our clothes in a machine. The owner, who lived upstairs, heard us and came roaring down, her red hair wild, her face dark and scowling. "Who let you in? Can't you see I'm closed? You some of them peace marchers here to make trouble?" Then she noticed our clothes in the washer. "Oh, you've already paid and started."

Shelah and I apologized, "We're sorry for disturbing you. We need clean clothes. We're camping and walking every day to let people know the importance of global nuclear disarmament, and we're dusty and dirty."

The lady listened and grudgingly acknowledged that maybe her fears were unfounded. She said, "We have been warned that a bunch of no-good hippies were advancing on our town, and we'd better watch out." We sat and chatted while our clothes tumbled and spun. Others from our March peered in the windows, and the owner unlocked the front door. Some put their clothes in the machines and joined our conversation. Others left, saying, "We'll be back. Just want to check out the bakery up the street."

"The bakery's closed today," the laundromat lady said, "but I'll give them a call and say it's okay to open up for you." She dialed another number. "Now, I'm gonna call the police. Oh, whoa now, it's all right. I want him to come meet you." In a few minutes, Officer Duane D. Bond walked into the laundromat. He told us he was the only police officer in town. We asked him why the townfolks were so afraid of us. What had they heard about us? What could we do to fix that?

"Well," he was thoughtful as he leaned against the door jamb. "We'd heard that you were just a bunch of gypsies out of work and wandering across the country asking for handouts and messin' up places. And we thought there were more of you than there are of us."

We repeated some of what Shelah and I had explained to the laundromat lady. After a while he closed the conversation by radioing the police departments in small towns ahead so that we could safely be welcomed.

After a while, those who had gone to check out the bakery came back and reported, "We went to a saloon and the bartender was a woman. She owned the place, and she had baked pies and lined them up near the front windows. Strawberry pie!" They grinned and rubbed their bellies.

She told them she had been skittish about the marchers and said, "When the first of you came in, I just warned 'em they better behave or not stay. Why, they were just as nice as my own kin. Not a bit o' trouble. They really liked the strawberry pie, too. You people ain't what I thought you'd be."

That night, as I wrote in my journal, I thought about my son's concern over repetitive walking. No, the daily walking was not boring. From on foot I could move at a human pace, not the frenetic 10-miles-over-the-speed-limit driven race of normal life. Walking slowed us down and was our means of touching people along the route. Eventually we would arrive in Washington, DC, to gain attention from our political leaders. In the meantime, our March was a series of miracles, and I had time to notice them. The March broadened my perspective, heightened my awareness, deepened my appreciation. We were "walking for our lives." A prayer in action. Not boring at all.

If you can't find a shower, a hose will do.

CHAPTER 14

Iowa!

Independence Day in Iowa! What could feel more red, white and blue than that? We had crossed over the Missouri River from Nebraska into Iowa and camped near Council Bluffs. We were 1,500 miles from New York, about the same distance as the length of the Great Wall of China.

Some of us walked in the Fourth of July parade, waved, smiled and flashed the peace sign. Our mayor Diane, in her brimmed red hat, sat up in the convertible with the mayor of Council Bluffs. The rest of us stood along the curbs together with the townspeople and cheered.

We were guests that afternoon at the annual barbecue in the city park. A Norman Rockwell scene: gingham covered tables laden with big bright bowls of potato salad, corn on the cob, tomatoes, summer beans, pickles. Men stood at smoky barbeques turning burgers and ribs. Children raced around or played baseball. Picnic tables with their attached benches stood in the shade, covered with cakes with red, white and blue icing that left our teeth and tongues blue, cupcakes with tiny American flags, dozens of fruit pies with latticed top crusts. It was too hot for Jell-O. I drifted around, sipped cold lemonade from a quart canning jar, and chatted with salt-of-the-earth Iowans.

In Lewis, the Rev. Melvin Ammon of the Methodist Congregational Church had been laying the groundwork for our arrival on July 9. He had heard of our recycling program in which we collected aluminum cans and glass bottles as well as paper along the road. An entire barn-load of newspapers awaited our arrival. He also gave us unlimited use of the church copy machine. The women in town held a bake sale and gave us the proceeds.

More than 60 people from Cass County came to our campsite outside Lewis to meet us and ask questions. Our mayor, Diane, and theirs, Bob Worth, exchanged keys to the cities; the 61st peace tree was planted, and the ceremony included everyone, marchers and locals, singing together. Someone brought Kool-Aid because it was invented in a downtown Lewis drugstore in 1900.

In exchange for their learning the history of The Peace March, a local historian told us the story of Hitchcock House, a station on the Underground Railroad. Mr. Hitchcock entertained guests upstairs while the very slaves for whom his guests were searching hid in the basement. This story reminded me of those I'd heard about my Great-Great Grandfather John Rankin of Ripley, Ohio, who was a leader in the Underground Railroad there. He, his wife and nine sons rescued, hid, and led to safety, slaves who had escaped across the Ohio River from Kentucky. As we walked from Lewis to Des Moines, along one of many Underground Railroad routes, I thought of these heroic measures my ancestors and Mr. Hitchcock had taken on behalf of others -- not unlike us, who were marching for peace.

We covered 25 miles from Lewis to our next stop, Lake Anita. Only a fraction of those who started completed the entire distance in that heat. At the end of a long, hot afternoon, I watched 50 of our marchers stride into the state park, continue across the grass, past the bath houses, down the broad steps, across the beach and directly into the shallow lake. Their flags still waving, they trooped and shouted their way into the water.

That evening, Gene Gordon and his Shakespeare thespians presented their version of *Twelfth Night*. We in the audience sat along the broad steps and the beach as the actors performed on the floating platform at the edge of Lake Anita. In thrift store costumes and having altered the script to reflect The March, Gene and his group were a hilarious hit.

Several months earlier, staff-writer Kathleen Hendricks, in a *Los Angeles Times* article, had segregated marchers into four categories: anarchists who disliked any form of structure, purists who walked every single day all the way, pragmatists who balanced working and walking with practical rest periods, and vacationers who had lots of fun. I fell somewhere between pragmatist and vacationer, but lately I had veered toward the latter. I had attended an opera, two weddings, toured historic sites, visited museums, and enjoyed a picnic. The mayor of Grinnell invited me to an evening of Bingo.

All my life I had assumed that the Midwest was a flat, empty wasteland. On my map, Iowa was colored drab tan. So I was totally surprised by the exciting architecture of the Des Moines Art Center, designed by the world-renowned architects Eero Saarinen and I. M. Pei. It was airy and light, with floor-to-ceiling windows in the lobby. In the courtyard, I saw a Carl Milles' bronze figure balancing on one toe, stretching joyously upward, just as I sometimes felt. Years earlier I had seen, in a Milles sculpture garden near Stockholm, his "Sunsinger," a figure with feet securely on the ground, but whose body and extended arms honored the sun, the spheres. As a marcher for peace now, I reached, as the sculpture did, to something beyond. I wasn't sure just what. Peace in the world, peace within myself. Months after Des Moines, in New York City, I listened to Paul Winter's soaring soprano sax wail the musical version of "Sunsinger," and wept in awe at the evidence of unity in our lives.

Two towns west of Iowa City, I noticed a playbill advertising *Madame Butterfly* to be performed on the University of Iowa campus in Hancher Auditorium. "Why not?" In spite of wearing rumpled (but clean!) March clothes, I went to the box office on the Friday of the performance. Only a few isolated seats were left, and I was hesitating when a young man approached. He had five tickets he could not use that evening. First balcony, front row, center. The next day five of us happily whistled Puccini arias as we swung along the highway.

To attend two weddings within a month while walking across

America is not as unusual as one might think. Several of us left The March for a few days to attend a wedding, greet a new grandchild, deal with a family emergency, undergo an appendectomy. Life went on; children were launched; marriages dissolved. Mary and Franklin Folsom celebrated their 50th wedding anniversary. In May, I had flown from Denver to Rhode Island for the wedding of my son John to Holly Harper.

The second wedding I attended was on July 27, on the grounds of Coralville Northwest Junior High School where Karen Anderson and James Smith were married. They had met several years ago while doing peace work in Santa Monica, joined The Peace March together, and invited all of Peace City to their celebration. The bride had fresh wildflowers braided into her hair, wore a simple flower print cotton skirt, a white, lace-edged blouse and was barefoot. The groom wore a new white shirt with clean Levis. Five hundred guests formed a singing circle around the newlyweds. The Peace March kitchen staff prepared a three-tier cake, garlanded with fresh flowers.

Living History Farms, in Urbandale, near Des Moines, is an outdoor museum documenting life from early Iowa Indian times to the 20th century. We camped among the trees and toured the various exhibits, including a 1925 farmhouse which, with its wooden steps and broad porches, reminded me of my grandmother's home in Portland, Oregon.

Across the street was a large commercial motel. Shelah and I knew it would have a swimming pool and, therefore, showers. We needed showers. We brushed our hair, checked for lettuce in our teeth, took our towels and shampoo, and walked right into and through the lobby as though we belonged there. I reminded Shelah of what my mother had often said, "Walk with dignity and no one will notice." The showers were delicious! In our clean shirts and shorts and sandals, we looked like everyone else so we sat at an outdoor table for a while and ordered two glasses of Chardonnay. We felt like mischievous interlopers.

Sue Guist, who wrote a book about The March, *Peace Like a River*, spoke about Des Moines:

> *We had an emergency call for church speakers.*
> *Shelah, Donna and I drove to the Friends Meeting House*
> *where chaos reigned. Nine-thirty at night, milling around*

hot and tired, we watched the advance team sort out marchers and speaker requests.

Someone gave us an address. Shelah drove, Donna read the directions, I cheered from the back seat. We got into some pretty spooky neighborhoods, close to midnight, and I thought maybe we should find a motel and call them in the morning, but finally we found Father Bob Schoemann's big old-fashioned brick house on East Ninth Street. Several marchers were there already. Air conditioning! Bathtubs. Linen cupboards full of plush towels. Good as home!

In the morning we went to our assigned churches. Mine was in a beautiful park-like setting, a former publisher's mansion.

Donna and Shelah raised a lot of money at their church.

Sue concluded that poor, ethnic groups were more supportive of The March than the wealthy.

"That may be true," I said. "People who feel disenfranchised need change, and they see us as possible leaders in their cause. The comfortable are—well, comfortable. We need to convince them that they, too, are just as vulnerable to nuclear destruction as are those with less money." I remembered that, in the Peace Academy bus, I had read an article about a "confederation of pragmatic, progressive businessmen dedicated to making the world safe for millionaires. Step one: no more nukes."

In the afternoon, Father Bob took us to a barbecue that included entertainment by local musicians followed by square dancing at 8:30. Sue wondered, "Are people really nicer here than they are on the coasts?" She added, "I don't see how they could fake it, town after town."

In mid-July, the Peace March arrived in Newton. At my January going-away party in San Mateo, friends Jane and David Carr had told me about this pretty Midwestern town where they had lived for a while. "You'll love it!" they had exclaimed. And they were right.

Newton was *so Iowan!* White frame houses sat on lawns that flowed uninterrupted down the blocks, flourishes of red geraniums in window boxes and on porches. It looked proud and neat.

I heard one marcher ask, "Do they scrub the streets in Newton?"

It was a Grant Wood picture town: sharp details, simplified forms, solid flat black shade beneath dark green oak trees, the geometric shapes in hard-edge relief against the ultimate green of corn fields. Heavy bright white clouds pinned against extra-blue sky.

I met a man who was painting a picket fence and asked him why so many houses were painted white. He straightened up to face me, "Because that's the color houses are s'pposed to be. They're s'pposed to be white, and barns are s'pposed to be red."

Oh.

I learned later that the iron in red pigment makes it last longer.

When we marched from the west along Highway 6, with the afternoon sun raising heat rash on the backs of my legs, we were greeted by signs mounted on a cyclone fence, "Welcome, Great Peace March." Farther along, on a grassy median strip, women crisp in summer cottons and men grinning as they extended their hands, told us of the medical clinic up the street where we could have our blisters treated. They offered us icy juice in paper cups too pretty to throw away. The Episcopal minister invited us to visit, "Any time. Now. Tomorrow. Come back if you can." A grandfather clasped my hands and said, "I hope you won't have to be fighting global nuclear arms when you're 81." His voice cracked, and he looked down. I later wished I'd hugged him as I wanted to, but forgave myself by saying, Iowans seemed more reserved than Californians.

On front porches that spanned the width of their houses, folks sat on wooden chairs and fanned themselves as they watched us trudge by. Every single person smiled and waved. So did we. I felt like a hometown hero and flashed the peace sign. Some porches held four generations. Several of the people came down to shake hands; some had cameras. Children at Kool-Aid stands offered eight ounces of coolness for five cents. Once I was offered a beer. The American flag flew everywhere. It was a red-white-and-blue day!

I almost forgot my burning legs as I paused to approach one porch. A stout man rose to greet me. The two women looked hesitant. I had heard that small-town folks sometimes greeted a stranger thinking, "Wonder just what this one wants." I stopped at the base of the steps and the quiet gentleman nodded and murmured, "You're doin' a good thing. God bless you." The women relaxed as the man announced, "I'm just a dumb truck driver, so I'm wonderin' at these trucks I been seein' goin' past here. I thought you was walkin'!"

I explained that more than 650 people were with The Peace March now and that we had about 100 support vehicles, four semis just for food and food preparation, another six to haul gear. We owned four porta-potty trailers plus old school buses and converted bread trucks that housed our Peace City services that included a new Performing Arts Center bus, the child care center, schools, mayor's office, medical center, media office, community interaction, speakers' bureau, vehicle maintenance, mail room, and security team. Our infrastructure had grown to more than 30 offices in all. The inquisitive trucker seemed to appreciate the complexity of moving a town each day. He said, "I wish I hadn't splintered my leg in an accident 'cause I'd sure enjoy goin' along with you for a while. But maybe we'll see you at the jazz concert tonight."

Jazz concert?

"Sure." He looked pleased to tell me, "We have a band shell down in the park."

At a corner closer to the center of town, we were handed half-sheets printed with a schedule of services and events: a softball game, a coupon for an ice cream cone, the city pool and showers. Jazz concert at 8 o'clock. What a welcome! And what a contrast to the fear we had encountered in Elm Creek, Nebraska. Our reputation must have been improving.

Our campsite was in Holland Park. Shelah and I set up our tent in a cool, shady, green glen, gathered our supplies and clean clothes and headed for the showers. In the nearby natural amphitheater, Fred Maytag Bowl, we'd later lounge on the grass to hear the Des Moines Jazz Orchestra play Errol Garner's *Misty*, and I'd remember the 1960s dancing parties my family had enjoyed. Sometimes I missed those days.

Fred Maytag had lived in Newton. He'd given more than a band shell to his hometown. Fred Bergmann had invented the washing machine in 1898 and improved and patented it in 1904. Then in 1907 Maytag partnered with an inventor who turned out a new kind of hand-powered machine. In 1911, they added an electric motor, and in 1922, they turned the agitator upside down and revolutionized the washing machine industry. Fred Maytag was responsible for marketing the machines. In 1986, Maytag was the largest employer in town, with more than 1,500 employees. I was fascinated to learn this history from a man who had worked 33 years for the Maytag Company and now shared a bench with me on the lawn of the Jasper County Court House. I was a long way from home.

I asked him, "Do you think about nuclear weapons? Do you feel threatened by them?"

"No, I don't. I'm livin' a quiet and peaceful life. You got a good cause, though. Hope you do some good."

A young family, a wholesome and neat mother and dad and eight-year-old son, walked by and smiled. I got up to walk with them. They told me they lived in Newton "because it's 10 times better than Des Moines. It is the best place to raise kids. We don't have to worry about their safety. It's like most Midwestern towns in that people live here most of their lives. People here are stable." I thought of the fluidity of the California population. Their son Brad hugged me goodbye, and I gave him a squeeze when he said, "I love you already."

From Newton, we walked along roads bordered by deep pink clover and wispy white Queen Anne's Lace. We were scheduled to meet a Russian Peace Delegation in Davenport on July 31. On August 6, we would honor Hiroshima Day in President Reagan's hometown of Dixon, Illinois. By the time we reached Chicago, we'd be two-thirds of the way through our nine-month commitment.

We marchers were walking to save Newton, Iowa, as well as all the small towns I could think of. "Every step is a step for peace," for Coquille, Oregon where I was a child, for Hillsborough, California, our sons' growing up home, for Oregon City where my father matured, for Rifle, Colorado, where I learned the history of barbed wire. So many small towns… all over the world. I had chosen a job all right when I'd said I wanted:

> *Peace on the mountain,*
> *Peace in the valley,*
> *Peace in our hearts,*
> *And piece of the action.*

Until I had been there, I had always thought of Amana as freezers.

Not any more. While the seven Amana Villages had a population of 1,600, the corporation employed 4,000. The people, mostly of German descent, annually hosted thousands of tourists in the woolen mills, craft shops and restaurants. Shelah and I read a brochure and learned that their original villages were established in Germany in 1714. Persecuted for their religious beliefs, they fled in 1843 and settled near Buffalo, New York. When they needed more land, they moved to Iowa in 1855. Today the community based on religious faith and spirit thrives.

Beneath an oak tree in South Amana, we enjoyed a picnic of apricot bread, jack cheese and elderberry wine. All of these delicacies were made locally and were a vast improvement over our usual beige March food. Not to denigrate The March food. Even Sharon Gonzalez, a leader in the kitchen said, "The food on The March is of great variety, some of it even recognizable." It was wholesome, but it could not compare with apricot bread baked in the Amana ovens.

The March arrived in Davenport in time to meet 47 Soviets who were on a Peace Cruise traveling the Mississippi River on the Delta Queen paddle boat with an American peace group. Russian cosmonaut Gregory Grechko shook my hand and said, "I like you, my American friend." I watched Russian and American children exchange gifts of pictures and flowers. The logo for the Mississippi Peace Cruise included the bow of the Pushkin, a Volga River boat, and the stern of the River Queen. The message was, "We are all in the same boat."

On August first, the *Los Angeles Times* published Kathleen Hendrix' report about that day in Davenport, Iowa:

> On Wednesday, The Great Peace March met the Mississippi Peace Cruise in what the local papers proclaimed on the front pages as the Crossroads of Peace.
>
> The Delta Queen pulled into port at Davenport, Iowa, with 47 Soviets and 130 Americans on board. They were on a seven-day cruise from St. Paul, Minn., to St. Louis, Mo.
>
> At the morning dockside ceremonies, Peace City's honorary mayor, Diane Clark, made welcoming remarks, as did the other four local mayors. Davenport Mayor

Thomas Hart welcomed The March representatives along with the Peace Cruise, and invited the delegation to a backyard picnic lunch he hosted at his home.

Meanwhile, most of the marchers were walking 14 miles from Wilton to Walcott where they would be bused to the events on the Mississippi.

In the afternoon when the bulk of the marchers arrived on the dock, Mayor Diane presented handmade keys to Peace City to the representatives of six Soviet cities. Marchers planted a maple tree on the bank of the Mississippi in honor of the Soviets, the 87th Tree of Peace planted on The March, accompanied with a hand-carved plaque, this time in Russian.

The Soviet and American cruise members climbed back on board and hung over the rails while the marchers began quietly to sing, "Give Peace a Chance." They stood there, hands raised in the peace sign, swaying gently and the passengers of the river boat did the same, calling out, "We love you." The band played, "This Land Is Your Land." From the delegation on the Delta Queen came balloons, streamers, post cards. Pam Abdo, a Davenport teacher, cried joyfully to a marcher next to her, "Isn't this fantastic? God bless you. It's not often you see people who practice what they preach."

The whistle blew. The band struck up another song and the Delta Queen was on her way, leaving a momentarily lonely looking group of people in its wake.

That same day, Admiral Gene LaRoque (ret), director of the Washington-based Center for Defense Information, visited The March to remind us, "If you ever think while you're marching that maybe it's not worthwhile, remember you're doing nothing less than saving life on this planet." I hoped he'd return to the Pentagon and tell others that same statement.

The South Amana Volunteer Fire Department, when they learned we'd not had showers for six days, brought their hose truck to our campsite and sprayed us. Ministers in Oakland brought 45 gallons of ice cream; a farmer delivered 700 pounds of freshly picked corn. On a Saturday, 250 local people waited for us under trees on the lawn of the Tiffin Methodist Church and joined us as "Marchers for the Day," for the final hot five-mile stretch. The March turned into a parade of 500 for the final mile in Coralville. On the school lawn, the community band played marches and dance music.

Ann and Dick Edelman paused in their dance for Ann to express changes she's noted in herself. "I've stopped worrying about whether everyone on The March keeps up a middle-class image," she said. "I've started considering myself part of a whole that reflects all of society."

I chimed in, "And I believe that we Over-50s generally have become more accepting."

In Davenport, Shelah and I stayed for a night in the home of clay artist Isabel Bloom. She recommended that we visit the John Deere Museum, so we went to see the evolution of the plow. From a rough-pronged stick pushed or dragged to furrow the soil, to the huge mechanical green monsters with multiple disks, the principle is still the same: make a slot for seeds or seedlings. Maybe a metaphor for planting seeds of peace.

By the time The March reached Iowa, I had discovered the Andrew Carnegie Libraries. Dave Miller showed one of them to me the day I rode with him to shop for another old school bus. He had become the bus shopper for The March. He also wrote articles for his hometown paper and, in his search for a quiet place to write, had found the Carnegie Libraries. They were clean, serene, and had chairs! And tables, bathrooms and drinking fountains. The wind didn't blow papers; the rain didn't destroy them. From then on, several times a month, I went with Dave to the libraries. We talked with the librarians about The Peace March, wrote our feature stories, sometimes leaned over to check our facts with each other, and then went directly to the post office to mail our dispatches. So easy! The libraries seemed to be everywhere! Later I learned that between 1881 and 1919, philanthropist Andrew Carnegie had funded 2,500 libraries to be built in small towns across the country from the Atlantic Seaboard to California.

On August first, a sparkling bright day, The Great Peace March crossed the Mississippi River. Our last campsite in Iowa melted away, just as another one appeared across the river in Illinois.

President Ronald Reagan's boyhood home in Dixon, Illinois.

CHAPTER 15

A Breeze Through the Windy City

Laura, our day leader, put the whistle to her lips and blew. When we heard the blast everybody froze. Stopped mid-stride, as if turned to stone. Cars drove by us; horns honked; we stayed immobile for several minutes. In a piece of street theater to illustrate life interrupted by a nuclear bomb, we stood motionless halfway across the I-280 bridge that spanned the Mississippi River from Davenport, Iowa, to East Moline, Illinois. An eerie silence held among us until the second signal sounded, and we resumed walking. We came back to life. Symbolically. For me, it felt like rising from the dead, a moment of miracle. We moved onward toward Chicago, hoping to have a real effect there.

Along the way, we arrived in Ronald Reagan's hometown of Dixon on August 6, Hiroshima Day. Folks rocked on their porches, sat on the front steps or stood in their store doorways to nod a greeting. Some just watched, and some waved at us and smiled cautiously, politely. It certainly wasn't the enthusiasm we'd felt in Newton, Iowa, but Dixon was conservative, Republican, and loyal to Ronald Reagan, their native son, who was then president of the United States.

On the courthouse lawn, where we sat eating our brown bag lunches, I stretched to wipe a shred of lettuce off my fingers onto my socks, the closest thing to a napkin I had at that moment. The Rev. Thomas Shepard, standing on the courthouse steps, described what had happened 41 years earlier when the United States dropped atom bombs on Hiroshima and Nagasaki in 1945. Massive weapons with shocking effects wreaked instant destruction and death. As he spoke, church bells began to toll, and he halted his speech. He stopped mid-sentence, standing as still as the Dixon air. We froze in place, as we had on the bridge over the Mississippi River. We stopped chewing gum, stopped scratching, stopped talking or walking. I halted, my right hand still on my sock, and peeked up sideways to see if anyone was moving, shifting from an uncomfortable position. Everyone was motionless except one man, who tilted his water bottle a little so water wouldn't run down his shirtfront. People walking by stopped and stood for moment, perhaps wondering what was happening, perhaps knowing and joining us.

Did they know that August 6 not only was Hiroshima Day, but it also marked the end of the Soviet Test Ban? The USSR had waited 18 months for the United States to stop nuclear testing. This was their action, not just words. The USA responded with its own action: it stepped up testing in Nevada. Once the agreement ended, the Soviets would no longer bind themselves to suspending nuclear testing. I thought of August 6 and August 9 of 1945, the summer I graduated from high school, when the total United States atomic arsenal, which pre-dated nuclear weapons, had been detonated in Japan. That autumn, when I went away to college, we believed there were no more atomic weapons in the world. I didn't worry then about nuclear annihilation; I was shopping for school clothes.

The bells tolled again. The moment of profound stillness passed, and life resumed. I cuffed my socks to hide the lettuce smear and remained seated on the lawn in Dixon, lost in the enormity of the nuclear weapons threat.

We left the courthouse lawn to walk over to Ronald Reagan's childhood home. Dixon was full of pretty, white, wooden Victorian homes standing firmly on their green neatly mowed plots, fronted by oaks and bordered by brightly colored annuals. On one lawn, I noted a sign, "Home of Ronald Reagan," and a flagpole. We ceremoniously presented a peace tree and wooden plaque to be added to the Reagan landscape. "At a later date," the mayor said.

That evening, to honor those lost in the bombings of Hiroshima and Nagasaki, we lit small candle lanterns and floated them on the Rock River. I remember the lonely look of the candles on the silver water. Bright, but so small as they bobbed away downstream. Like our March, bright but small? Would we light up enough awareness to have a lasting impact?

We grew increasingly excited, as well as apprehensive, about Chicago. It would be our largest city so far, and advance teams came back to The March to announce there were no TV and radio interviews set up yet. We needed media coverage to gain attention in a large city. This was not Elmwood, Nebraska! However, we were pleased to learn that 75 churches and synagogues had scheduled March speakers. That was a relief. Evan Conroy, at 23 the youngest board member, said, "In Chicago, either we are going to become a very large movement or a small group of very dedicated people."

We arrived in La Grange, a Chicago suburb, on the campus of Bethlehem Center, administered by the Sisters of St. Joseph. The entire community of sisters had walked out to the roadway and formed a reception line. As we turned into the grounds, the sisters embraced us, took our hands, thanked and welcomed us, telling us how thrilled they were to have us there. The tears in their eyes caught us by surprise and overwhelmed us. I had tears in my eyes, too, at the sincerity of these gracious women.

We awakened at three in the morning to walk into Chicago on time for several scheduled events. In South Chicago we were encouraged by black families who hung out windows in their red-brick ghetto. Drivers stopped along the street to honk and cheer and call, "God bless you all." They shook our hands, wished us well, and thanked us for our efforts. I was so encouraged that I took the hand of a woman standing on the curb and said, "Come on! Just a block if you can't do more. Come walk with us in The Great Peace March!" Her strong, warm hand clasped mine, and we sauntered down the street, swinging our hands together—mine tanned almost as dark as hers. At the end of her brief walk, she hugged me and said, "You'll just have to go for me. I got childrens to care for."

We headed for the Loop in the downtown commercial area, whooping and cheering, calling out to bystanders. Businessmen in gray three-piece suits were silent, looked annoyed, and ignored us. "I never felt so invisible in my life," said marcher Ellen Murphy, 49, from San Diego, as she spoke of The March through the Loop at noon. "The onlookers weren't hostile or unfriendly. They looked right at us and didn't see us."

I looked at the indifferent bystanders and wanted to go shake them awake. Instead, I asked a man walking next to me, "What's the matter with these city people? Don't they understand?"

"This doesn't surprise me," said Bob Hurlbut, an electrical engineer who had taken the day off to march with his wife, daughter, and neighbor. "Everybody's asleep, walking around in a coma, totally unaware—or they're too inhibited to show anything."

In Lincoln Park, Studs Terkel, 1985 Pulitzer Prize winner for *The Good War*, told us he thought people were interested and sympathetic. "I know this March represents the deep-seated values of the great many. But when it comes to making the connection with daily life, we're up against banality, the evil of banality. The American society has to make up its mind if it has a life wish or a death wish. I've got a life wish. That's why I like The March." Later, he reassured us that even though we were a minority, eventually more and more would speak out. I wanted to believe him.

Near Buckingham Fountain in Grant Park, Chicago Mayor Harold Washington welcomed The March and reminded us that Chicago was the largest nuclear-free zone in the United States. Twenty marchers who named themselves "Wild Wimmin for Peace" sang songs that spoke of violence against women as violence against Mother Earth. Speakers from Hollywood, political figures, and our mayor, Diane, spoke. An hour or so full of speeches and music. We had developed a rally pattern. We only needed more ralliers!

At the Chicago Peace Museum, Shelah and I met director Mary Ann Filbin, who smiled and told us The Great Peace March was having an impact, although it was not as overtly dramatic in the windy city as in some other locations. I had the sense that Chicago was a fairly sophisticated town politically as a lot of organizations that did peace work were headquartered there. Mary Ann said our March had helped add new names to local peace group rosters, recruits inspired by face-to-face contact. I hoped she was right.

After three days, we walked out of Chicago and contemplated

the effect we had in big cities. We had learned that large cities were, for the most part, not the places to draw large crowds. Individual contacts, the hopeful message that one person can make a difference by getting involved, by writing their lawmakers, was The March's greatest strength. I was reminded of the statement by Dr. Helen Caldicott, Australian pediatrician and founder of Physicians for Social Responsibility, who said the United States is *not* a really great country. It *could* be, she insisted, but not until its citizens became better informed and more responsible participants. She advocated that no one should graduate from school without having had a basic education in the history of the nuclear age. "It's as important as washing your hands after you go to the bathroom," she said.

We remembered our excitement, only a week earlier, about entering Chicago, where we'd hoped to create a groundswell of demands for global nuclear disarmament. Now, we were, as Evan had suggested, a small group of very dedicated people who felt somewhat powerless, but then I remembered what Margaret Mead had said, "Never doubt that a small group of thoughtful, committed citizens can change the world. Indeed, it is the only thing that ever has."

I wondered how we would change the world. What would happen in Philadelphia? Would New York even notice us at all?

Peace tree planting, Imka with the plaque; Mayor of Peace City, Diane, in her red hat.

CHAPTER 16

Peace in the Murder Capital of America

Our campsite on August 19 lay beneath cottonwood trees in an undulating grassy meadow. Across a meandering park road lay a white sand beach. With breakers along the shore, a body of blue water stretched to the horizon. Children and adults built sand castles. A lifeguard called to a swimmer who was too far out. Walkers strolled the water's edge looking for bright pebbles and tiny donut-shaped fossils. It was a disorienting scene. Way off in the hazy distance, the sun was setting over the Chicago skyline! We were not on the sandy beaches of the Pacific Ocean, but in Gary, Indiana, on the shores of Lake Michigan.

What might have come to mind in 1986 when anyone thought of Gary, Indiana? The song from *Music Man*? High crime? Steel mills?

Black population? Right, all of that. But I was completely caught unaware by the natural beauty of this area. I had no idea. My preconceptions were not inaccurate, just incomplete.

In the 1980s, Gary had the reputation of being the "Murder Capital of America." Security around the campsite was strengthened; the Vietnam veterans who were on The March patrolled the perimeters, and we set up our tents in tight villages. We were alert for strangers who might wander unattended through Peace City, and, at the same time, we invited townspeople to visit and conducted our usual tours of our campsite. Local squad cars dotted the nearby parking lots. I didn't feel comfortable enough to wander alone down the beach.

Yes, there were steel mills. We stopped on the way from Hammond, Indiana, to Gary at the U.S. Steel plant to hear trade union officials declare that even though military spending had increased dramatically over the recent decade, the amount of steel used by the military had decreased. Since 1973, the steel shipped to ordnance and other military markets had dropped 71 percent and now represented less than half of 1 percent of total steel shipments. There simply wasn't much steel in missiles and "Star Wars." As for "Star Wars," a $1-trillion defense plan promoted by Strategic Defense Initiative in 1983 to protect the United States from nuclear missiles, we showed our opinion by cutting round four- to six-inch holes in black thrift store umbrellas. A billion dollar leaky umbrella. "Not much protection," we said.

Unemployment in northwest Indiana was high. Third generation steel workers walked along with us and demanded that we bring their plight to the attention of the federal government when we reached Washington, DC.

I resented their demands. We had enough to do. Then, as I listened, I began seeing connections between government spending and citizen poverty. Peace and justice. I began to reflect on larger social issues and realized I'd had a blinkered view of the world. The farmers in the Midwest had told us of the foreclosures on their family farms and their need for support from the government. The banner, "FARMS NOT ARMS," that the Nebraska Peace group had given us, made more sense to me now. Imagine how our quality of life might change if our taxes were spent on the basic needs—not the greed—of segments of our population. When we looked at each other with compassion and empathy, instead of "what's in it for me?" entire programs could be developed. It sounded true to me that there could be no peace without love and justice. It seemed as though we would have to do nothing short of changing our way of thinking. We needed to be more cooperative and less competitive. I recalled Mother's saying, "Value people not by what they have, but by who they are." Small citizen groups can effect change, but we needed political clout. How could we get that? Deep in thought, not knowing the answers, I walked along.

More than 75 percent of the population in Gary was black. Clusters of exuberant black youth on bicycles wheeled by our camp. They waved and watched us as bright smiles lit up their shiny faces. Beach path joggers flashed the peace sign to us.

At dusk, Mayor Richard Hatcher and our Peace City mayor exchanged keys to the cities. Congresswoman Katie Hall welcomed The Great Peace March with ceremonial formality. Someone read a proclamation. Talented musicians Darryl Purpose, Collective Vision and Wild Wimmin for Peace played for us and led a sing-along. Townspeople offered prayers. They called us "noble people." A group of gospel singers joined us. On a mild summer's night beneath a full moon, on the beach only a few yards from the surf, folks from town swayed with us to the enveloping sounds of soaring gospel singing.

Marquette Park in Gary is within the Indiana Dunes National Lakeshore Park. Fellow marcher Wally McCamat of Coos Bay, Oregon, gazed out over the dunes and murmured, "Reminds me of home." I agreed. The sand dunes in southwestern Oregon were impressive. However, the area within Indiana Dunes Park may have been the most unusual ecological system in the world. The very word Ecology was invented along these shores when Henry Cowles (1891-1936), professor of botany at University of Chicago until 1934, and his students conducted extensive field research in this region.

In these sand dunes I learned to admire the cottonwood tree. I had known that in New Mexico and Arizona, it was the preferred wood for carving Kachina dolls, but here I learned that when the topography of the dunes changed and covered lower cottonwood branches, they actually turned to roots. As the dunes changed again and exposed the roots, they adjusted back into branches. Another lesson in adaptability.

Thanks to the Ice Age, environments had collided and deposited remnants of the past. The result was some strange combinations of plants that attracted Dr. Cowles' interest. Southern dogwood and arctic bearberry grew side by side with plains flowers and prickly cactus.

In 1986, Indiana was a manufacturing state. The Calumet District in the northwest quadrant boasted one of the most gigantic industrial concentrations in the world. In addition to manufacture of heavy machinery, electrical supplies and transportation equipment, more than 60 percent of the building limestone used in the United States was supplied by quarries in the Hoosier State.

At a brunch for 25 of us hosted by Michigan City peace groups, psychologist Sky Schultz sat next to me. We talked about the industrial component of Indiana, and he told me he made films about the relationship between man and his environment. Following the brunch, he brought his film, *Common Miracles* to our campsite. The film, 27 minutes long, dramatized the natural wonders of our world, the fragility of our air, water and soil—the foundations for a healthy life in a healthy environment. It demonstrated the connection between society's ills and society's lack of understanding and appreciation of the wonders of nature. "The source of health is within reach," he concluded. I thought of the angry unemployed steel workers, the crime in Gary, Indiana, the heavy exploitation of natural resources in this corner of our country and wondered at the possible connections.

A few days later, in a small-town Carnegie Library, marcher Dave Miller, who had introduced me to these library oases, and I wrote our reports to our hometown papers. We were snug, cool and clean as we typed. Two fourth-grade girls were there, too. They had noticed us and wrote their thoughts. Shyly, walking with their shoulders touching each other for courage, they approached me, smiled, and handed me pieces of binder paper.

They had written, "We think the peace walkers make good decisions and friends along the way. We hope we can help them in their walk for freedom. One day we hope our kids can live in a world of peace and not be afraid of the Bombs. We are the new Generation and want to live with peace and freedom. Thank you. Your friends, Janys Flemming and Jennifer Huthes"

Today, in 2011, almost exactly 25 years later, I wonder if Janys and

Jennifer remember that afternoon when they wrote those important words. I remember them. I remember that day. And 10 more days in Indiana. We had fabulous farm suppers brought to us by people in La Porte, New Carlisle, South Bend, Elkhart, Bristol, Shipshewana, Lagrange and Angola.

From South Bend, I wrote home to tell my families that Shelah and I set up the tent on the 50-yard line of the Notre Dame football field. I also told them that Notre Dame had the best showers so far. They were large, warm, private, and had soap and shampoo dispensers and hooks for our towels and clothes.

Elkhart was known as the band instrument manufacturing capital of the nation. It was a cheerful, flower-laden town that had a park with picnic tables—covered with pies. For us! Some of us bypassed dinner and went straight to pie.

In Shipshewana, the high school marching band led us to our campsite. They were so full of pep and energy. They buoyed us that last hot mile to tables in the shade where gallons of lemonade awaited us. This, after all, *was* The March I'd ultimately signed up for. I thought of the diversity within our ranks mirrored in the wide diversity of our country, even just in Indiana, where one day we would see abandoned steel mills and idle unemployed men and women and the next, a park full of pies.

In real rural America.

CHAPTER 17

A Good Day for a Walk

When everything went right, I worked two days a week and walked three. The other two were for whatever came along. One week I was able to walk three days plus two more! It's difficult to say just what was the best part of any week, but *one* of the best parts was the walking. I had known this earlier in The Peace March, but now, after six months, I was even more aware of the delights of our being "on the road."

By September, we had reached Ohio, our 10th state since leaving Los Angeles on March 1. We had 76 days left before arrival in Washington, DC, on November 15. As I walked along, I felt especially grateful for the opportunity to see our vast country from on foot and hoped it would still be here for the grandchildren to see as I had.

The day we awakened on the shores of Crooked Lake at the La Grange County Fairgrounds the sun rose my favorite color, orange, above clumpy trees. Mist rose off the glossy pewter lake—no frost as there had been the previous dawn. The grass was dewy, but short, so our shoes got wet, not drenched. I found two plastic bread bags to slip on over my socks before putting on shoes. Walking with wet feet makes the skin soft. Soft skin, blisters.

I hauled my rolled sleeping bag and pad down to their stacks near the gear trucks and listened to early risers recommending breakfast. By the time I got to the serving tables, the oatmeal was gone. That was alright, so was the honey. I chose scrambled eggs, which were fluffy and not burned. The whole-grain bread tasted as nutritious as it looked, and there was real butter! A marcher urged, "Hurry and get a banana. No brown spots today."

The fragrance of good coffee wafted out of the back of a nearby van. A young woman from Santa Cruz, California, Shawneee—who spelled her name with three e's—was on The March with her two beautiful young children. Shawneee dressed in layers of colorful garments accessorized with beaded jewelry and a decorated crocheted hat. In recent weeks, she had begun to brew and serve fresh coffee. For 15 cents, she filled my orange plastic mug. Back at the tent, I sat in the doorway to gaze out over the lake and enjoy breakfast. I lifted the mug in salute to the sun, and noted, "Cousins! The mug and sun are the same bright color!"

Marchers who carried the flags gathered by 7 o'clock to lead us on the next 16-mile hike. Lagging spirits were buoyed when they followed the American, United Nations and state flags. In addition, we had the tall Japanese prayer banner carried near the Buddhist monk who beat his drum and chanted his prayer-mantra for peace during the daily walks. Several creative flags and banners of bright designs were held aloft by their owners. I had always loved a parade. Now I was part of one!

In a narrow file along the left side of Ohio State Highway 20-A, we faced the sun. When cars honked, our right hands automatically rose in a wave or peace sign. We could do that and smile without interrupting a conversation. I strode along with Bea Novobilski, a retired psychiatric social worker from Carpinteria, near Santa Barbara, California. We pointed out to each other the corn stalks crisping in the sun. We had been watching corn since its green infancy in eastern Colorado.

Bright pink fluffs dotted green fields extending to the barns on the horizon. We laughed at literally being "in fields of clover." In Ohio the barns were no longer always red; they could be just as white as the pristine farmhouses. When they were red, barns often displayed decorative painted hex signs on their doorways. Above the barn doors were neatly lettered family names and dates ranging from 1875 through 1983. Usually the family names included "& Sons." Our favorite was "M. J. Johnson & Daughters."

Musing about the Johnson family prompted Bea and me to talk about her daughters and my daughters-in-law, but mostly we talked of the sense of freedom we enjoyed. We talked about being old enough to have done all that our families and society required of us, yet being young and healthy enough to do what we chose and alert enough to make choices. I recalled telling my sons, when they were teenagers, that to have freedom, they must be responsible, that the two went together. Bea and I decided that we were acting responsibly by protesting nuclear armaments. So it was alright to feel so free.

Bea remembered a Chinese proverb: "If there is righteousness in the heart, there will be harmony in the home. If there is harmony in the home, there will be order in the nation. When there is order in the nation, there will be peace in the world."

We thought The Peace March might have spawned 650 compulsive wanderers. Not all who wander are lost. Maybe we'd become pilgrims. We knew first hand about experiencing hardship and deprivation while discovering spiritual growth along the way. We had the opportunity to stretch and grow, and talked about how any path of life allows that. We had slowed down enough so lessons could be integrated within us, but we were too close to see those changes clearly. Now, 25 years later, I can look back and see how each of us was a pilgrim. I learned that it is my response to what life brings that creates the difference between my journey and someone else's. The process of transformation happens all along the way. The March was walking me, and I only glimpsed my internal changes. Bea and I agreed that a pilgrim is one who passes through life in search of some high goal. Freedom from global nuclear destruction: Does that qualify as a high goal? "What *shall* we do after Washington?" we asked.

By the time we'd covered four miles and reached the first porta-potty stop, we had drawn no conclusions except, "What a jubilant day!" I remembered what author-activist Ken Kesey had said, "The answer is never the answer. What's really interesting is the mystery." Another reason our March was so interesting. How we kept going was sometimes a mystery.

A local farmer sliced watermelon on the hood of his pickup truck.

With the sweet sticky juice running down our wrists, we walked on.

Within the next few miles, I chatted with a farmer who offered pears from his tree. "They're green and hard, but sweet," he said as he handed us his gift. He was right, they were crisp as apples. I asked him what he thought of our March. "I thought you'd be a bunch of hippies screamin' an' hollerin'."

I told him others in other states had thought similarly.

He continued, "Well, I'm glad to see you're not, and I think you've got a good idea. I'm going to tell my wife to write our senator this afternoon to tell him to quit voting to spend more money on weapons. We folks need some of that money right here, and anyway, there are already plenty of nuclear bombs."

I finished the pear just in time. A horse-drawn Amish cart with a sign on its side that read "Home Baked Goods" was stopped on the roadside. The chocolate oatmeal cookies were so rich, it took three of us to finish the first one. The others after that were easier. I hardly had room for the oranges offered at the next rest stop.

Frogs and black crickets sang their songs as we walked. Flocks of small birds swooped across our path. We stepped over an assortment of flattened animals, victims of highway traffic. At the lunch stop, we sat in the shade among friends, grown close to one another over these months, and listened to marchers Bob Alei and Steve Bingham. They had just returned from Boston where they had visited with Helen and Bill Caldicott. Helen, after all her work to establish Physicians for Social Responsibility, felt disenfranchised and exhausted. Bill suggested that Peace March headquarters be established in Washington, DC, so that constant lobbying could take place. The gravity of our pilgrimage became clear. This, I was again reminded, was not just a stroll through the early morning sunshine. I was reflecting upon our simple life, close to the earth, with its many pleasures, and my commitment to the peace movement, when Bea dug a paper out of her day-pack.

"Have you read this yet?" She handed me a quote from Albert Einstein which said, "Strange is our situation here upon earth. Each of us comes for a short visit, not knowing why, yet sometimes seeming to divine a purpose. From the standpoint of daily life, however, there is one thing we do know: that man is here for the sake of other men... for the countless unknown souls with whose fate we are connected by a bond of sympathy." I felt as though Einstein were speaking for me when he said, "Many times a day I realize how my own outer and inner life is built upon the labors of my fellow men, both living and deceased, and how earnestly I must exert myself in order to give in return as much as I have received and am still receiving."

Marcher Sam Wolfe at the end of a long day.

CHAPTER 18

Nice Neighborhood You Have Here!

At that time of the walk, Jane Zacharias Love was married to my son Sam, and they were parents of her son, Zac, and their son and daughter together, Derek and Caitlin. For eight years Jane's parents, Mary and Ed Zacharias, had asked me to visit them in their home in Poland, Ohio, not far from Youngstown. In 1986, I did. I walked from the Pacific Coast to get there. And on September 20, I sat in Jane's girlhood bedroom, which was as pretty as the pale pink roses in the silver and crystal pitcher atop the antique mahogany dresser. The ecru eyelet bed linens were a far cry from the bag in which I had been sleeping for over six months.

The Great Peace Marchers had reached Youngstown and were camped in Wick Park for the weekend. But my tent-mate, Shelah, and

I were doing a special Marcher in the Home. We were not guests of strangers, but of family! I felt very much at home, not only because I was happy to see Mary and Ed, but because Poland, Ohio, was to Youngstown what San Mateo and Hillsborough were to San Francisco—beautiful, affluent communities. I sighed and prayed, "Please protect beautiful neighborhoods from nuclear annihilation."

Shelah and I went for a walk around town. Founded in 1794 as Town One, Range One of Connecticut's Western Reserve land, Poland predated Youngstown. We learned "the village" was 1.2 square miles, all land. I liked best that William Holman McGuffey, who wrote the *McGuffey Readers*, lived in Poland. Published between 1836 and 1960, over 122 million copies helped teach youngsters, including my parents, to read.

In Jane's bedroom, I looked up to the wall above her desk to see pictures of my grandchildren. Over 2,000 miles away, I felt connected to them and to home. Just a week ago I had been back to the San Francisco Bay Area for the first time since having left on February 14. I missed the marchers' entrance into Cleveland because Shelah drove me to the airport that day. Forty-five hundred peace activists joined to walk for a day. On the bridge over the Cuyahoga River, 5,000 people, when given the signal, stopped in their tracks for three minutes. The police turned on their sirens and patrolled up and down The March column to dramatize again, as we had on the bridge across the Mississippi and in Dixon, Indiana, that should a nuclear war take place, everything would just stop.

But I didn't enter Cleveland that day. I was going home. It felt something akin to how I had felt going home from college for the first time, perhaps for Thanksgiving. It took less than five hours to fly back over the stretch of land that had taken us six months to walk. I sat on the plane and marveled at the luxury of what used to be an ordinary experience. An airline meal had never tasted so good: cold apple juice, tiny precisely shaped scallops over nice rice with green peas that were actually green, topped by a few slivers of orange carrots and black olives that had been quartered! I ate the salad because it tasted good: lettuce and shrimp, crisp and flavorful, a red cherry tomato for garnish. The carrot cake was a tidy 2-inch cube with icing. Everything was served in dainty dishes; even the miniscule salt and pepper containers amused me.

All this while I was flying westward over our country toward my family. We flew across Lake Michigan, across the Mississippi and Missouri rivers. I thought I recognized the Quad Cities and Omaha. The sight of lumpy Utah beneath scattered columns of clouds thrilled me. A road meandered off toward the south through a small hamlet, roofs, possibly tin, glistened in the sun. The grey ribbon that unfurled nearby must have been a flat, slow river.

I didn't like to think of this land blackened and destroyed. I had no marchers nearby with whom to share these thoughts, so I told them to my little green journal. How many times had I flown over this terrain really loving it as I did now? I wondered if I would be content to do anything other than try to save it. To campaign for peaceful resolutions in the world, in our nation, in our families, I resolved to become more informed. A few months back, in Nebraska, I was certain in my conviction, so didn't feel the necessity to attend films and lectures in the Peace Academy. Now I felt that I must absorb as much information as possible. I'd already decided, now I had to play the game.

What had I learned during The Peace March? How had it changed me? First, I could speak with calm and confidence—even when I was unprepared—to groups. I was more comfortable in a greater variety of situations. I was closer to being myself, more inner-directed than outwardly influenced. Not as much of a people pleaser. I'd learned that too much chocolate and nuts made my gums feel inflamed. On the other hand, if I walked 15 miles a day I could eat lots of ice cream and not gain weight. I was closer to being able to express my feelings. Now all I had to do was learn to recognize what my feelings were.

I was quietly, ecstatically in love with our earth. I was sad that we polluted the air and water, trashed the earth, and violated the gifts of nature—the colors, light, shadows, warmth and coolness, fragrances, textures, the stillness of dawn gathering energy from the sun to get through another day.

Suddenly we were landing. The salt flats in south San Francisco Bay had never before been such lovely deep russet colors. Over Foster City, I looked for the Meis van der Rohe building because the plans and photos of it had been in the Chicago Museum of Contemporary Art in August and so had I.

Before The March I had rented my house and sold the car, so I stayed with a neighbor, who drove me to a car rental agency. I was free to keep a dental appointment, to see friends from Africa who were visiting in Marin County, to visit my mother in Oregon for two days, to be with local friends.

But I was going home primarily to attend the West Coast Reception for Holly and John Love who had been married in Rhode Island in May. John's father hosted an elegant party for them in his home in San Francisco. I wore my bright mustard-colored silk MOG (Mother of the Groom) dress and lapped up the affection of family and friends.

Daughter-in-law Jane hugged me close and whispered, "I'm so proud of you."

Sam, who in February when I was leaving for The March had said, "Walk in the middle of the pack, Mom. It's safer there," now said, "When The March fell apart outside Barstow, I told my friends you'd stay and finish even if you had to walk alone."

Their father, Jim, said, "I admire your dedication, Donna, but surely there's a better way to get what you want."

I asked him for suggestions. He threw up his hands, took a step back, and said, "Oh, far be it from me to try to tell you what to do!"

They asked about my feet and shoes. My feet were fine. I wore out a pair of shoes about every thousand miles.

"How many miles do you *really* walk each day?" "How can 650 people walk along highways?" I explained that we walked 15 to 25 miles a day, and they couldn't imagine that. I told them we walked along secondary roads. "Oh, blue roads. Like John Steinbeck's *Travels with Charlie,* and understood.

Mostly, though, friends on the Peninsula could not fathom my dedication to global nuclear disarmament. Most didn't ask about the experiences, the sensations of The March, our achievements, the reception in the Midwest. They said I had a great tan and asked about blisters. I was ready to discourse on my commitment, but answered, "Yes, most of the blistered feet are healed. Our skin has become tough." Some were honestly interested in my comments. Some listened politely with a glazed look on their faces. Some changed the subject. And some thinly disguised their hostility toward one of their own who would venture outside their comfort zone. I think they noticed that I had changed. I felt more open-minded, less judgmental than I had been six months earlier. These changes probably made some of them uncomfortable. Comfort seemed of paramount importance to those who lived in warm, dry houses and had shoes for any occasion. And hot water, dining rooms, toilets. I empathized with the fright some felt when confronted with the reality of nuclear threats. They didn't want to think about the fragility of their perceived security. It wasn't a pleasant topic of conversation.

As Connie says on page 172 in her book:

> *Obstacles to accepting a new idea are very real. But there is additional resistance to dealing with the threat of nuclear weapons. It is an enormously frightening and overwhelming issue which forces us to look at death—not only our personal death, but death of the entire planet, of everyone and everything we know. The presence of The Great Peace March brought the issue out into the open in communities across the country, and the marchers were showing, by their presence and commitment, that others needn't sit by helplessly while governments manufacture weapons for our possible extermination.*

After I'd been in San Mateo a few days, I checked with the renters, Mike Krukow and his family. Mike was pitcher for the San Francisco Giants, and I wanted to tell him about the rooting section on The March. I had first discovered it in a laundromat one rest day in Indiana when I noticed a group of marchers watching a baseball game. I asked one of the young men, "Who's pitching?" and when he said, "Mike Krukow," I said, "Oh, good."

The marcher asked, "Oh, do you like baseball?"

"I like Mike Krukow. He lives in my house."

"Oh! Lucky you! Say, do you think he'd send us some Giants hats? We root for the Giants every chance we get."

So, when I found Mike, I passed on the request and took a dozen Giants baseball caps back to The March with me. Every time I went into a laundromat and saw the rooting section, I laughed, slid down a wall to sit on the floor with them and cheered my hometown team.

When Shelah and I arrived in Poland, Ohio, I told Mary and Ed about the visit back to California, showed them photos of the West

Coast Reception and our mutual grandchildren. Those grandchildren were a primary reason I was on The March. I felt that doing away with nuclear bombs would not guarantee peace, but stepping back from nuclear war would buy us time to begin to save the planet for our, for all, grandchildren. Ed and Mary wanted to hear about The March and invited friends who also were interested to come have coffee and cake with us.

Shelah and I found frilly baskets of feminine soaps, shampoos, and lotions in the vintage green and black tiled bathroom upstairs. We took long luxurious baths, climbed into our most presentable March clothes, put on our earrings and came downstairs. We were to have birthday cake! September 21 was my 59th birthday, and we had a special celebration at the dining table set with flowers and candles and lovely food. Mary gave me a small enamel box, one I carefully packed away in a sock during The March. It now sits on a window sill where I see it daily.

The next morning, up in Jane's room, I sat at her desk, stared out the mullioned windows at the tree-shaded lawns and wrote an article for the *San Mateo Times*. I felt sheltered. If I stayed too long, I'd run the risk of getting soft, comfortable, lethargic. When Shelah popped her head in and asked, "Are you about ready to go back to The March?" I nodded and said, "Yes, let's stop by a post office on the way so I can mail this piece."

We got into Shelah's car, and she said, "I feel like we're going home."

Marcher Unity in Diversity.

CHAPTER 19

Nothing Can Stop Us Now

In spite of the tensions and turmoil within The March, we persevered. A community has been defined as a group of people who meet each other without the usual defenses and who value the diversity among themselves. Author Scott Peck has written, "Communities often arise spontaneously amid a crisis, but they seldom last. Once the crisis is over, they tend to dissolve."

Perhaps The March survived because there was almost always a crisis, but I think The March persisted because many who were responsible and mature worked at keeping it going. Maybe it had something to do with the consensus form of government, the policy of inclusiveness, and respect for the rights of individuals. Walking and camping forged strong bonds. As the months passed, that bonding had strengthened in spite of, or maybe because of, our diversity.

The encouragement we received along the way gave us spirit and kept us going, exhausted though many of us were. A Pennsylvania dentist met some marchers in Colorado. When The March reached Philadelphia, he and his staff came to camp to clean teeth for free. He said, "I've never been a joiner, but I want to participate in this. I've written my legislators several times. The March has had a very positive effect on me."

In her book, Connie wrote:

> The effect of the GPM on those who interacted with us was evident in the earliest days. "Bible Bob" came to heckle us in Los Angeles when The March began. Through a loudspeaker on his panel truck he kept up a constant harangue, promoting his fundamentalist view of the world's troubles—and criticizing The March. For several days Bible Bob followed our column and preached to us— and against our mission. But we were courteous, and Bible Bob began to listen some and talk less. When he bade us

farewell as we headed into the desert, he called, "Bless
you, brothers and sisters. God loves you." Then he warned
us to "avoid fornication because it weakens the legs." We
chuckled for months about that switch in attitude. "Oh,
oh, tired legs? What have you been up to? Remember
what Bible Bob said!"

At 1:30 one morning in rural Iowa, rock star Jackson Browne came
to camp. About 50 bleary-eyed marchers assembled to hear Browne sing
and tell them, "I think the issues of hunger and weapons are so closely
related that when you start a song about hunger, it will end up about
weapons and vice versa. Keep going. People will hear you."

The following night, in Iowa City, Senator Tom Harkin told us that
peace is not through military strength, but strength is through peace.
"Instead of wishing for peace and preparing for war," he said, "it's time
we started seeking peace by preparing for peace." He pointed out that we
marchers were doing just that.

A marcher reported, "I parked my van in front of a bakery. When
I got back, I found it completely filled with loaves of bread!"

In late fall, over 50 massage therapists came to our site for the first
ever "Massage for Peace."

A March supporter said, "I got a feeling of hope for the first time
in maybe 20 years that people were going to make a difference, and
that maybe somewhere I could fit in this process." I thanked her for
her contribution and invited her to walk with us for a mile or so. She
regretfully declined; she had things at home she had to do.

Connie wrote, "Guest speakers were good for morale. Sometimes
it was easy to feel that the country didn't know and didn't care that
every day several hundred people with a cause were packing up their
belongings and their town to travel 15 or 20 miles down the road. Guest
speakers assured us that we hadn't been forgotten, that what we were
doing was indeed important and appreciated."

Yoko Ono, Jesse Jackson, Daniel Ellsberg, Hollywood stars, mayors,
senators, governors came to tell us we gave hope. Mayor Hatcher of Gary,
Indiana, said, "I will tell my three young daughters that someone cares
about their having a place in this world when they grow up."

In mid-September, schools were back in session. When we passed by, church bells rang and hundreds of children poured out of the schools to welcome us. One school served lunch and the children ate with us, asked us questions and begged us to stop war. The fourth-grade teacher told me, "This was an experience they will never forget. It was a highlight of the school year." With tears in our eyes, we looked over the heads of those children out on the grass with the walkers. I ached to guarantee that we'd be successful in halting the nuclear arms race. "It's all so pointless," we choked up and held each other's hands.

These acts of support and encouragement fueled our determination. And we needed all the support we could get if we were going to make a lasting impact on the attitudes of citizens across America.

The little book, *The Hundredth Monkey*, was passed around. It is a story about monkeys on an island near Japan. Food for them was airdropped and landed in sand. One monkey took his food to the sea to wash it. Others imitated him. After the hundredth monkey washed sand off his food, monkeys on another, nearby but separate island, began to wash their food, too. The theory is that a threshold number of people working for peace or global nuclear disarmament, or equality and justice, or the environment, creates a force field that spreads, through some intangible means, to create a collective leap forward in consciousness. The Peace Marchers worked and walked toward this goal. More and more people joined The March as we proceeded toward Washington, DC.

Nothing was going to stop us now.

Hinton Harrison painted his face, wore a big Peace hat, and rode his unicycle across America.

CHAPTER 20

Where'm I Gonna Live When I Get Home?*

The campsite near Pittsburgh was in Shenley Park, a beautiful place to rest after five days walking, mostly in cold driving rain, from Youngstown, Ohio. Our legs were not used to the ups and downs of the Allegheny Mountains; the terrain since Denver had been a long downward slope, and our thighs ached as we walked into Pittsburgh.

One of the marchers had a brother who played violin in the Pittsburgh Symphony. As a special treat, he arranged for 150 marchers to attend the Saturday evening performance. We washed our hair (in cold showers), dressed in our cleanest clothes and sat in good balcony seats. Patrons in pearls looked with curiosity and disapproval at us, but during

*A Billy Ray Cyrus ballad familiar to me because we dance to it in fitness class, 2011.

the program, a host announced our presence and welcomed "members of The Great Peace March. They have walked from Los Angeles to be here." We stood to receive enthusiastic applause. I wondered if my proper friends back home might have thought, "Tsk. Tsk. Wearing walking shoes to the symphony!" At that moment, stylish clothes didn't seem as important as the music.

Sitting in the semi-darkness of the Symphony Hall, being swept along with the music was such a contrast to some of our days.

Sometimes it was almost just too hard. The physical exhaustion, the aching muscles and tired feet, the beige food and the constant coping with the elements. Then there was the noise. In the night, the roar of the generators that powered the cold-food-storage trailer. There was the traffic along the highways, the incessant voices, the motorcycle riders who cruised our campgrounds just looking at us.

The constant stress was compounded by so many people, so many different kinds of people who didn't really know each other very well, all living like nomads in a non-nomadic culture. We lacked common standards; we lacked privacy. When we ate in the rain, our salads floated. If our jackets or our faded pastel tents leaked, we got wet. When it rained several days in a row, envelopes stuck shut and stamps stuck together, our tents grew mildew, and we put on wet shoes.

Not everyone was discouraged by internal conflicts. For some, The March produced transformation in their personal lives; they had become softer, more understanding, more peaceful—and healthier. Those who spoke positively were often those who chose to walk alone, either way ahead of the main body of The March column or way behind. To be alone for awhile, away from the constant talk of how things should be run, was important in keeping emotional health. One of the reasons I enjoyed the adventure of The Peace March was that Shelah and I were away, in her car, doing advance work on Tuesdays and Thursdays.

On those days I didn't watch the "potatoes" lolling round beneath the trucks, smoking, playing guitars, admiring each other's weird haircuts. I didn't see them crowding onto the bus needed for transporting workers to the next campsite. They pre-empted seats when they could have ridden in their own bus.

One night a young marcher with the security team smelled smoke, the "wrong" kind of smoke. He boarded their bus, found a smoldering duffel bag of pot, and dragged it out. Drugs were disallowed on The March. Those potatoes left the next day.

New Frontier, a Pennsylvania magazine, said, "Despite, or maybe because of their diversity, the marchers try to hear each other out when they're making plans, thus getting a glimpse of what a truly peaceful world would be like." If we, living in these conditions, could glimpse real peace, we truly would have made progress.

I thought of the contentious problems on The March and the attempted peaceful solutions. It seemed to me there was a difference between peaceful solution and acquiescence to avoid conflict. I had to admit I was an avoider. All my life, it'd been "peace at any price." Now I realized that to achieve true peace required not only acceptance, but hard work, not avoidance. I'd have to face difficult issues and people in order to gain the peace that Gandhi taught.

September in Pennsylvania was one of my favorite times on The March. The small towns and villages with their houses built of fieldstones and rough-hewn logs, some with plaques noting their founding in the 18th century, were charming. The maple leaves were golden, the air crisp, clear and sometimes golden itself. Frost sparkled on the seams of our tents in the mornings as we crawled out to start another day. In the evenings, I watched the sky turn to riotous reds and oranges. One such late day, Shelah and I lay on the ground and propped our heads on rolled sleeping bags. If colors could sing, it would have been a massive, sky-wide chorus. I mused, "How can I stay home after a year like this? I think I'll be a gypsy for a few years. I could continue to rent out the house, but where would I go when I needed to be back in San Mateo? I'd still want to spend time with my families."

We pointed out a swath of passionate apricot pinks. Then I thought of that space downstairs, the "bonus room" that had bunk beds, an upright piano, and Marty's old drum set. "Shelah," I said and sat up. "I have a spare room on the first floor in my house. What if I make that into a coming home space for me! I could ask son Sam. He's a really good contractor. Maybe he'd build it, and I'll have it painted these colors of peachy Pennsylvania sunsets." I was so excited that night that I wrote a postcard to Sam to ask him if he'd help after The Peace March was over. He wrote back, "After the Giants baseball season, when Mike Krukow and his family have moved out of the upstairs, Will Clark has moved out of downstairs, and you are home, we can get started. Maybe right after Christmas."

By the time we had only 45 days left, we had walked 3,135 miles and set up and taken down the tents 158 times. As The March walked through rolling rural scenery, past rusting abandoned steel mills, across rivers, and through towns with quaint names—Harmony, Economy, Reading, Hershey—I spent hours dreaming and planning "The Mouse House." It would be small, about 400 square feet, enough for an eight-foot kitchen, a bathroom, a walk-in closet and a hide-a-bed. A coming-home space that would allow me to go out and come back, the hand on the yo-yo string. I planned to get a really good shower head.

I was tired of searching for showers. Yet we spent an inordinate amount of time and energy finding them. I didn't like taking a cold sponge-off at our water trough on a crisp fall day and had taken enough cold showers. I yearned for warm, clean, private showers that drained well.

School gymnasiums provided lots of hot water, but we were too many people all at once. In a small town in Ohio, two of us had sought showers at a senior citizen center housed in a former middle school and the director said, yes. They were fine, private showers. In Bedford, Pennsylvania, Shelah and I negotiated with a motel clerk and agreed to pay $5 each for showers the next morning. We would bring our own soap and towels. He would allow up to 10 marchers.

The next day was a rest day. Five of us drove through the rain, eagerly looking forward to being clean. At the desk we were greeted in a frigid manner with the news that all rooms had been reserved and there was no possibility of our using any of them for two hours. I felt sure someone's mind had been changed and felt frustrated at being discriminated against for no good reason. We all piled back into Shelah's car and before I was through fuming, she turned into another motel entrance, popped out, and pushed through the office door. In only a few minutes, she returned, striding victoriously, a big grin on her face.

"It's okay. Three of us can shower now and more when the first ones are through. This, however, is not a motel. It *was* a motel. Now it's the local Army Recruiting Station. Come on!"

In Gettysburg, Shelah, Mim and I shopped the Goodwill Store, still a new experience for me. Mim had been in the fashion industry in Hollywood before The March and, with her help, I was outfitted in a perfect-fit, $2 peachy sweatshirt. "To match the sunsets," Shelah said. I wore it out of the store, feeling like a new woman. Mim bought a colorful, practical sunhat. In a nearby antique shop, I found some clay marbles, reportedly of the "pre-revolutionary era." We ate ice cream cones and returned to the campsite without having viewed the Gettysburg battlefield. Battlefields, no matter how historic, were not really our preferred choice for tourism.

Near Harrisburg, The March walked through Carlisle, home of the Army War College. At the gates, we had a short demonstration and "die-in." We dropped to the ground as if killed by a bomb. As we lay inert, with a slow drumbeat as background, a woman marcher read a moving narrative. The stoic guards at the college watched without any display of emotion, but marchers cried, and a few civilians watched and wept.

Across the country, truckers had been helpful. They radioed back to let others know the peace marchers were along the roadside. They helped pull stuck gear-trailers out of the mud. They rolled down their windows, waved and blasted their horns. One bright day, as we swung along a road paralleling a major highway, a trucker rolled down his window, gave us the finger, and growled at the top of his voice, "You oughta do that in Russia!"

We waved back, raised our fingers in the peace sign, and in a second, I heard, "That's a great idea!" Up and down our column the idea flashed like lightening. That evening several marchers offered to go down to Washington to pursue the idea. The next Monday, Allan Alfeldt, a graduate student from California, and Carlos de la Fuente, a retired Los Angeles Municipal judge, left to visit our State Department. When they proposed the idea of a Peace Walk in Russia, they were told, "Oh, that's not possible. Logistically impossible."

Allan and Carlos replied, "Yes, we've been hearing that for about eight months, and here we are."

They went over to the Soviet Embassy. First Attaché Anatoly Khrustalev said, "That *is* a good idea, but you'll have to talk with the

Central Peace Committee. They organize peace demonstrations in the Soviet Union."

"Okay, we'll go see them. Where are they?"

"In Moscow."

In January, after The March was finished and Christmas over, Carlos and Allan flew to Moscow.

But in the meantime, we still had to finish what we'd started over seven months ago when The March had left Los Angeles. Now long meetings were devoted to discussions about what we would do in Washington, DC. Over 119 proposals were posted on porta-potty doors. Connie Fledderjohann lists some of them in *The Great Peace March*: *organize a nationwide teach-in at public and private schools, colleges and universities; set off large-scale fireworks on November 15 that would dramatize visually and audibly the firepower of World War I, World War II, and present-day world nuclear arsenals; march around the world, carrying symbols of peace, perhaps crossing the oceans on Greenpeace ships; petition for a constitutional amendment banning nuclear weapons; send aloft 54,000 black balloons, one for each nuclear weapon on earth; join with existing projects to encourage conversion of military facilities to peaceful uses.*

Some suggestions were whimsical. Someone suggested the marchers enter Washington walking backward; another wanted a citizens' arrest of President Reagan. Nineteen voted to participate in an armed revolution, if Reagan's arrest became part of The Great Peace March plan.

Outside Harrisburg, Pennsylvania, Mitch Snyder, a peace activist and advocate for the homeless, and Philip Berrigan, a Catholic priest deeply involved in anti-war movements, joined The March at a lunch break. We sat in school bleachers and listened as they urged us to plan a civil disobedience demonstration in Washington, DC. Some of us roared approval, but I hoped The March meetings would come up with another plan. Several Marchers wanted to bypass New York and head to Washington and demonstrate immediately. However, events had been planned in New York, and people from across America were planning to meet us on November 15. We stuck to the original schedule.

One evening when I saw a meeting in a meadow, I wandered over to join the hundred or so marchers. I thought perhaps some constructive ideas about "After DC" might be forthcoming. Wrong! The major topic was, "Can we afford to buy paper plates so the dishwashers won't have to work on rest days?"

I walked away. That was not the question I wanted answered. The real challenge was creating and living peace.

As we plodded through sparkling autumn days, I imagined The Mouse House with pretty peachy painted walls, white wooden shutters, fluffy bath towels, and a drawer full of new white socks.

Parading across the Brooklyn Bridge in New York.

CHAPTER 21

New York! New York!

Just before dawn on October 23, I heard a clear, strong voice belting out the show tune *New York! New York!*. With unprecedented alacrity, marchers were up and out. Tents came down. There was excited shouting back and forth, "Today's the day!" "Can't wait to walk into New York!" "Lemme borrow your hairbrush. Gotta look good!" Oatmeal was washed down. We were headed for our easternmost city to take a bite out of the Big Apple!

In addition to the crackling excitement, there were choices to be made. Phil Donahue, who hosted a popular nationwide daytime TV show, invited 200 marchers to fill the studio that very morning. Selected marchers would be interviewed and the rest would be the audience. A fine publicity opportunity. Diane Clark, already wearing her red mayor's hat, asked me, "You *are* going to be on *The Phil Donahue Show*, aren't you? If you want to go, be over by that tree at 5 o'clock in the morning. A bus will be there to take everyone." It was tempting, but I answered, "I'd rather walk. I'll enter New York on foot over the George Washington Bridge." It was a good choice. Over 800 of us lined up in Leonia, New Jersey, and trooped behind the many flags that seemed to have multiplied and grown taller overnight. Beneath the bridge a lone sloop swung on its anchor. "It's the Clearwater! It's Pete Seeger's boat! There he is!" Many of us swerved over to the railing to wave and shout to our loyal, dedicated supporter who had more than once huddled with us in a Town Hall Tent to sing as rain poured onto our campsites.

"Someday," I said wistfully to the marcher next to me, "someday I'm going to sail on that boat. Up the Hudson River."

But, this day, it's New York! Circling down the bridge exit onto Manhattan, we were greeted by local peace groups and handed large red apples. Casey Kasem told us he had completed a four-hour fund-raiser for The March. School children cheered. New York City and state officials welcomed us with speeches that extolled our virtues and guaranteed their support. After the speeches, the women of Riverside Church served us a picnic lunch. We sat across the street in the plaza surrounding Grant's tomb to enjoy the food, and I ate the apple we'd received.

There was no ticker-tape parade. No crowds cheering along elegant 57th and tacky 42nd streets. But through Harlem, across Manhattan, on poor and proud 125th Street, we loped along and received our warmest response. Some marchers sang and exchanged encouragement with people who stood and looked with disbelief when we replied, "All the way from Los Angeles and going to Washington, DC. We'll be there November 15. Come on, walk awhile with us." And they did.

In the huge St. John the Divine Episcopal Cathedral, Bishop Paul Moore and other local religious leaders held a service to honor The Peace Marchers. I recognized Paul Winter's soaring saxophone. The joy brought tears down my face, and I had to fish out my bandana. Paul Winter was my favorite musician, and he and I were in the same space! I stood to see if there were any empty seats closer to the front. The entire nave was jammed with people. I sat down and wept. Not out of frustration, but with a profound feeling of connection and gratitude.

A friend next to me took my hand and said, "We cry tears of joy, of gratitude, frustration, and exhaustion. There are no words to capture the essence of The March so we cry instead." I squeezed her hand, sniffed and nodded.

Outside, after the service, a marcher asked me, "Want to camp on Randall's Island? Or do you want to stay with us here at St. John the Divine? It's more conveniently located than an island in the East River."

I had heard that the old stadium on Randall's Island had warm showers and that the view of the New York skyline would be great. "But whatever happened to the Central Park plan?" I asked. "That's where I want to camp."

"Well," a shrug and an answer, "Mayor Koch isn't one of our fans and doesn't want marchers in Manhattan, so officials have disallowed our camping there. Just as well. Central Park is such a target for anti-everything demonstrations."

"Okay," I swallowed my disappointment. "I'll go to Randall's Island."

That evening I lay with my head propped on a duffle of clothes in the doorway of the tent and gazed westward at Manhattan shining in the soft autumn haze. After a very satisfactory shower, I snuggled down in the sleeping bag, blew a kiss toward the skyline and couldn't hold my eyes open a moment longer.

Next morning, we gathered behind the flags, trooped over the Triborough Bridge back to Manhattan, through Central Park, and on to Dag Hammarskjold Plaza at the United Nations Building. I found it difficult to really believe we had come so far. More than 3,200 miles in 237 days. At the United Nations Rally, there were more speeches. Yoko Ono was poignant; Jesse Jackson, a spellbinder. Others. My friend Bea and I decided that we'd had enough speeches and walked up to 53rd Street and across toward Fifth Avenue. I recalled my delight in the little 50-foot-wide pocket park tucked between tall buildings.

I told Bea, "Years ago I spent several meditative hours sitting alone there." I had sat with tea and listened to the water cascading down the sheer wall at the rear of the cobbled fairyland in the center of one of the world's largest and busiest cities.

Just as I was speaking, there it was, still protected by delicate trees. A number of ladies were sitting to rest and chat, some with tea from the tiny catering stand in a rear corner. Bea and I shared a muffin, and before I continued with reminiscences, a woman leaned toward us. "Are you with that Peace March?"

We were quickly surrounded by women who pulled their chairs close and asked all sorts of questions about us and about The March. They shared their dreams and fears, told us of their grandchildren and asked about ours. I showed them the badge with the photograph of Derek and Caitlin, the grandchildren I hoped to save from nuclear annihilation. We gave the women Peace March brochures and left them sitting beneath the lacy tree branches in that tiny oasis where the waterfall drowned out traffic jangle.

"Now, where are we headed?" Bea asked.

It didn't really make any difference. "I don't exactly know, but we are not tourists who don't know where we've been. We are travelers who don't know where we're going," I responded. When we spied a poster announcing an exhibit of American Folk Art in the lower level of the IBM Building, we veered in through the revolving door. We were still orienting ourselves when three women looked over at us. We smiled, and they said they were visiting from Maryland to see this particular exhibit and asked, "Aren't you with The Great Peace March!" One thought she'd seen me on *The Phil Donahue Show*. "No, that was Jolene. We are often mistaken for each other." We answered their questions—"How many pairs of shoes have you worn out? Where do you sleep? What can we do to protest nuclear weapons? What do your families think of your doing this?"—and gave them copies of our brochures. One wanted our autographs. Two of them promised to walk into Washington with us.

Outreach in the IBM Building. Maybe we should have gone upstairs.

But we had an appointment. We scanned the exhibit and relished memories of places we'd visited and were now seeing represented in folk art. We admired quilts like those we'd seen in Amish counties in Iowa and Pennsylvania. I noted the Ammi Phillips' "Girl in a Red Dress," similar to one on a wall at an inn in Lancaster County, Pennsylvania. This girl held a small dog; the other had a cat.

We caught a bus downtown, got off and found Pete's Tavern at 18th and Irving. It's Old New York. O. Henry sat in the second booth and wrote *Gift of the Magi*. We sat there, in that same tall dark booth, at an ancient wooden table and had a glass of wine with Phoebe and Kem Edwards. In the 1950s, these durable friends with their young family lived in San Mateo, around the corner from the young Love family. We had stayed in touch since they'd moved east. Two Love sons had shared college holidays with the Edwards family. In that old booth we sat and talked about old times. "Remember our weeks at the beach in Capitola! Between us we had eight children under the age of 6! Four Edwards girls and four Love boys. How'd we survive that week!"

Phoebe laughed. "Easy. First, they were good kids, and remember with dinner we always had a large glass of wine."

Phoebe and Kem treated us not only to dinner in Pete's Tavern, but to an off-Broadway production of a new musical *Brownstone*. Even better than that, they took us home with them to Fair Haven, New Jersey. That night Bea and I sighed audibly as we slipped into beds with smooth white sheets.

Sunday morning, we washed our hair in a wonderful old-fashioned yellow-and-black tile upstairs bathroom. Phoebe and Kem took us to their local Episcopal church where the congregation was invited to meet us after the service and listen to our comments. In that warm old church with brick floors, I listened to the footfalls and thought of all the steps that had been taken for us to get there. I told Bea, "I feel more peace here than at any of those high pitched rallies in New York."

"Me, too." she nodded.

After church we drove out to Sandy Hook to dip our hands into the Atlantic Ocean. We had made it from "sea to shining sea!" I still had with me a tiny vial of Pacific beach sand and slowly emptied it into the ruffles at our feet.

That evening, TV screens broadcast, not the triumphs of The Great Peace March, but the sixth game of the 1986 World Series between the Boston Red Sox and the New York Mets, which was played in Shea Stadium. We four rooted for the Mets and jumped to our feet when the Red Sox' first baseman, Bill Buckner, fumbled a grounder in the 11th inning of the sixth game and the Mets won 6-5.

Monday the seventh game was postponed due to rain; Phoebe and Kem went to work while Bea and I stayed home. We read the paper, baked chocolate-chip cookies, fixed dinner, set the table with real silver flatware and real china on a real dining room table. On October 27, the Mets won the series, 4-3. Phoebe and Kem took Bea and me, clean and refreshed, back to Stanten Island, where The Peace March was camped for two days.

Marchers spread out across New York to speak in schools. Now we were interviewed and covered by the media. *People* magazine ran a 12-page spread of Jeff Share's panoramic photos. *The Daily News,* front-page coverage. TV programs and radio station news gave The Peace March major attention.

The children of The March climbed the Statue of Liberty and learned more about why we were marching.

Marchers' shoes, after 3,700 miles, on the White House fence.

CHAPTER 22

We Did It

With 18 days left, The March struggled with driving rain during the days, below-zero nights and flooded campsites. Entire busloads of people arrived to walk the last miles with us. Peace groups from across the nation, families who had hosted us for Marcher in the Home, some families of marchers and individuals. They walked a week or a day with us until we were in Washington.

There were moments of encouragement and glory. At the campsite on the Princeton campus, Yoko Ono and her son, Sean, visited again.

Marchers surrounded them in the Big Blue Town Hall Tent as she spoke in her soft whispery voice of her admiration for our efforts. In Philadelphia, 5,000 people came to the rally, and the next night, more came to sing along with Graham Nash of Crosby, Stills and Nash and Peter Yarrow of Peter, Paul and Mary. Feisty 83-year-old Maggie Kuhn, founder of Gray Panthers, urged us, "Tell the people to remember, 54 cents out of every tax dollar goes to military spending." Swarthmore College in Pennsylvania welcomed us and provided archival space for hundreds of pounds of Peace March news articles and memorabilia.

Across the country, I had been in awe of our country's natural beauty. In Delaware, in the Du Pont family gardens at Longwood, Shelah and I wandered for an hour in beautiful surroundings created by humans. I liked the sweeping lawn that once was a pasture where cows had grazed. As we walked back to Shelah's car, I stopped to admire a display of tiles in a shop window.

"Let's go in!" I said and opened the door. We were the only customers. The walls and cases were covered with tiles for bathrooms, kitchens, floors and counters. They looked gorgeous to me. I held one with scattered wildflowers and imagined it in The Mouse House.

The young woman clerk asked, "You are on The Peace March, aren't you! Oh, I'd love to be a part of that."

I gave her a copy of our schedule and asked, "Could you come for a day? You'd be welcome to walk with us, share our lunch, get a taste of The March. Lots of people do that. The contribution is $15, and we'll drive you back to your starting point."

She clutched my arm and exclaimed, "Yes! Oh yes, I can! I'll be there Tuesday!" She paused, then touched the lovely tile I still held. "Would you like to have this? And, you, Shelah, please choose one. I want to give you a souvenir." Twenty-five years later, that tile is still with me, used beneath the teapot on the dining table. I ordered eight small flowered accent tiles from her that I would use in The Mouse House in January. I love recalling those few minutes in that tile store.

Seven cold and soggy miserable nights in Maryland. We camped in the parking lot of the Baltimore Orioles where the stadium protected us from the worst of the wind. I had a cold. Another night our campsite was marshy. Shelah had told me she expected an artist friend to meet The March and join for the last few days. He had been at an art show in the

South where he had exhibited a three-dimensional piece of art he called "My Nuclear Home," which demonstrated that the nuclear equivalent of 16,000 sticks of dynamite exists for each person on earth. He would find The Peace March wherever it was.

I sat shivering in the tent the evening Shelah announced, "He's here! He has a dry, warm van. Bring your sleeping bag and come with me." I also grabbed Kleenex (actually a roll of toilet paper) and followed her through the rain until she knocked on the door of a green Chevy van.

"Dale!" she shouted. "Open up. Here's my tent-mate. She has a cold. She needs to sleep in a warm place. She can sleep on the floor in here."

Dale grinned down at us and said, "Hi. Hi, Donna. Come on in. You too, Shelah. I've made some popcorn. Want some?" We climbed up, and I jammed my sleeping bag at the end of his bunk across the back. Our friend Bea was sitting in the driver's seat, writing in her journal, getting warm. I sat down and looked around. Dale was not a big man, but he was dynamic. His blue eyes sparkled, his white hair shone. In his Birkenstocks and Levis, he moved gracefully about the small space.

"Is this marine hardware?" I asked. "I've seen this style before."

Dale's face lit up. "Oh, do you know boats?"

"A little. My brother has a boat and my father always had one. He used to go deep-sea fishing to get away from the phone. He was a small-town doctor and was at everyone's beck and call. Mother used this kind of hardware in some cupboard doors in their dining room."

"What's the name of your brother's boat?"

"It's the Ingrid Princess. A motor-sailer. About 38 feet, I think. Brown sails. They sail up and down the Pacific coast from Alaska to Baja."

"Ah, yes," Dale passed more popcorn and thought for a moment. "Was her name... hmm... Dianne? They were from Oregon?"

"Yes! Dianne and David Rankin! He's my youngest brother. How in the world do you know them?"

"Met them at the water faucet on the beach at Cabo San Lucas." He twinkled and ate another mouthful of popcorn.

I could hardly believe it. "Oh, I wish I had my word processor and some paper. I'd write a letter right this minute to Dave and Dianne to tell them that out in the middle of a flooded campsite in Maryland I've met a man who knows them! I have felt so far from home for months now and here you are, a direct connection to my brother and sister-in-law."

Dale reached up over my head to open a storage space, and I could see his belly button in the gap between his shirt and Levi's. He pulled down a small portable typewriter, latched a tiny hinged table next to me, found some paper and said, "Here you are. We can mail it tomorrow."

I think I half fell in love with Dale at that instant. After he gave my aching legs a massage, I was hooked. For the remaining few days of The March, I sometimes slept in the tent and sometimes in the van. In a few days I'd forgotten my cold.

On the morning of November 14, almost 2,000 marchers met the crowds of people who wanted to walk into Washington with us. Shoulder-to-shoulder, we lined up on the grass along the border between Delaware and Washington, DC. Some carried banners. The press was there. We hooked arms and in unison chanted the names of all 15 states we had crossed. Then, with one step, we crossed into Washington, DC.

"We did it! We did it!" we chanted and hugged each other. Some wept. Bea and I leaned together, and I shouted, "You see, *anything* is possible! They said we couldn't do it, and we did it." One step at a time.

AT&T had set up phone booths where marchers could call home for free. I found an empty one and happily dialed son Sam and Jane's number. I knew she'd be home with their children, Derek and Caitlin. "We made it!" I hollered.

"I know!" Jane replied. "I can see you on TV. Yes, *you!* You are at a phone booth, and we are talking, and you are on TV right here in Santa Rosa, California! We are so proud of you, Donna!"

I peered around and waved at the TV camera.

Later that afternoon, as many were setting up their tents on grounds of St. Paul's Theological College and masses of marchers surged about, Shelah and I checked into the small Radisson Henley Park Hotel that I had noted in a *Sunset* magazine ad way back in January when I was preparing for The March. It was a "just in case" that we were glad to use. Several other marchers joined us so that ultimately we were in three rooms. I draped our tent's rain cover over the four-poster bed because I'd always wanted a canopied bed. Someone ordered pizza, and someone else produced wine, and we had a picnic on the carpeted floor. I lay on the canopied bed and sampled the contents of a box of chocolates.

"Ooooh, this is the way to live! This is The March I signed up for!"

Dale found us, came in, looked around at the over-crowded space, and said, "I'm going to get another room." He cocked his head. "And I'll be right back to get you," and pointed a jaunty index finger at me.

The next morning, showered and shampooed, we joined a throng of 15,000 to make the final walk down Lexington Avenue. Behind the flags and banners, the Veterans led the silent procession. Next came the Over-Fifties who had come the entire way. Then others who were part of the original 400. Then everyone else. The group was eight abreast, from curb to curb, over 2½-miles long. As we began our slow, measured, quiet entrance into our capital, Oliver, the young man with the dreadlocks and no shoes, appeared from nowhere and hooked my arm into his. He wore a warm jacket and shoes—no socks, but shoes. Other anarchists walked beside other Over-Fifties. "To protect you in case there's any violent reaction from the crowds," Oliver said.

When we reached Meridian Park for the first of three rallies, he bent to hug me. He smelled of soap. "Good luck," he said. "Maybe see ya."

I patted his chest and told him, "Thanks, Oliver. You go to school."

As the speeches by consumer advocate Ralph Nader, the Rev. Jesse Jackson, Casey Kasem, music by Holly Near and Peter Yarrow, ceremonies, interviews and tearful goodbyes filled the day, I was dazed by the fact that we had finally arrived. That it was over. That we had been on the road for 261 days and traveled on foot 3,706.8 miles. Sue Guist grabbed and hugged me. "This is surely a 17-hanky day, isn't it!" I sniffed, wiped my nose, shrugged and grinned. Some feelings I just couldn't define, let alone express in words.

We were distressed to learn that the United States conducted a major nuclear weapons test in the Nevada desert that very day. News services reported that shock waves shuddered the upper levels of some Las Vegas buildings. When we heard about the test, we stopped along our route, formed a huge circle, stood silent for a moment and then yelled, "We're still here!"

Several marchers said they never expected the tests to end with our March into Washington, but The March would not end with Washington.

The *Washington Post* quoted me, "This is the beginning,' said Donna Love, from San Mateo, Calif., who said she marched for the sake of her grandchildren. 'We have people's attention. Now the work begins.'"

Carole Schmidt, 25, who had worked in Fisc & Disc, agreed, "The only thing that's over is the walking."

At the Lincoln Memorial, peace lovers were reflected in the pool. From mid-afternoon until after dark, we and our guests were welcomed, acclaimed and urged onward by astronomer and television personality Carl Sagan; Yogesh Gandhi, a controversial figure who claimed to be a relative of Mohandas Gandhi; physicist Michio Kaku; pediatrician and author Benjamin Spock, and Daniel Ellsberg. Pete Seeger again arrived as did actress Lindsey Wagner and actress Betty Thomas. As the evening progressed, thousands of candles were lit from one another, carrying the flame of Hiroshima to the very heart of the government we had tried to touch.

For the last time, Shelah and I set up the tent and crawled in. Tomorrow? We'd think about that tomorrow.

It began as many others. For the last time we awakened to the gong and songs of the reliable wakeup call of Bill Thompson, a teacher from Redwood City, California. I pulled on the long underwear again and the same old rust-colored cords, shrugged into my dependable grey wool sweater, pinned on the picture of the grandchildren. Rummaging around, I found some socks, not quite showing daylight through the heel weave. The Avia shoes, purchased in September, had some wear left on them. Our excitement and good humor soared even as tents, crisp with frost, were rolled and bagged for the last time. I ran the gauntlet of friendly faces and heartfelt hugs, taking care of morning errands and all the time feeling deeply how much we would miss each other after this day. Many faces were bright with tears. Even members of the press became swept up in the high emotion, sometimes forgetting to turn off their tape recorders as interviews morphed into personal conversations.

For a few moments, I stood near the kitchen trailer to gaze at our group. I felt as though I were studying an illustration from Chaucer's *The Canterbury Tales,* with our unsophisticated musical instruments, layers of scarves, hats, capes and caps, the sense of camaraderie, the jests and jokes, similar to those shared among the pilgrims along their way to Canterbury. I liked the feeling of being connected to pilgrimages of the past. The Great Peace March had a place in the strand of pilgrimages. Yet it was unique: the largest group of people ever to traverse a continent to promote peace.

Diverse as our group was, summarizing became almost impossible.

I asked Dick Edelman, a Los Angeles psychiatrist and one of the 400 who stayed from beginning to end, for his comments. "The March had nothing to do with the ending of global arms buildup," he said. "It had to do with raising the consciousness of millions of Americans. And we did that."

I asked Billy Lieb, the marcher with whom I visited the fourth-grade classroom in Salt Lake City, what he thought was most important about The March. He was quick to reply, "Just getting here in spite of all the logistic problems and that we are virtually leaderless. We have done what we set out to do. We got here."

Ann Edelman exclaimed, "It's what has happened to us! The March has changed each of us. We have learned to live respectfully and peacefully. Knowing that, sometimes I'm so happy I think I'll just burst."

Others echoed Ann. I was among those who believed that we started out to make changes "out there" and finished by changing our own truths and hearts. I felt opened, broadened and deepened, more confident and quieter, but more willing to speak out, than I had a year ago. More connected with the earth. More connected with God. I believed that anything was possible. Faith over fear. As Oliver had said, things usually work out.

Shelah said she was not sad to see The March end. She was among many who were planning to form small educational groups that would travel to promote peace issues. She and psychological counselor Sky Shultz of Hawaii and Indiana were planning workshops to empower those who felt helpless in the face of governmental determination to escalate the nuclear arms race.

"I am angry," Shelah frowned. "Those farmers who have owned their farms for generations are being forced to relinquish their heritage. People throughout the world are starving and the farmers' grain rests in silos unused. Money needed to save the farms is used to support the military. None of it makes sense. It is sick."

With tears, Bea Novobilsky sighed, "I'm just tired. I'm tired of these interminable lines. Tired of rice. Tired of the wind blowing the lettuce off my plate. Tired of being cold. I'm ready to go home and get a degree in anthropology."

Carole Schmidt, who knew the finances of The March, said, "We did it. And we did it for less than $900,000. Originally it was supposed to cost $20 million, and we did it for less than $1 million. Pretty fantastic."

We all had been asked what we were going to do now that The March was finished. I overheard two women standing in the shower room at the Baltimore Orioles stadium sharing a foot rest on a wooden stool as they shaved their legs. "What are you and John going to do?" one asked.

"We'll stay in Washington for a while," answered the other. "No, not to work for peace, to work for money. We have spent it all on this mission and need to accrue more before we can go anywhere. How about you?"

The woman responded, "We'll just tune our way back to California and then see what happens." Her husband was a piano tuner.

Several marchers were planning to join the three-week long Florida March after Christmas. Carlos de la Fuenta, a Los Angeles attorney, on The March from the start, was eagerly working on the plan for the 1987 peace walk in the Soviet Union.

I took Dale's hand and asked for his comments. He recalled a scene from the classic movie *Harold and Maude*. "Remember when the young boy gives Maude the ring, and she accepts it, admires it, expresses her appreciation, and throws it over her shoulder into the San Francisco Bay? She explained, 'Now I'll always know where it is.'

" 'But,' Harold moans, 'I love you.'

" 'Wonderful. Now go out and love the world,' Maude urged him.

"So," Dale recommended, tapping his heart, "We will always know where The March is, and we can now go out and love the world."

Donna Love, thinking *Now what?*

CHAPTER 23

And Then

On November 16, the first day after The Great Peace March ended, Shelah and I stood at the rear of her jaunty little red car, still parked on the grounds of Catholic University in Washington, DC. The trunk was open, and we stared at the accumulation of papers, memorabilia and detritus collected on our way across country. The rolled tent and sleeping bags lay on the ground at our feet; the four green plastic milk crates in which we'd stored our meager wardrobes for nine months were stacked to one side. We were quiet as we cleaned out the trunk and loaded it again.

Then Shelah asked, "Well, what would you like to do?"

"I've never seen the Shenandoah Valley." I answered. "Is that close?"

"Maybe. Let's go get some water." We shut the trunk, took our water bottles over to the kitchen-trailer warm-water spigot to fill them, and said goodbye again to marchers. We all looked dazed and lost. Several asked, "Do you have room to take me to New York?" or "Where are you going? Could I come, too?" "I need to get to Florida. How about a lift?"

"We don't know where we are going," we said. The car was loaded. We didn't have room to take anyone with us.

We wandered back to the car, got in, and sat there. Drank our warm water.

"Before The Peace March," I said, "I never knew how comforting plain warm water could be. A nice cup of warm water… so soothing. Don't you think so?"

"Yes, soothing. Okay," she turned. "Let's make a plan. Where's that map? I wonder if Dale wants to go along with us. Let's drive over to where he parked his van."

A week earlier, Dale had set up his "Nuclear Home" on the lawn of Lafayette Park and was now methodically taking it apart and stacking the pieces in his art-trailer. The day was dull, overcast and cold. He paused when he saw us, rubbed his hands together, and gave us each a big hug. His bright eyes shown blue below his bushy white eyebrows. "So, my ladies, what shall we do today? Perhaps a little drive?" He seemed ready for anything.

I offered, "I have a cousin just outside Atlanta. I think we could stay with him and his wife."

Shelah said, "Sounds good to me. We can see what's on the way, get to Atlanta, and then turn right toward California."

Dale said he'd like to travel along with us. He'd stay in his van. "Anyone want to stay with me?" He wiggled his eyebrows suggestively and chuckled.

We told him we wanted to sightsee along the way and would meet him at prearranged places every few days. Shelah drove; I read the map; we headed south. We drove through a part of the Shenandoah Valley but missed the National Park. At the Blue Ridge Mountains National Park, the gate was locked and covered with icicles. Cold blue sparkles everywhere. The air hurt our lungs. Shelah took a picture of me next to the sign, and we jumped back into the car. Gatlinburg, Tennessee, was full of craft shops. I went straight to the baskets. "Buy small or ship it home," Shelah admonished. I bought one, humped in the center to keep eggs from rolling around. In Qualla, North Carolina, at the Cherokee museum and craft shop, I bought a small white oak Cherokee market basket and filled it with snacks. Twenty-five years later, they both sit on a high shelf in my home, full of beach shells. We stayed in modest motels or found Dale and set up the tent next to his van. I saw a phone booth and called my cousin Don Onthank.

"Hey, Cuz! The March is over and three of us are headed your way. Could my tent-mate and I stay overnight with you and Joan?"

"Sure, Cuz! Of course, you may stay with us. We'd love to have you. I want to hear all about your Peace March. We'll have everything ready for you when you get here. Hurry up!"

In Boswell, Georgia, a suburb of Atlanta, he met us on the front porch and eagerly ushered us into their guest room. "You'll have a bathroom all to yourselves." Did he appreciate what a luxury that was?

We cleaned up, met Don and Joan in their living room and answered questions until our wine glasses were empty. I think we unsettled their conservative, traditional routine with our open road, whatever-happens-is-okay attitude. Joan said, "I can't imagine brushing my teeth outdoors among so many people. People I hardly know."

The next morning, Don hugged me goodbye and whispered, "I am proud of you, Cuz. I wish I could have been there with you."

Shelah and I met Dale and from Atlanta the three of us drove across Alabama, Mississippi, and Louisiana, sometimes in pouring rain along roads we didn't know and couldn't find on the map. One black night we stopped for gas and asked the attendant for a nearby motel.

"Ain't no motels here, Ma'm. This ain't even a town. Your best bet is to ask the fathers at the Catholic Church. It's only a few miles down the road. Cain't miss it." I asked him to call first. He dialed and gave the receiver to Shelah. She talked a few minutes.

"It's okay," Shelah told me. "We don't have to sleep in the car. We can roll out our sleeping bags in their spare room. Here, let's buy this box of tea and a package of cookies to take to them."

Dale said he'd park around back of the gas station and see us later the next afternoon. "In New Orleans. Near the visitor information office."

When we knocked, a young smiling priest in black slacks, white T-shirt, and black stocking feet opened the door and invited us into their comfortable masculine brown living room. "I'll just leave our sleeping bags here in the hallway," I said.

In front of the bright fire, Shelah and I answered questions about The Peace March. I almost fell asleep on the floor near the fire so I excused myself. In the spare bedroom, I sighed contentedly as I snuggled down into the sleeping bag. I had grown to love that bag! Shelah stayed up most of the night talking peace with the two priests. The next morning, she told me one had said, "It will take more reflection before I can accept the nuclear arms issue you advocate so well. It's hard for a Goldwater-Reagan Republican to change spots. I'll keep trying." They invited us to stay until Sunday to speak to their congregation, but we declined.

When we met Dale in New Orleans, where he had been before, he played tour guide and showed us the Latin Quarter. As we walked around admiring the lacy iron railings, he teased me about my attitudes regarding height. Ever since eighth grade, I'd been self-conscious about being tall. In group photos, I'd always had to stand in the back. Now, here I was, charmed by Dale, who not only was shorter than I, he walked in the gutter while I walked on the sidewalk beside him. He held my hand and chuckled wisely up at me. "See? Does it really matter?" I dissolved in laughter and learned again that the packaging of a person is not as important as the contents.

Dinner was hot spicy rice and fish. Along our walk on Bourbon Street, we heard jazz drifting out through doorways. We stayed two days, just wandering around.

By Thanksgiving Day, we were in East Texas at a truck stop. Before we went in to dinner, I collected the tiny orange pumpkin I'd bought and a stubby orange candle. The dining room was surprisingly busy for a family holiday, but we found a table, ordered the day's special, and immediately dispersed to freshen up. In the cavernous bathroom, Shelah and I washed our hands and faces, brushed our hair, straightened our clothes, and pinched our cheeks pink. In that moment, I thought that from then on, for the rest of my life, I'd probably not dress up, but settle for cleanup. Back in the dining room, we set the candle in the ashtray and lit it, put the little pumpkin next to it in the center of the table, grasped each other's hands, and said our own brief silent grace. People at the next table noted my red sweatshirt with *Great Peace March* across the front and my father's summary statement across the back. The man leaned over and asked, "Just what does that say there on the back of your shirt?"

"Oh," I smiled. "That's what my father said when I told him I was going to walk across the United States. He said, 'That's the God damnedest dumbest thing I've ever heard of' but he ran it all together the way it's printed."

His wife brightened. "Were y'all on that Peace March? I've heard a' that! Well, God bless ya. Enjoy your suppa." We did. Dale asked for more hot gravy. We cleaned our plates just as the waitress brought big pieces of pumpkin pie topped with whipped cream.

"Did we order pie?" I asked.

The waitress said, "These are from the people who were sitting over at that table. It's their treat."

On across Texas. Forever. We camped, sat around and sang, hiked, collected fragrant sage, played loud music, had picnics. Sometimes I rode with Dale, sometimes with Shelah. We weren't in any hurry for this trip to end. I suppose some would say now that we were decompressing, reorienting, re-entering real life. Shelah was still planning to meet Sky Shultz after Christmas to begin their educational tours. Dale explained his desire to make movies. He'd call his film company, "Pretty Good Pictures for Peace."

I wasn't sure what would be next for me. "I'll set up a slide show and do talks," I said.

"And, where would you like to do that?" asked Dale with his usual mischievous twinkle.

"I'm not quite sure," I answered, "but I have to go to San Mateo for Christmas and to build the Mouse House."

"Well," Dale tossed a pebble toward a cactus, "I have a slide projector if you'd like to come to Santa Barbara with me."

"I guess I'd better come to Santa Barbara then."

He tossed a pebble toward me.

I lay back on the desert and sighed, "I like the life we are in right at this moment, these days on the road. No matter how broad and flat and dry Texas is, I like it." We drove across New Mexico. And Arizona. Finally, we arrived in California.

We pulled off at a rest stop and transferred my gear to Dale's van. Shelah would turn toward Los Angeles where she was going to see her mother and daughter. Before she drove away, she choked up and said, "You promise to stay in touch, right?" We gave each other hugs, The Great Peace March equivalent to "hi" and "goodbye." I would miss Shelah. We had been together since Colorado, every day, and had never had a moment of tension. She was one of the best friends I would ever have.

"Yes. And you come stay with us," Dale and I said simultaneously. I went with him to his home in the hills above Santa Barbara.

I got a car, a red one similar to Shelah's. During the following months, I occasionally drove north to San Mateo. My four sons and their families lived in the San Francisco Bay Area, and I needed to see them as well as the people who rented the main part of my house. On the lower level, my son Sam built a small coming-home space, The Mouse House, in peachy Pennsylvania sunset colors with white shutters, just as I had envisioned it. I spent time in San Mateo whenever I wished and didn't disturb the people who rented upstairs.

Life with Dale continued. I walked four miles down to the beach to lie on the sand in the sun. I shared his spacious one-room hand-crafted cabin for weeks at a time, bought an old pine dresser with a lovely patina, a pine table, added a chair and a bright-red file cabinet. The word processor sat on the table below a window that faced across a canyon covered with eucalyptus trees. Dale created art in his studio by burnishing patterns onto large sheets of copper and using acids to add various colors. We set up his booth at art shows, and I met his artistic friends. I joined a writers group and wrote rambling stories that I read to him. He was a kind listener, made a few suggestions, and over time my writing became more focused.

We remained close to peace marchers and to peace issues. I scheduled slide shows with student groups, civic and church groups, any group anywhere in Santa Barbara, the San Francisco Bay Area, and north to Eugene, Florence and Portland. I'd go to anyone who asked me to speak about The Great Peace March and the transition from homemaker to peace-maker. At my son John's invitation, I spoke one noon to Apple employees. The San Mateo Soroptomists named me Woman of the Year. The Giraffe Project, which recognized people willing to stick their necks out for the common good, wrote complimentary articles about me. Rather fitting, I thought, given my totem. I was interviewed on radio and TV.

Meanwhile, The Peace Walk in Russia was taking shape. Two hundred thirty Americans were to walk with 200 Soviets from Leningrad (now St. Petersburg) to Moscow in June and July of 1987. In April, when I applied, I was told I was too late but they'd put me on the waiting list. Maybe someone would drop out. I'd wait. I checked my passport; it would still be valid in June. I waterproofed my hiking boots, just in case.

THE SOVIET-AMERICAN PEACE WALK

June 14—July 8, 1987
Leningrad (St. Petersburg) to Moscow, Russia
USSR

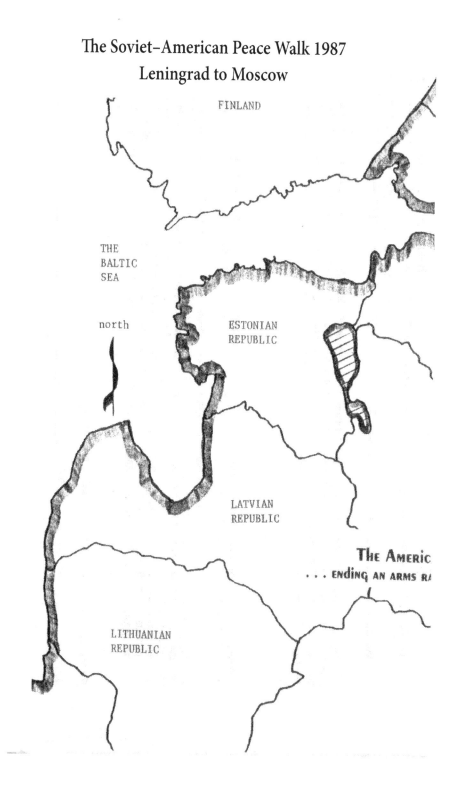

The Soviet–American Peace Walk 1987
Leningrad to Moscow

FINLAND

THE
BALTIC
SEA

north

ESTONIAN
REPUBLIC

LATVIAN
REPUBLIC

The Americ
. . . ending an arms r/

LITHUANIAN
REPUBLIC

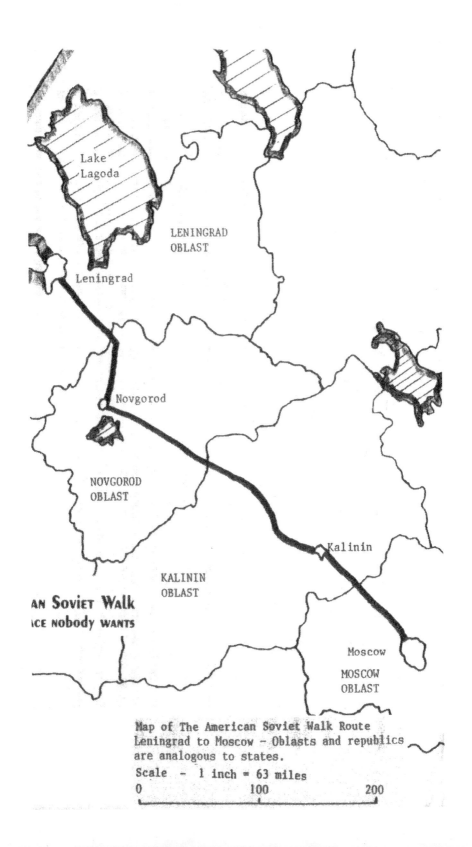

Lake
Lagoda

LENINGRAD
OBLAST

Leningrad

Novgorod

NOVGOROD
OBLAST

Kalinin

KALININ
OBLAST

AN SOVIET WALk
ICE NObody wANTS

Moscow

MOSCOW
OBLAST

Map of The American Soviet Walk Route
Leningrad to Moscow - Oblasts and republics
are analogous to states.

Scale - 1 inch = 63 miles

0   100   200

Marchers in four regions of the United States.

CHAPTER 24

"You Oughta Do That in Russia"

Saturday morning, June 13, 1987, before 7, the phone rang and Dale reached across me to answer.

"Yes, she's right here." He handed me the phone, his eyes big, and mouthed, "It's a man."

I blinked myself awake, "Hello, this is Donna."

"Hi, this is Uldis. Remember me from The Peace March?"

"Yes, I do, Uldis, and you are working on The Peace Walk in Russia. How is that going? Aren't you about ready to leave?"

"Yes, we are, but there is a problem. One of the applicants has dropped out, and we'd like to fill her spot. Could you meet us at Dulles airport in Washington at 10 tomorrow morning?"

I'd been chosen. Accepted. I've always loved that feeling of being invited. I could hear Rhoda, one of the peace marchers who had read Shakespeare across the United States, calling, "Come on, Donna. Go with us."

"Yes! Yes! I'll get a flight out this evening and be there. This is fantastic news, Uldis. But, what about the papers and forms I need to fill out?"

"Oh that. Well, you can do them when you get here. Glad you can come. Have a good flight. See you tomorrow morning."

"Thank you. Thank you, Uldis. Bye."

Dale took the receiver from me and replaced it on the night stand and stayed right there, stretched across me. His eyes sparkled with excitement. I grabbed him, and we shouted together, "She's going! I'm going! She's going!" On our knees, we bounced around on the bed, holding on to each other and laughing, shouting, ecstatic until we fell into a heap, two grey-haired kids, giggling.

"Well," he climbed down off the bed, "we have lots to do today. I'll look up the airlines and get you a ticket."

"And I'll start packing. Oh, I'll need some balloons to hand out to children. Do you want breakfast now? Would a banana do for the moment? Where's that green suitcase that's also a backpack?"

I paused and Dale looked up from the phone book. "Thank you," I said, "for your enthusiasm, for your happiness for me, for being here. Such gifts."

He touched my face. "Have you forgotten that I love you?"

"No, I never forget. It's the greatest gift of all," and touched his hand that touched my face.

I peeled a banana, poked most of it in his mouth and popped the rest into mine.

I knew that my friend and peace marcher Jacquelyn Smith of Carmel was going. We had talked about being tent-mates. So I gave her a call to let her know I would be in Washington, DC, the next morning, and to ask her if she still wanted us to share a tent.

Her answer was immediate and unconditional: "Yes! I'd love that."

"All right, then," I replied. "See you tomorrow!"

I called Mother. After she listened, she said, "Don't call attention to yourself, Donna. You don't want to end up spending the night in a Russian jail."

Late that afternoon, we were ready. As we left the cabin, I picked up a red ink pad and peace dove stamp and crammed them into my pocket. On the way to the airport, we stopped by a party store, and I bought a ball of narrow, red ribbon and a gross of white balloons printed with an American flag. I told the checker why I was buying them, and she looked at me with sad eyes. "You'll go to Russia, and we'll never see you again."

We arrived at the airport early, time for a glass of wine and dinner. Dale gave me one of his cameras and a lesson in photography, then handed me a bag from Longs Drug Store. "Open it." Inside was $200 worth of film, some red heart balloons and sparkly red sticker hearts. He danced around, blowing bubbles and making me laugh. We hugged each other, and he murmured, "You go for me, honey." I boarded a United Airlines plane at 7:55 p.m. and watched out the window at him waving, blowing bubbles, and flashing me the peace sign until the plane taxied out to the runway.

I had time to think about how this Peace Walk had started. In October with the trucker in Pennsylvania who rolled down his window and growled, "You oughta do that in Russia!" A few days later a few, four, I think, marchers drove down to Washington, DC, to begin negotiations with the Soviet Peace Committee. Among the marchers were retired Los Angeles Municipal Judge Carlos de la Fuente, 49, and UC Irvine graduate student Allan Affeldt, 27, who became the president of International Peace Walks, Inc. The agreement between the Soviet and American organizations was signed in February. Two hundred thirty Americans were going; each had to come up with $2,500. A staff of 10, housed in an abandoned yacht club in Newport, California, had ironed out the details. And we were going. I was going! I couldn't imagine all the work—the compromises, the misunderstandings, the patience—that had gone into making this possible. Margaret Meade had to be right: Social changes are made by a small group of dedicated people.

I wished I'd applied and been accepted earlier so I could have attended the training sessions in Leesburg, Virginia, a suburb of Washington, DC. They had studied Russian culture and recent history, attended lectures on the arms race and American/Soviet relations. They'd learned a popular little Russian song: "May there always be sunshine, May there always be blue skies, May there always be mama, May there always be me"—in Russian.

I'd have to ask Jackie to fill me in. I wasn't even sure that my name would be on the roster. Oh, well. I sent up a prayer of gratitude and drifted off to sleep.

At 5:43 the next morning the plane landed at Dulles. I wandered around the airport looking at the shops, then found Aeroflot gate near Pan American. A sunny window ledge was a good place for a nap. When I wakened I saw piles of boxes of posters, T-shirts and IBM supplies, as well as mounds of camping gear. Then the familiar faces and shapes of peace marchers. Porta-potty Bob. Anne and Dick Edelman, with whom I'd walked many days as we read our newspaper submissions to each other. Mim, who had taken me thrift store shopping in Pennsylvania. Allan Affeldt, who now was organizer of IPW (International Peace Walks) and therefore of the Soviet-American Peace Walk. Billie, who was with me in the fourth-grade classroom in Salt Lake City. Jeff Share, the award-winning photographer. Jackie Smith with whom I'd share a tent for the next several weeks. Of the 230 walkers who were going to Russia, about 80 were from The Great Peace March. Some I hadn't seen for seven months. Everyone was elated. We hugged each other and talked about walking together again.

Some talked about a protest walk in New England in August and September.

"There's a two-month walk in New Zealand that starts about July 20. Want to go?"

"Maybe next year Soviets will come to the United States for a Peace Walk."

The traditional Russian welcome; a smile, round bread and salt.

CHAPTER 25

Leningrad

From Washington, DC, to Leningrad was a long flight, but it felt like a long party. The entire plane was filled with walkers. We roamed up and down the aisles, sat on the arms of seats and hung over the backs talking excitedly about our next three weeks. This "Walk for Peace" was to be the largest exchange in history between citizens of our two countries: 230 Americans and 200 Soviets. We would walk 300 miles from Leningrad south to Moscow, two of the largest cities in the Republic of Russia. "That's about the distance from San Francisco to Santa Barbara," Jackie said.

She and I sat together and reminisced about The Great Peace March and life since it had ended seven months ago on November 15, 1986. In anticipation of tenting together, we sorted out our personal preferences.

"I wake up, sit up, get dressed and am out fairly quickly." I said. "I don't even brush my hair until I'm standing up outside the tent. "How about you?"

"Well," Jackie laughed. "You'll probably beat me to smithereens. I like to lie there, stretch, peek through the little tent window to check the weather outside, decide what to wear, and have a leisurely start to the day."

We'll be fine, I thought. Jackie was cheerful, smart, easy to be around. We agreed that if anything, anything at all, was bothering us, we'd talk and not let it grow out of proportion. We'd practice peace principles, the basics of which seemed to be respect and communication.

We landed June 15 at 4:30 in the afternoon. Customs did not open our luggage, only x-rayed it; an act of trust we noticed and appreciated. Activists from the Leningrad Peace Committee and some of the Soviet walkers surrounded us. They gave us flowers, spoke carefully when they said, "Good afternoon. How are you?" and hooked arms with us as we walked together to the big red buses that would take us to the Repin Hotel and campground. I felt royally welcomed.

Premier Gorbachev had sent a letter in which he recognized the importance of our Peace Walk. The political atmosphere of *glasnost* (openness) and *perestroika* (restructuring) contributed to our warm reception. We would, indeed, be treated as citizen diplomats. I knew that we would be eating in restaurants, hotels, and out in fields and forests as we wended our way southeast to Moscow. We'd sleep in college dorms, resorts, hotels, and in our tents. Bus numbers were on our identification tags; mine was Bus 6. The pre-planning seemed thorough. Maybe best of all, we were guaranteed showers at least on alternate days.

I learned to call the main language "Russian" and the people "Soviets." Over the 11 time zones of the USSR, 100 languages were in use, but the main one was Russian. All 15 Soviet Republics were represented on The Walk and to call all their citizens Russians would have been like calling everyone in the United States "Texans."

When the buses from the airport arrived at the Repin Hotel and parked, we were shown our campsite. It wasn't a place to set up tents, as I'd expected. A grove of birch trees protected little playhouse-sized recreation trailers—stat wagons, they're called—where Jackie and I found a clutch of wildflowers inserted in the door-pull of ours. It was immaculate inside, complete with a glass pitcher of water, filmy lace curtains at the little windows and reading lights by the beds. We sat down at the miniscule table and beamed at each other. "Let's just stay here and play house," she said.

But, no, outside we heard accordion music and laughter, shouts of glee. We left our gear in the house-trailer and joined hundreds of people folk-dancing in the parking lot. Two hundred Soviets, representing the 15 Republics of the Soviet Union, danced with 230 of us Americans. Dinner that evening was in the hotel dining room. White tablecloths, fabric napkins, crystal stemware, gold-rimmed china plates. Four courses. A quartet played off to the side. This was nothing like the dinners on The Great Peace March, when our salads floated in rainwater.

Franklin Folsom, the eldest on The Great Peace March and on this Peace Walk in Russia, wrote, "When we arrived in the Soviet Union, we were overwhelmed with the most generous and thoughtful hospitality. And the walkers, a great many of whom seemed to be more interested in personal relationships than in politics, were astonished by the individual outpourings of friendship they encountered at every turn. And there was continuous evidence of the expansion of Socialist democracy under the popular policy of glasnost."

Our awe and excitement didn't keep us from sleeping. Tomorrow we would tour various "enterprises."

Donna Love and a Soviet woman walked several miles together on the highway south of Leningrad.

CHAPTER 26

Tours, Tea Boxes, and Teeming Multitudes

The next morning, we split into groups to board the buses which took us to electric plants, a steel mill, a shoe factory, two textile plants, a tool fabrication plant, a children's clothing plant and a porcelain manufacturing plant. We had hot lunches served family style with the workers at long wooden tables. Thousands of Russians saw Americans that day, sometimes for the first time in their lives. They gave us gifts. I still treasure a small decorated ceramic bowl that reminds me of the woman worker with bright blue eyes who, smiling, offered it as a gift.

In the afternoon, instead of taking the boat excursion along the rivers and canals of Leningrad, Jackie wanted to meet a young Russian rock musician who had visited her in her hometown of Carmel. She had made an appointment with him to meet at the statue in front of the Hermitage Museum. I had, in the mid-1970s, been in Leningrad (St

Petersburg) and toured the Neva River (our guide had pronounced it "da Neeva Reeva,"), so I went with Jackie and waited for her friend in the huge cobbled square that fronted one of the world's oldest and largest museums. Established in 1764 by Catherine the Great and opened to the public in 1852, The Hermitage houses one of the largest collections of paintings in the world.

We didn't wait long before Sieva came loping toward us. He hugged Jackie and bowed a little before shaking my hand. He looked like so many young musicians: shaggy hair, untucked shirt, black high-top Converse shoes, big grin.

"Come, come with me. My mother wants to meet you. I will take you to her. In our home. She is waiting for you. I hope you don't mind." His English was very clear and had a bit of a British accent.

Mind? This is what I wanted, to visit a home. I felt honored to be invited. He led us to the street car, and we clacked along through neighborhoods of big drab grey block apartment houses. I recalled that Leningrad had suffered severely during World War II. All these utilitarian buildings were post-war.

Upstairs, along a dusky hall, Sieva opened a brown wooden door, and we stepped into a crowded room hung with drying laundry. Ducking under it, we found his mother, a small plump woman, sitting in a deep dark-brown overstuffed chair, smiling serenely, her hands in her lap. Light streamed in the open window behind her. Symphonic music came from somewhere. A radio or CD? I breathed in the aromas of strong laundry soap and vegetable soup.

His mother extended both hands to grasp Jackie's. Sieva said, "She is blind so she'll want to touch your face. I hope that is alright with you." When I met her, we touched each other's cheeks, and both of us chuckled.

While our host put water for tea on the stove in the small kitchen, I looked around the living room. Artful posters advertising the Bolshoi Ballet were tacked to the walls. Classics—Pushkin, Shakespeare, Mark Twain—filled the bookshelves that lined the living room. Also on the shelves, dozens of Celestial Seasonings Tea boxes! Empty.

"What are the tea boxes for?" I asked.

"Oh," Sieva smiled. "When I was in Carmel visiting Jackie, she gave me boxes of tea to bring back to my mother. There are sayings on the boxes, and I learned to read them. Such lovely English phrases. And I listen to BBC [British Broadcasting Company)] I practiced until now I can understand and speak English pretty well. Don't you think so?"

Yes, I thought so. I also concluded that although living conditions were crowded and by some American standards, poor, the cultural enrichments such as music, art, drama, ballet, literature and poetry, seemed more important in Leningrad, at least in this one family, than in more lavish homes in America. I wondered at our differences in values.

That day, Jackie and I missed not only a tour of the rivers and canals of Leningrad, but also a walk to Piskarevskoye Memorial Cemetery. The wreath-laying ceremonies honored over 1,117,000 victims who died between 1941 and 1944 during the 872-day Nazi siege of Leningrad and are buried in mass graves. We weren't involved in greeting people along the route, and we didn't visit the Lenin Memorial Museum. But visiting Sieva and his mother in their home was worth it. He accompanied us on the streetcar back to the door of the hotel and courteously bid us good evening. We returned in time for another lavish dinner at 8:30. The sun was still up; we would have twilight until after midnight. These were the White Nights, close to the summer solstice.

During the next three days, we saw what must have been every attraction in Leningrad—the city founded by Peter the Great—palaces, parks, museums, monuments, cultural centers, farms, concerts, schools and greenhouses. Ever since the siege of Leningrad, when citizens starved to death, greenhouses have dotted the landscape of gardens and parks. Tomatoes, cucumbers, cabbages, green onions and lettuces are grown year round.

"We will not starve again," one of the Russian walkers told me. He reminded me of Scarlet O'Hara in *Gone With the Wind*, when she returned to her family's devastated plantation after the American Civil War and proclaimed, "As God is my witness, I shall never be hungry again."

Buffy Boesan, a nun from Colorado, beamed, "I'm counting. Nine rallies and six concerts in the first week. I figure if there's a mike, it's a rally. And there's always a mike. I wonder what today will bring."

It would bring fine meals, that we could count on. The catering team that accompanied The Walk set up an Army mess tent and served elegant midday meals in fields of wildflowers or in groves of birch trees. In the rain, they constructed dining pavilions of new fragrant plywood and clear plastic overhead, with white damask cloths on the long plank tables. Breakfast, dinner, and supper were feasts with cheese blintzes, cabbage rolls, soups, roasted meats, garden vegetables—and always fresh flowers centered on the tables.

Everywhere we went, the streets were lined with crowds. We received bouquets of flowers and little gifts. Children gave us pictures they had drawn. I thought that the "enterprises" where we saw thousands of workers, probably belonged to the Soviet Peace Committee, and were sanctioned by the government, but not part of the government. Workers probably paid dues to the committee. I suspected that when some event such as the Soviet American Peace Walk happened, all the employees of the plant got off work for part of the day. As a result, large crowds would be visible at the street corners and squares for the rallies. I wrote in my journal, "I am having a hard time figuring out how so many people can be so organized: the banners, flags, flowers, buttons. How do so many people in so many places all have the same grins, waves, gifts and displays? I concluded that the Central Organizing Committee must be very well in place and everyone very responsive to the directives. Americans are not that way; we are more amorphous, less structured, more spontaneous.

One day I sat on a park bench and blew up balloons. A girl about high-school age sat next to me to help. Children gathered around, and we tied inflated balloons to their wrists. Parents beamed.

When I took out my peace dove stamp and red ink pad, everyone stuck their hands out to get stamped. Students extended their notebooks, men, their caps; young girls wanted their faces stamped, and women held their baby's bare feet out. I got the sense they thought I was blessing them.

Holding out the peace dove stamp, I asked the girl, "Do you know the name for this bird?"

She nodded brightly and answered, "Yes, I know."

"Good," I said. "What is it?"

"It's a pigeon."

At every crossroad, people lined up and shook our hands and chanted, "*Mir y druzhba*"—sometimes weeping when they weren't smiling, expressing their unfeigned delight at seeing a large body of

Americans who, like themselves, wanted to end all war.

At each village and town, and at one big collective farm, the local officials greeted us. Almost always they told of the sufferings of their community during World War II. Along the way, local choruses and dance groups in beautiful costumes entertained us—the first Americans that many of them had ever seen. And always a lovely young woman in local costume offered us a round loaf of bread with a dish of salt in the center—an ancient symbolic act of hospitality.

There were no porta-potties. Instead, we were welcome to use the bathroom in any of the homes along the way. We were to approach a house and ask for the *too-al-y-et*. One morning I did just that. Several women who were standing by the front gate broke into big smiles, and one ushered me into the house, through the front room and around a corner to a closed door—with a window in it. Crisp lacey curtains provided some privacy. I entered what felt like an immaculate outhouse, only it was in the house. A broad wooden bench with a lidded hole in it was the toilet. The waste dropped down to some dark place under the house. Squares of toilet paper nestled in a basket. I noted fresh flowers, Queen Anne's lace and daisies in a porcelain pitcher sitting on a small old chest of drawers, framed photos on the wall and no washbowl. A small window shrouded with more lace curtains, provided ventilation and natural light. I learned later that beneath the house, separated from the waste tank, was a manger for a few goats, a cow, some chickens. The house shelters the animals, and the animals' bodies provide warmth that rises through the floorboards of the home. The combined animal and human waste was used to fertilize the gardens. I wondered why there was no unpleasant odor. Only a mild farm aroma.

When I returned to the women at the front of the house, one showed me the sink in the kitchen where I washed my hands. The women had set a small table with a white tablecloth, tea and cookies and had brought chairs out from the house. They invited me to sit down with two of them while the rest hovered around, chattering and rummaging in their pockets. We showed each other pictures of our grandchildren, and one gave me a packet of flower seeds. I gave them balloons and an entire sheet of the sparkly heart stickers that Dale had handed me in Santa Barbara. I dug my Polaroid camera out, and we took photos of each other and clustered together to watch the images emerge. I gave the photos to them. We laughed at everything and exchanged hugs. I showed them how to do a group hug. I was a foot taller than any of them.

Novgorod, south of Leningrad 189 kilometers (113.4 miles) along Highway M10, is an ancient city. Already in 859, it was reportedly a major station on the trade route between the Baltics and Byzantium. An historically important cultural center, it was never invaded during the Mongol invasion of Russia because the attackers would have become bogged down in the marshes that surrounded the city. It was occupied, however, in the early 1940s, by the Germans who systematically destroyed the historic monuments and all but 40 of 2,536 stone buildings. They used the central cathedral to stable their horses. Liberated by Allied forces in January of 1944, the city has gradually restored the old buildings. When we were there in 1987, 200 church buildings existed, only one of which, an Orthodox, was operating. A young Russian told me, "It is not natural to go to church."

At the time we were there, the population of Novgorod was 229,000. Over a 100,000 people came to greet us at the rally at Russian Millennium Monument park. There was no mistaking the excitement among the people. They were witnessing in their midst, an unprecedented eruption of Americans who, by their very presence, were saying that they did not agree with the belligerent foreign policy of the Reagan Administration.

In Novgorod, the oldest Russian city, it fell to Franklin, the oldest walker, to represent the Americans. His eloquent speech brought roars of approval. Franklin prophesied, "The day will come when Soviet and American citizens will no longer need to march against armaments which are the common enemy of both our peoples."

At one point, I was so crushed by enthusiastic Russians, I almost panicked. I couldn't see any Americans, except Franklin far away on the speakers' platform. I struggled for a moment with my balance, until a tall Russian I recognized as a peace walker took my arm and guided me to a spot where we had a bit of room to breathe. I examined the name tag he wore and showed him mine. He was Peter Ganea. He seemed not much older than my sons, maybe in his late 30s, and he spoke English.

The crowds walked with us to the buses parked on the south edge of town. Television cameras were everywhere. Microphones were shoved toward us. All I could say in Russian was *mir y drushba*, peace and friendship. As we boarded a bus, Peter sat down beside me. We would become friends.

Each day we rode buses through sparsely populated areas. As we approached the northern edge of a town, we got out and walked along the highway. As we walked, people on the roadsides joined us. Some came in delegations—wearing the uniform or emblems of their sports clubs, schools, committees—and waited patiently, even for hours in the rain, to join The Peace Walk. Many of the children were dressed in red, white, and blue—a tribute to our national colors. We became a river of humanity several kilometers in length. Flowing. The destination was the process. A woman sporting a plain cloth coat, a bandana and a shy smile, took my hand, held it and walked a mile or so. She spoke a little English, and our conversation ranged from our children to mosquitoes (Jackie said they were "as big as Volkswagens") to the beauty of the birch forests, to the arms race. Our concerns were similar and mutual. At the head of our mass were an American carrying a Soviet flag and a Soviet carrying the American flag. Others carried banners that stated: "End the Arms Race that Nobody Wants," "Give Peace a Chance," "It's Our Move"—in Russian and in English. Many walkers carried paper USA-USSR souvenir flags.

Police controlled traffic so we had one lane of the highway. Cars and trucks slowed as the drivers waved, much as had occurred the previous year on The Great Peace March. I counted and concluded there were 24 trucks for every car, and every truck was painted army green. With no competition in Russia, there was no need for bright advertising on the trucks.

As we passed small wooden houses sitting in flower gardens surrounded by wooden picket fences, women dashed out of their doors, wiping their hands on their aprons. They paused to gather flowers to give to us. They held up their children for us to touch and their icons to bless us. *Babushkas* (grandmothers), their metallic front teeth glinting in the sunshine, dragged wooden chairs to the edge of the road to sit close enough to shake our hands. A water glass of flowers sat on one chair.

Old veterans in their mismatched slacks and jackets, campaign ribbons decorating their breast pockets, sat on low walls or benches and waved to us. One old gentleman stood as I passed by. I almost didn't notice him, but I realized what I'd seen, so turned back and walked over to him. He gazed at me with tears rolling down his face, took my hand in both of his and didn't let go for a long moment. I motioned that I'd give him a hug. He sucked in his breath and opened his arms.

Oh, how I wished President Reagan could see this!

A typical lunch in a restaurant.

CHAPTER 27

Ask and Ye Shall Receive

Four hundred thirty of us had clambered onto the big red buses to ride south through the rural area to the next village. On these buses we had time to rest, to finish conversations started during the walks, maybe to sing songs. Peter and I sat together and compared our teaching experiences. He taught math and English to college level students in Kishinev, Moldova, and I had worked with dyslexic students in San Mateo, California. In a while, I became aware of the conversation in the seats right behind us. Our American leader, Allan Affeldt, was talking with his Walk counterpart, Igor Filin, Executive Secretary of the Soviet Peace Committee. I heard Igor say, in his heavily accented, proper English, "Allan, tell me, is everything going well with your people? Are they pleased with this experience?"

"Why, yes, Igor, they are. The hospitality, the preparations you have made, the scheduling of events is impressive. And these Austrian buses are amazing. Many walkers have commented on the newness of the teeth-brushing stations and clever water systems in the campgrounds."

"Good," said Igor. "We want to do all we can for your comfort."

"Well, I think everyone is as comfortable as they can be." Allan paused. "But, I will say one thing, if I may. You know, many of the American walkers are from California and are used to having fresh fruit. They like fruit or juice at breakfast, for snacks and at the midday meal. Maybe not so much in the evening. The vegetables have been good. The potatoes, cabbage, onions, carrots, the green beans are all good. And the tomatoes. What other vegetables are available?"

I looked sideways at Peter. He gave me a quiet little smile, slightly lifted his shoulder, and nudged me with his elbow. He was listening, too. I heard Igor's "Hmm. Fruit. Vegetables," and could imagine him taking notes.

That night we slept in college dorms. The wire bedsprings were so saggy that Jackie and I put the mattresses on the floor and slept well. The next morning when we entered the vast dining room, huge bowls heaped with oranges sat on small round tables covered with blue cloths. Along with the usual breakfast of coffee, tea, breads, cheeses, tomatoes and cucumber slices, entire stalks of ripe bananas lay down the center of each table. I hooted with delight and shoved a banana into my pocket. Luncheon, or rather one o'clock dinner, was a four-course meal of soup, green salad, an entree of meat, boiled potatoes with parsley and green beans. That was pretty normal. But for dessert, instead of the usual cake, we were served strawberries in bowls of cream.

"Pictures!" we squealed. "We need pictures of this! Put a berry on your spoon. Okay, open your mouth. Look at me. Who at home would believe this!"

At the evening meal, there were artichokes! They needed melted butter and were a little tough, but with salt, they passed the scrutiny of appreciative walkers. I showed Peter how to pull each leaf through his teeth. He tried it and was polite, but said. "I think I'll wait for an artichoke in California," As though he had a chance on his meager teacher's salary to travel from Moldova to the United States.

Later, at the folk dancing around a bonfire in an open field, I asked Allan how all that fresh fruit and the artichokes had magically appeared at mealtime.

He looked as incredulous as I felt, shrugged his shoulders and raised his hands to the heavens. "They flew it in last night from Israel."

Imagine! Artichokes grown in Israel rather than Castroville, the small town in central California renowned as the "Artichoke Capital of the World." The bananas, the oranges, and the berries. All flown in overnight so we Californians would be happy!

I wandered around until I found Igor to thank him. He was surrounded by smiling Americans shaking his hand, clapping him on the back, and rubbing their bellies.

Donna Love and Anne Edelman of Los Angeles, walking for our lives.

CHAPTER 28

Notes from the Little Green Journal

"I think I'll stay quietly here in the dorm at this Pioneer Camp (a youth camp similar to a Boy Scout camp). I'm in an eight-bed room overlooking some of our faded Peace March tents set up in the yard. We have had a pleasant luncheon of salted fish and cucumber slices followed by chicken noodle soup, dark and light bread. Then bananas and pineapple chunks in juice. Finally, the entree: meat, potatoes, peas and tea. If I were a vegetarian, I could have had tasty breaded cabbage patties.

"I feel at ease now. It took a couple of weeks. When I felt the gears shift yesterday, I asked Gene Gordon if he felt the same and he said, 'Yes, I do. It's a better rhythm now.' I guess my Peace March friend Gret is fine; at the Lenin Memorial yesterday, she spoke to me at length about her little romance with her Soviet English teacher friend, Bob.

"This morning I felt like dancing in the parking lot with the women. I stood there for several minutes feeling shy, then took a breath and stepped out to enjoy dancing in a small group. When I returned to the sidelines, one of our interpreters came to say, 'I think you are a good dancer.' What a change from the dances in high school where I often slouched against a wall trying to look invisible or retreated to the girls' bathroom where I could hide my shame at being a self-conscious awkward wallflower.

"When a Soviet woman came over, dipped in a small bow, and asked me to dance, I declined, but she looked disappointed and those standing nearby encouraged me to accept her invitation. I was sure I would feel weird dancing with a woman, but remembered that most of their men had been killed in World War II. Without men, and loving to dance, they danced with one another. So I accepted, and although my steps weren't perfect, they were good enough, and I had fun and felt giddy. At the conclusion, she escorted me back to my place and repeated her little bow.

"From the parking lot, I was directed along the road from the camp out to the main Leningrad-Moscow highway, where I saw only a small number of marchers walking toward the south. They looked like people I knew so I started out, and Gret joined me. We walked along waving in Great Peace March style, past the police guard station, until finally one of the security cars came along, and we were waved across to the right side of the road to their car. Though we didn't know why they wanted us to, Gret and I obediently climbed into the car, but the others insisted on walking to the next campsite. We were dropped off and told to wait on the roadside for Bus 11. Of course, we did. We waved exuberantly to the first 10 buses as they sped past. Bus 11 had only men! Nice, helpful, informative, cheerful Soviet men.

"Later, after the reception and speeches in another small town I was on my regular bus, Bus 6, sitting, as usual, in front of our leader, Alan Affeldt, and his Soviet counterpart. I could overhear some of their conversation: 'We have a problem,' said Igor. 'Your Americans walk off down the road, and it gives our security people lots of problems. Your Americans leave their luggages behind and then expect us to find them. Your Americans must learn to be responsible for themselves.' It sounded like a father talking to his children.

"Our having walked along the highway was not the only problem. Arranging for 5,000 tickets to the rock concert in Moscow on July 4 is another. Many of us feel that if the Soviet Peace Committee has sole control of the tickets, only those who are owed favors will get them. We want not just privileged people attending the rock concert, but ordinary citizens such as those we have been meeting along the way."

On another page in my journal, I wrote, "I wonder when the Russians sleep these summer nights. It's 10 o'clock, and I can see well enough with the light coming in the window, and it's raining."

An enthusiastic Soviet greeting two American peace walkers.

CHAPTER 29

Who is Our Enemy?

Sitting with Peter on the bus, I asked him what he thought were differences between Americans and Soviets.

"You want your freedoms, we thrive on discipline," he answered.

"Yes, I can see that. What else? I think that Americans learn perseverance and Russians learn patience."

"I think Americans demand a lot of life, and we require little. Some music, a child, security, a little vodka."

We traded ideas. Americans feared alteration of their lifestyle; Soviets feared another war. To Soviets, individual pursuits looked like selfishness. Americans valued self-expression, and Soviets embraced collectivism. American competition versus Russian cooperation. Americans strove to create the future; Russians struggled with the pain of the past. We had Uncle Sam; they had Mother Russia. With Americans, money talks. With Soviets, Mama (Mother Russia) talks.

Rhoda heard us and leaned across the aisle. "Don't forget the two cultural negotiating styles. The Soviets set up an immediate boundary. We have to find the crack in the wall, and then they give everything they can. Americans are flexible in their negotiating until they hit the brick wall, and then they hold firm to their boundary." She added, "We *are* in this together and there's *no* problem we can't solve with respect and affection."

Gene, in the seat ahead, peered around and said, "I notice the Russians serve coffee at the end of breakfast, and we serve it first. That's crucial!"

Allan poked his head over the back of my seat and said, "Impossible is just a state of mind. We need to negotiate, and we can do that if we respect the logic and reasons for our different stances." He grinned. "Sometimes it seems like one of us is playing chess and the other, checkers."

I wrote a list of these differences into my little green book and all these years later, still treasure that hour in which Peter and I and the others, worked to understand each other.

North of Valdai, we climbed down off the buses to walk into town. The traffic control guards arranged themselves, as usual, along our route, waving their arms, clearing motorists and onlookers like scattering chickens. After the welcoming speeches and ceremony, I visited several classrooms in primary and secondary schools because I was interested in the teaching materials. In every classroom, Lenin leered down from his place on the front wall. I wondered if we'd ever see George Washington and Vladimir Lenin side-by-side on classroom walls.

In the primary school, I noticed workbook pages headed with *Mir,* one of the few Russian words I knew: Peace. When I looked at the secondary-school materials, sure enough, the first lessons in the books were about peace.

I asked the teacher if this were the real lesson or the material put out so visiting Americans would see it. The teacher tilted her head and looked perplexed. I asked again, "Do you really teach a unit on peace?"

She nodded and said, "Why, yes, we do. At the beginning of every school term. Don't you?"

The teacher asked a small girl—about eight years old—to recite what she had learned. She stood shyly by her seat. "*Nyet, nyet.* Come to the front," the teacher insisted. The child looked at her classmates and at the five of us visiting peace walkers, and with gathering force and speed, she said:

I vant to laugh and not to cry.
I vant to live and not to die
I vant vorld peace and doves to fly...

The poem was very long. Before the end, I was wiping tears from my face.

Having talked with the teachers, I shouldn't have been surprised to see brides at the base of war memorials. Every village, town and city has a war memorial. Brides, still in their white bridal dresses and veils, are accompanied by their grooms and parents as they go immediately from the wedding to the local war memorial and place their bouquets there. They then pledge to devote a portion of their adult lives to creating peace.

And these were the people whom we Americans have feared and declared our enemy!

The most fearsome individuals I'd met were the big women in loose cotton dresses who attended the public baths in Kalinin. About 100 of us went in buses, a police escort stopping traffic along the way, to the baths. We walked in, women to the right, men to the left, and were shown to the lockers, handed a large white rough linen-type towel, and told to take off our clothes. When we were wrapped, a woman gave us the tour. There was a steam room, a wooden sauna, a hot tub and a cold plunge. Also showers. All, except the cold-pool plunge, were in a maze of very hot rooms in an area I recall as larger than a basketball gymnasium. We were guided from one experience to the next and given cups of water to drink. The big women had wet leafy birch switches, and, as we stood stark naked, they obligingly whipped our backs and legs, laughing at our yelping and gasping. Some of us took advantage of everything available. I couldn't bring myself to jump into the icy cold plunge, but shivered and shrieked in the cold showers. After a couple of hours, we were clean, pink, and refreshed. As a final treat, we were invited to sit in a lounge and drink fruit juices. I can't recall when I felt so vibrantly healthy.

I'm not certain how all that water was heated for the public baths, but I did learn that when I asked at a hotel for a shower, I would need to wait for 45 minutes. Beneath the wooden bath house, which was built on a slope behind the hotel, was a fire over which a large tub of water sat. I think that the hot water was pumped up to the shower above. That system required someone to fill the vats and someone to stoke the fires. Was there no end to Russian hospitality! No wonder we were called citizen-diplomats. We were treated as honored guests. At least, that's how I felt.

One evening, after only a few rehearsals, I was on stage in a play. That was very unusual for me. As a senior in high school, I had a walk-on part as a Native American boy, dressed in fringed "deerskin," with my dark hair in long braids. I walked on, held up my hand in greeting, grunted, "Ho!" and stood in the back row with the other tall students. Usually, when a play was produced in school, I was a stage manager, the prompter, someone behind the scenes—too self-conscious to be in front of an audience.

But in a Russian high-school theater, I was in a play. Well, maybe a skit. I don't recall all the details, but I played a lady, her shoulders draped with a colorful fringed shawl, who entered stage right, crossed to a small round table and sat down in one of two chairs. She arranged her long skirt to cover her hiking shoes. Just that—walking across the stage and sitting down, thinking it's my chance to practice my Katherine Hepburn stride—took courage. I remembered what Mother had so often said, "Walk with dignity, and no one will notice if everything is not just perfect."

In a moment, a tall, good-looking gentleman in a trench coat came on stage, greeted me, pulled me up for an embrace, and then we both sat down. The rest of the cast entertained us as though we were in a bistro. There were musicians, tumblers—I don't remember all of them. The gentleman and I smiled at each other, held hands, looked like lovers. We were among couples who danced together on a pretend dance floor. By that point in the performance, I felt a lot better. I was able to play my part, and found that I enjoyed pretending. Neither the gentleman nor I said a single word. He was Russian. He looked like a KGB officer in his trench coat. In fact, he was KGB, one of several who accompanied our Peace Walk. "For security reasons, to protect us," some Soviet officials had told us.

A few days after the play, the gentleman asked me to meet him in a hotel lounge for a glass of wine. I didn't, but sometimes wish I had. We could have celebrated my theatrical debut.

Children were eager to pose. Donna Love in Red Square, Moscow, near St Basil's Cathedral.

CHAPTER 30

Moscow

After so many drizzly days and smaller towns—Pushkin, Tosno, Novgorod, Valdai, Kalinin, Klin, others—we arrived in Moscow on the sunny afternoon of July 1. We entered the city on a sleek, modern riverboat, following a four-hour cruise down the Moscow River. During those four hours Sallie and Alan Gratch and I became good friends. They told me of their life in Evanston. "We've lived in the same old house since our children were babies. It's near the campus. I wish you could see our area; it's lovely."

"But I have seen your neighborhood. Our third son John went to Northwestern. Maybe I've walked by your house!"

Sallie told of her dream to establish an association of American and Soviet Jewish women. "I think we can do it. Certainly the Jewish women here yearn for it."

A huge crowd, waving colorful balloons and peace placards, lined the dock fronting the picturesque passenger terminal. Other greeters cheered from the steps and rails of the old port building, while a naval guard snapped to attention. A full week of activities awaited us in the capital city—sightseeing and wandering about unrestricted, sessions with Soviet officials and peace organizations, dances and folk festivals, and new friends. New friends, always, wherever we went.

Once we were checked into the Solnetchny Hotel, Jackie and I wanted to see the subway terminals. We walked to the nearest metro entrance, watching little shapeless women in dark gray attire using twig brooms to sweep streets that, to us, already looked clean. We had heard of the stations' museum-quality art, but were in no way prepared for what we found. We'd get on the subway car, ride, watch the people, say little, and get off at the next stop. There, we'd stand in awe, then get back on and get off at the next station, time after time. We saw about 30 of more than 100 such platforms. At every station, we were stunned by the beauty, the elegance of polished marble on the floors, walls and ceilings. Everywhere! Begun in the 1930s, the underground was the USSR's largest civilian construction project, with stations built as "people's palaces." The art included bas-reliefs, friezes, marble and bronze statues, stained-glass windows and endless mosaics made with glass, marble and granite in good Byzantine fashion. Some of the themes were sports, industry, agriculture, warfare and idealizations of historic characters and their victories. The portrayal of the heroically laboring working class included various Soviet ethnicities and, of course, The Revolution. I could have spent an entire day riding the metro and admiring the stations.

Jackie and I, the only Americans we could see on the subway cars and in the stations, felt comfortable among ordinary Muscovites. After all, we were in a sophisticated city with a varied population, and without our daypacks we almost blended right in.

On July 4, one year after we'd walked in the Independence Day parade in Council Bluffs, Iowa, we stood in the afternoon sunshine outside Ismailovo Stadium. We hadn't yet been told that an hour before the concert, at least 50 army trucks had unloaded hundreds of soldiers who marched double time into the stadium and retreated out of sight where they stood guard. Troops of uniformed police and KGB men in business suits completed the high-profile security force. Hundreds of volunteers and soldiers uniformed as student athletes remained in the stadium to make sure the crowd behaved. I'm glad I hadn't seen that demonstration of control, which was probably based on the fear that Americans would get too wild.

Someone shouted, "We made it! All the way to Moscow!" I remembered the morning of November 15, 1986, only 10 months ago, when we on The Great Peace March had stepped across the line from Maryland into Washington, DC. We had shouted, "We made it," had fallen into each other's arms and let the tears—of exhaustion, joy and anticipated separation—flow.

In the Russian Republic, between Leningrad and Moscow, we had covered 360 miles in 24 days. Sixteen of those days, we bused and walked an average of 9 miles. We had arrived in Moscow, having already achieved our goal of demonstrating that Soviets and Americans can live well together, even in cold, rainy weather and unfamiliar circumstances.

Suddenly a 35-piece Soviet jazz band began playing *When the Saints Go Marching In,* and I jerked back to the present. We followed the band into the stadium to roaring, continuous applause and paraded around the track. Just like the Olympics—it was a heady experience! More than 25,000 fans had come to be a part of the world's first rock concert featuring American and Soviet performers. From the United States were Carlos Santana, James Taylor, Bonnie Raitt and the Doobie Brothers. From the Soviet Union were the popular rock group Avtograf, along with folk and jazz ensembles Pakrovsky and Nazareff. I wondered if Jackie's friend, Sieva, might be there. Later Jackie heard from Sieva that he, in Leningrad, had watched the concert on TV.

The marathon seven-hour concert could not have taken place

without a $580,000 donation from Apple's Steve Wozniak and the expertise of San Francisco impresario Bill Graham, who had put the concert together in six weeks. "A miracle," he said. "The waiting list for telephones here is five years. We got ours in two days, but only for local calls. When we told them we needed international lines, we got those the next day. People tell us only the KGB gets that kind of service.

"I've been skeptical about world peace for the past few years," Bill Graham continued, "but this has really changed my mind. The arms race is keeping these people in the Dark Ages. They want peace even more than the Americans do."

With flags flying, music filling the air, and masses of blue and white balloons in the grandstands spelling out *MIR* and PEACE, the concert was a fitting finale to the scheduled events on The Walk.

Jolene DeLisa and I, friends since we had met on The Great Peace March, sat on the grass for about an hour of the concert. I asked her how long she wanted to stay.

"Oh, until about now," she answered. We stood up and worked our slow way to an exit. A young man stopped us and said, "You're not leaving are you? Tickets for the floor were running 200 rubles [$280], which was very expensive. The average monthly pay in Russia is 200 rubles. How can you leave now!"

We explained that our 60-year-old ears just couldn't take the volume. After a Doobie Brothers hit, I looked around and saw exuberant Soviets hugging any American within arm's reach. When we spied two Soviet women we knew, we invited them to join us and walked a few blocks to a nice old hotel for tea and talk. In the lobby, we were tempted by an exhibit of amber jewelry. A salesperson came to help us as I fingered luminous golden necklaces and earrings. Under other circumstances, I probably would have bought something, but with our two new Soviet friends waiting, I carefully lay the necklace back onto its black velvet, and we turned to sit down in a cozy corner near tall windows. From another room, we could hear a string quartet playing softly. I liked this music better than thumping, driving rock music. We four mature women chatted as though we were neighbors about everything from pasta to peace. One of them reminded us again of their fear of war. "In the Great Patriotic War, we lost almost all our men, and so many women and children. Over 27 million, half of the world's war casualties died in

Russia. Please, I beg of you, do not forget us," she said. We exchanged addresses and promised to keep in touch.

I thought of something one of our leaders, Joe Kinczel, had written. "America and the Soviet Union have often related to each other by threats rather than dialogue. Our walk offers an opportunity for individuals of both nations to engage each other in dialogue that can positively transform the ways in which we see each other. We believe that our example of trust and cooperation can influence our societies and governments." Four women at the tea table might lead to many more at the peace table.

United Press International ran a headline on July 5: "U.S. Stars Rock Socks Off Moscow Soviet Groups." Did the writer know how important our socks had been to us? I imagined all the walkers in the stadium shouting "hooray!" and taking off their socks to toss into the air, much as graduates toss their mortar boards at commencement ceremonies.

On July 5, the day after the rock concert in the stadium, some of us visited Novodevichy Monastery, just south of Moscow. In the Middle Ages, the 15th to 17th centuries, widows without children to care for them lived in the convent, as well as unmarried 18-year-old girls, including members of the royal families. A czar's daughter brought her servants, wore her own clothes, and had houses constructed. The inhabitants seldom left their houses or rooms, devoting much time to embroidering. Girls from poor families wore black habits and did the more difficult work. A Soviet walker told me, "A church was built for every victory." Today the golden onion domes atop a cluster of tall structures in the configuration of an orthodox cross gleam above the tree-lined streets.

The sanctuary was filled with candles, shadows, old ladies, and peace walkers. The Orthodox service lasted about two hours, full of music, incense and liturgy. When the bishop introduced us, blessed us, and told us that his believers prayed first for peace, I believed him. In that dusky church, ancient and hallowed, decorated in soft murals, I felt spirits, masses of them, hovering in all the corners. In a church of such antiquity, I felt the presence of countless good souls, and I was humbled. One small person in an endless stream of people who had prayed there.

I presented a banner of the Pentagon Ribbon to the congregation as a gift from women in Chehalis, Washington, and Virginia. Women on

The Great Peace March had asked peace lovers along our route to sign pale blue ribbons which were then attached to fabric to make a banner 1-yard wide and many yards long. This had been taken to the Pentagon as a plea for nuclear disarmament. But we had not left it with them. We shared pieces of it with Soviets to indicate that many Americans back home wanted peace, just as we did. In the Novodevichy Monastery, I felt like a bridge between dedicated American women and bereaved Soviet women, the aging widows whose husbands had died in World War II.

Red Square was originally a slum full of wooden shacks, a marketplace in the 1500s, and in the 20th Century, it had become a site for concerts and public festivals. The Soviet Peace Committee was nervous about our planned demonstration there. They were afraid the entire walk contingent would be arrested, and they might lose their jobs. But still they allowed it, and there was no crackdown. We were the first foreigners ever to legally demonstrate in Red Square.

On the day we paraded onto Red Square, in front of St. Basil's Cathedral and Lenin's tomb, all 430 of us joined hands and stretched out into a gigantic circle enclosing almost the entire 5.8-acre square in unity and love. We realized that our Walk would end in a few days, and many of us didn't want to leave. Holding on tight, we walked the perimeter and sang peace songs to each other. I looked around for Peter. "He *must* be here somewhere!" I cried out. Our human circle was a metaphor for the connection we Soviet and American walkers felt for each other.

In *Moscow News*, an English language weekly, Valentin Vasilyev asked our leader, Allan Affeldt, "Do all these different people together believe that a symbolic undertaking like your walk could really stop the arms race?"

"We are not so naive as all that," Allan replied. "Our aim is to help Americans break through the wall of prejudice and mistrust of the Soviet people. What we are trying to do is treat the disease, not its symptoms."

I recalled that Mark Twain said that travel is lethal to prejudice. Oh, if only more Americans and Soviets could visit each other as we were.

Maybe Southern California's Cathy Zheutlin would help. She had made a documentary about The Great Peace March, *Just One Step*, and she was in Russia filming again. I asked her about it. "This one will be an hour long," she said, "and be shown in both countries. We'll reach an audience of 80 million people in the USSR and many more millions in the USA."

Les Linderman was a contributing editor of *50 PLUS*, a magazine published in Chicago. In Moscow, he interviewed several of us Americans for an article to be in the October, 1987, issue.

He talked with Franklin Folsom, with Sallie Gratch, me, and others. Franklin told Les, "When I got up on the stage in Novgorod, my reaction was that I had never seen such a dense mass of humanity. Had someone fainted, they would have been held up by the pressure of people around them. I saw the contrast in the numbers of people who were coming to see us here compared to crowds we pulled last year in the United States. You know, most of the crowds in the United States were quite small."

Sallie told Les, "Of all the Soviets I have met, the ones I feel closest to are the ones who have just come up to me as I walked along. They sort of attach themselves to you. An 11-year-old girl walked with me and held my hand for two hours. The communication was all nonverbal because she didn't speak English, and I don't speak Russian, but it was very personal. The next day, she showed up at a rally and had notes for me from her parents. They were in Russian, but I had them translated. They said they hoped our two countries would always live in peace."

Sallie continued, "I walked out of a restaurant one day and a man asked me to sign his autograph book. The next day, 20 kilometers away, someone brought him to me. 'This man has been looking for you,' the interpreter said. He was a fireman, and he had got the day off and had *run* all the way to the next town. He brought me a present—pictures of his family and a book of Chekhov short stories. He was bursting with excitement, talking about what it meant to him that Americans had visited his town, and he had seen that we were just as he is—warm and giving and friendly. The atmosphere was very charged. Many of us on The Walk made friends with the Russians."

When Sallie returned home, she founded Project Kesher (*kesher* is a Hebrew word that means connection or linkage). Her dream of a coalition of Jewish women in the Soviet Union and in the United States came true. An entire generation of Jews in that country had forgotten their traditions, and Project Kesher re-established them.

Now, in 2011, according to their website, "across nine time zones from Russia to Ukraine, Belarus, Moldova, Georgia and Kazakhstan, and in Israel, Project Kesher transforms women's lives, restoring their Jewish identity and providing training in leadership and social activism. United by shared values, they are building civil society."

When Les asked me what I thought had been accomplished during The Peace Walk in Russia, I responded, "If I think of this as an introduction, it's a tremendous success. If I think we came here to understand the Russian mind, then I'm frustrated.

"For instance," I continued, "I asked a receptionist at the hotel in Moscow how to get someplace I knew was nearby. She said, 'That's impossible.'

"I said, 'When I go out to the street, do I go right or left?'

"She said, 'Perhaps you want to do that tomorrow.'

"I said, 'No, I'm going now,' and I began to walk away. She came around from behind her counter after me, put her arm around me, and walked me halfway there." I had no idea what prompted her to first discourage me and then to be particularly helpful, but I knew that, at that moment, I loved this hotel employee, this woman who had her arm around my waist.

"So I see the trip as an introduction," I said. "A chance to become familiar with each other. When The Great Peace March was in Elmwood, Nebraska, they closed the laundromat. There were more marchers than residents of that town, and they were afraid of us. After we talked for a while we got to know the owner, and she introduced us to the lone policeman of the town, and he radioed to police departments ahead to say we were okay. That's what getting familiar will do, and I think that is one mission of this peace walk.

"If we persevere, there is a crack, and then it splits wide to reveal an open heart."

I would remember the open hearts of the Soviets we had met during our brief time in Russia. At the airport, we pulled away with tears of sadness from perceived enemies who we now knew were friends.

Donna Love and Dale Clark circle dancing at Leadbetter Beach, Santa Barbara, California.

CHAPTER 31

Ten Minutes of Fame

In January of 1988, Dale and I were on one of the largest TV shows in Mexico City. *Todo El Mundo* was a program similar to the Johnny Carson Show, in which guests were interviewed and had a conversation with the host.

We had attended a Charlotte Selver workshop on Sensory Aware-ness in Barra de Navidad, a sandy little beach-side pueblo in the state of Jalisco in January of 1987. One evening, Charlotte asked Dale and me to speak to the group about The Great Peace March. Afterward Jorge Unikel asked us if we would go to Mexico City to be on a TV show with a huge viewing audience, as far north as San Jose, California.

"Oh, yes. *Si!* We'll be there. But we don't speak Spanish."

"That's alright," Jorge said. "We have simultaneous translation."

On the show, the host asked us questions: "How did you get interested in the Peace Movement?"

I told about meeting Connie in Greece. Dale told about his friend Shelah who joined The Peace March.

"The purpose of The March?" To alert people across the United States that we were all on the road to nuclear destruction.

We described the demographics of The March, told how The March had changed our lives, the response in Russia to our Peace Walk there, and what we were doing now.

"We're speaking to audiences about peace issues. Your television audience is our largest opportunity." We faced the cameras. "We'd like to show you something to demonstrate the size of the world's arsenal of nuclear weapons."

Dale and I had shopped for two metal buckets and 10,000 BBs. We found the buckets, but not the BBs. Instead, we bought two big blue Mexican enamelware cook pots and 10,000 dried pinto beans. In the hotel room we counted out enough beans to fill a drinking glass and continued to fill glasses and pour the beans into one of the pots until we had estimated the correct number. On TV, we explained that one bean equaled 15 atomic bombs, such as the two dropped on Hiroshima and Nagasaki. We dropped one bean into the empty pot. Clunk. Sixty beans equaled all World War II Allied traditional bombs plus the atomic bombs dropped on Hiroshima and Nagasaki. We poured 60 beans into the pot. Rat-a-tat-tat.

"Now," Dale said, "close your eyes and listen to the nuclear arsenal we have today."

I held one pot while he poured the rest of the 10,000 beans. They roared into the pot for an interminably long time.

When we were through, the host opened his eyes, took a big breath, and asked, "Tell us what we can do to help with this. Send me a list of suggestions, and I will share it over another program." I had the list with me and gave it to him (see page 283).

Dale thanked him; we shook hands, picked up our pots, smiled at the cameras and pushed through the doors into the warm evening. As we walked along, feeling 10-feet tall, a boisterous group of American boys pointed and hailed us. "Ma-a-a-n, tonight you really spilled the beans!"

We chuckled at our moment of fame and decided that we wanted our work to be well-known, but not our faces. Weeks later, when I got back home to San Mateo, my cleaning lady told me she had seen the show. Had she seen the subsequent show when the host shared the list of suggestions to promote peace? Yes, she had, and she had told her high school son who told his teacher who told his classes.

THE AMERICAN-SOVIET PEACE WALK

June 14—July 18, 1988

Washington, DC to San Francisco, CA
USA

American–Soviet Peace Walk 1988
Washington, D.C. to San Francisco, CA

San Francisco

Los Angeles

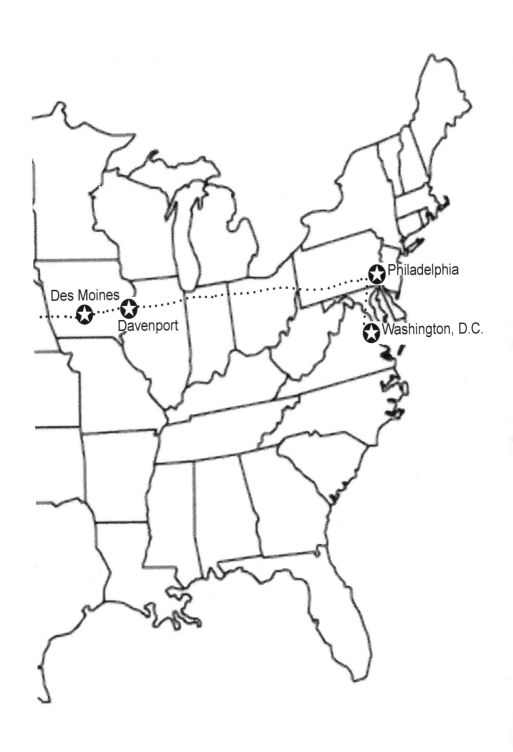

Des Moines

Davenport

Philadelphia

Washington, D.C.

Our Move

Logo of the American-Soviet Peace Walk in 1988.

CHAPTER 32

One More Time, With Feeling

For 34 days in June and July of 1988, Soviets invaded America. "The Russians are coming! The Russians are coming!"

Actually, they had been invited. When the 230 Americans had walked in Russia the year before, we had invited Soviets to come to the United States for a peace walk. It would be organized by the recently formed International Peace Walks, Inc. and be the grandchild of the 1986 Great Peace March for Global Nuclear Disarmament. One more time, I would be hitting the road and pitching my tent for peace.

Since I was the very last person to be accepted for The Peace Walk from Leningrad to Moscow, I made sure to be the first to sign up for the walk from Washington, DC, to San Francisco. I was excited to stand up tall near my own hometown of San Mateo, only 15 miles south of San Francisco, as a woman who walked for peace.

I had been an enthusiastic hiker for many years, but 1986 was the first year I had joined hundreds, sometimes thousands, to walk for a cause. These walks were changing my life. Now I was one of 140 preparing to greet 217 Soviets when they arrived in Washington on June 16.

We American walkers had arrived two days earlier for orientation. In the previous year, 1987, before going to Leningrad, the American participants had studied the cultural differences between our two countries. But I had not been present for the orientation. I had arrived from Santa Barbara at Dulles Airport in Washington the very morning of departure to Leningrad. Now I needed to learn everything I could. I looked forward to learning about Soviet communication styles. Oh, yes, we learned at lot of abstract information on that subject. But we received a stark first-hand example soon after their arrival. We discovered quickly that the Soviets would listen politely, intently, while we spoke, and then they all erupted at once and at the top of their voices, sharing their points of view. It was pandemonium for a while. Some of us, nervous and unsettled by all the shouting, left the meetings. Others of us, myself included, sat stunned at what appeared to be rage. Then, just as suddenly, our guests stopped to listen again. We smiled, laughed to cover our discomfort, and watched for the next outburst. It was something we needed to understand if we were to get along.

But before the Soviets arrived in Washington, we had time to listen to experts who were supposed to help us better understand these foreign guests with whom we would be sharing this important adventure. Vladimir Kilmenko, interpreter and USSR consultant, lectured on "Becoming a Citizen Diplomat." He, among others, reminded us of vast historic and cultural differences.

Psychologist Steven Kull offered the images of a motorboat and a sailboat to explore the distinctions between how Americans and Soviets view themselves.

> *Americans are like motorboats. We are inwardly motivated and emphasize our uniqueness and individuality. We assume that we are acting in an autonomous, inner-directed way, independent of external forces. We therefore tend to emphasize personal initiative and creativity over conformity and cooperation. For*

us, truth is an absolute perspective that we arrive at individually. We value one-to-one loyalties above group loyalties. For us, the bigger the entity, the weaker our allegiance to it.

I remembered a comment made in the 1960s by our insurance agent who was also a friend. "You'd be surprised how many people, people we know well, people we trust as friends who would never violate that trust, but would routinely try to manipulate large insurance companies into paying them more than a fair recompense."

Kull continued:

Soviets, on the other hand, are more like sailboats. Rather than being inner-directed, they are much more aware of the effects of the environment, metaphorically speaking, the wind and the movements of the sea. They stress the situation they are in as the causal factor in their behavior. For them, truth is derived more from social consensus than from an inward process. For them, group loyalty is preeminent, especially when dealing with foreigners.

In a hand-out on "Citizen Diplomacy," I read:

A major difference in our societies is described by anthropologist Edward Hall, who divides cultures into "high context" and "low context" types. Americans are a very low-context society. What is being said is more important than the larger context in which the message is being sent and received. We emphasize specificity of content, and because we are relatively unconcerned about context, we value the qualities of honesty, flexibility, and initiative. When confronted by a complex problem, we tend to want to break it down into its component parts.

The Soviet Union, on the other hand, is a very high-context culture. For Soviets, the setting in which a message is sent and received is as important as the message itself.

> *If we seek to break complex problems down, they tend to emphasize the general setting out of which complex problems emerge. It is nearly impossible to talk about a contemporary political issue with a Soviet official without the official at some point mentioning the heavy Soviet losses during World War II. Soviets emphasize the general over the particular, the sweep of history over the immediate political concerns. The Soviets know how to wait, something foreign to Americans whose whole political economy is predicated on taking the waiting out of wanting.*

The statements by Steven Kull and Edward Hall were rough generalizations, yet useful for Americans seeking to work with Soviets. They enabled us to understand the enormous differences in how Americans and Soviets perceived themselves. Respecting these differences between our cultures and value systems made it possible to build cooperation that could benefit both groups.

We citizen diplomats would endeavor to open channels of communication. We may not have been sure of what we would accomplish, but we were totally certain that doing something was better than doing nothing. I didn't feel as helpless as I had when I'd been at home teaching children basic skills of reading, writing, spelling, arithmetic and thinking. The thought of our earth, our children, our grandchildren being obliterated by man-made weapons had caused me nightmares. When flying over our nation, peering down at the terrain I'd walked and grown to love in a very personal way, I wept at the thought that we might exterminate all this that is our home. So, I could no longer do nothing about it. If I did nothing, the nuclear threat would become even more menacing.

How much more menacing could it become? We had enough nuclear weapons in 1988 to kill each other—the Soviets and the Americans—40 times. We could, with the current arsenals, duplicate World War II for 30,000 years! Those of us from the United States and from the Soviet Union who had chosen to participate in this event, would demonstrate our respect for each other by walking, singing, dancing, playing and feasting with each other. We had done all of this last year in Russia and would do it again across the United States. Maybe our governments might take notice.

A dynamic Soviet-American husband and wife team, Vladimir Padunov and Nancy Condee of Kennan Institute of Advanced Russian Studies, addressed us. Through street theater and lecture, they delineated cultural characteristics of Soviets. Padunov pointed out, "Soviet grandmothers have experienced three wars, three revolutions, and the horrors of Stalin. Of men born in 1921, 3 percent returned from the Great Patriotic War [WWII]."

"Look for the petty differences," recommended Vladimir Padunov. "Notice how Soviets strike a match away from themselves and how Americans strike it toward themselves. Then notice why. The Soviet wooden matches produce a large spark. Strike it toward you and there goes your sweater. Continue to look for small differences and wonder why."

At the end of the first day of lectures and seminars, I set up my tent among others on the grounds of Georgetown Visitation Convent and Preparatory School, adjacent to Georgetown University. I crept in and fell asleep. When I awoke I was surprised that with all the excitement, I could have slept at all. During the day, it was over 80 degrees and humid. And I, from coastal California, was not used to hot sticky weather.

The numbers were under the 200 Americans originally expected. Including the 60 workers upon whom we would all depend for smooth operations, we were 140. That meant only 80 walkers. Having fewer numbers did allow for more intimacy. Those of us who had met on The Great Peace March for Global Nuclear Disarmament in 1986 and again during The Peace Walk from Leningrad to Moscow in 1987, greeted each other with hugs, sometimes tears. It was coming home. It was family. It was emotionally exhausting.

Jolene DeLisa, 59, of Kona, Hawaii, while on The Great Peace March, had screeched, "This is like living in a loony bin!" Now, she was charmingly processing arriving walkers through the initial reception: identification badges, volumes of printed material to read, surveys to be completed, insurance releases to be signed. She directed registered walkers to the tenting area or to the cool beverages and cookies waiting on one of the dining tables in the shade of a pavilion tent.

This year we had dining tents, tables—even tablecloths. And chairs.

More like the refinements in Russia than on The Great Peace March.

Gene Gordon, once of Stanford and San Jose's radio station KKUP but for two recent years with the organization staff of International Peace Walks, was assisting new walkers he had recruited. It was Gene who, while walking the nine-month Great Peace March, had read 37 Shakespeare plays. Last year in the USSR, he had discovered the Soviets' broad appreciation for Shakespeare. Now, he said, "I can hardly wait for them to get here so we can read together!"

Allen Alfeldt, 29, President of International Peace Walks, Inc., announced, "The Soviet Peace Committee in Moscow is overwhelmed with Soviets wanting to come on The Walk. There are nearly 10 applicants for each available space. In response, we have offered 20 more spaces for the Soviets on The Walk in America." Until July 18, the end of The Peace Walk, each American Walker would adopt five Soviets. Americans would be available to help their adopted guests, would answer their questions, guide them, show them the ropes.

When the Soviets arrived, the campsite would be ready to welcome them. Their three-person tents, provided by International Peace Walks, would be arranged into *sosyedstvas* (neighborhoods) among American tents. An American walker went to the flower mart to buy masses of flowers to give to the Soviets upon their arrival. We hadn't forgotten the armloads of flowers bestowed upon us from cottage gardens while we were in Russia last summer. Someone brought balloons and small American flags to decorate the tents. In Sosyedstva Number 6, the one I was in, nine Americans and about 20 Soviets would become friendly neighbors.

I was eager for the Soviets to arrive. I so hoped to see Peter Ganea among them.

Peter Ganea of Moldova, USSR.

CHAPTER 33

Here They Come, Ready or Not

They'd be here tomorrow. The Soviets. How would they respond to us?

I read Dr. Dennis Haughton's *From Swords to Plowshares*, in which he wrote:

> *In general, the standard of living in the Soviet Union is much lower than in the United States, where we have been spoiled by abundant material wealth. Cars in the Soviet Union may easily cost three to four years' wages and years on a waiting list. Japanese VCRs are often not available at any cost. Some people may have to wait months or years to get a new apartment. A Soviet shopper visiting an American supermarket for the first time, might very well pass out with disbelief.*
>
> *Shopping Soviet style I have found meant standing in one line to see what is available, moving to another to pay*

for it, and finally waiting in a third to pick it up with your receipt.

On the other side of the coin, you can ride anywhere in any Soviet city comfortably, quickly, and safely for five kopecs (about seven cents). Monthly rent, utilities, and phone bills may only cost 18 rubles ($26)—total. The Soviet Constitution guarantees every citizen a 41-hour maximum work week, 100 percent health care, a home to live in, free education including college, paid vacations, and complete disability coverage and maintenance in old age.

The simplistic condemnation of one system by the other is becoming less acceptable as people on both sides become more informed. Without doubt, our preconceptions of each other are an unjust distortion of reality that has perpetuated the Iron Curtain of misunderstanding between our peoples for the last forty years.

I thought Dr. Haughton's comments worth remembering. I felt a little embarrassed that we Americans had a surfeit of goods, that we measured people by the value of their possessions rather than by their personal integrity, values and commitments.

The Soviets we were to greet included a member of the Supreme Soviet, a member of the Moscow Philharmonic, a textile factory worker from Moscow, a solo vocalist from the Leningrad choir, a librarian from the Lenin Library (the largest in the world), a factory mechanic from the Lithuanian Republic, the director of a physics laboratory in Uzbeck Republic and his 12-year-old son. We'd also meet an experimental biologist and a village school teacher from Armenia, a people's judge from Baku, a Lutheran pastor from the Latvian Republic, a cardiologist from Byelorussia, a factory worker from Turkmanian Republic, the secretary of the Diocese of Kalinan of the Russian Orthodox Church, and the Calgary Olympic Gold and Bronze Medalist in bobsled races, Latvian Janis Kipurs.

And maybe Peter Ganea, the high school science and English teacher from Kishinev, Moldova Republic, who last year had become my friend. When we had parted in the Soviet Union I had asked what I might send him and his family.

He had replied, "My daughter would love to have a Barbie doll."

"Of course," I thought. "Every girl in the world wants a Barbie doll." When I had gone to the toy store in San Mateo, owner Gordon Moore contributed the doll and a wardrobe of clothes. Both he and I were delighted at the thought of a girl in Moldova opening a gift from a toy store in California.

I had thought often about Peter during the past year whenever I gave slide show presentations about the Peace Walks. I'd show a picture of tall, dark haired, sturdy Peter and tell the following story about him. Peter offered to help set up my tent in the summer of 1987 while we walked in Russia. Since he had chosen to stay in the lodge that night, he had time to help carry my gear, tent and sleeping bag from the truck to the tent site. He and I arrived at the parking lot just as the rear door of the truck was lifted and the gear was being passed down. Americans automatically formed a bucket brigade to pass along and stack our bags. Peter, large, strong, young, stood to one side watching.

I called, "Peter, come here! You can help!"

I had noticed that he had to be invited by someone he perceived to have some authority. That was typical of many Soviets we met. Peter took his place next to me in the line and began passing. After a few minutes, obviously enjoying the rhythm and efficiency involved, Peter gave out a big belly laugh and exclaimed, "With American ingenuity and Soviet discipline, we can do *anything*!"

So it was that we American and Soviet peace walkers hoped to form a bucket brigade around the world, passing along what was needed to avoid global nuclear destruction, to build peace between our two nations.

At the end of The Peace Walk in Russia, General Secretary Mikhail Gorbachev had said, "This joint walk of Soviet and American citizens, the first of its kind (size) in the history of relations between the USSR and the USA, is a specific contribution to strengthening mutual confidence, understanding, and friendship, and it is a convincing example of citizen diplomacy in action."

The stage was set for more extraordinary joint events. Not only The Walk with Soviets in the United States in June-July, but a walk from Odessa to Kiev to Moscow from August 15 to September 18 that would include Americans. More International Peace Walks: 1989 in Georgia, USSR, and Georgia, USA, in 1990; a month's walk in the Pacific Northwest culminating in Seattle at the Goodwill Games matched by a walk in Turkic Republics including Tashkent, capital of the Uzbek Republic, sister city to Seattle. Meanwhile, a Midwestern educator was coordinating teacher exchanges between American and Soviet teachers. Another peace walker was setting up home exchanges in which entire families would stay with each other. Others were joining walks elsewhere: in Japan, in New England, in New Zealand. I was not the only one whose life was changing because of experiences on these walks. The evening before the Soviets were to arrive, several of us sat on the grass in the dark, gazing skyward. Gene Gordon sighed, "You know, the first words ever spoken from outer space were by the Soviet cosmonaut, Uri Gagarin. He looked back at our earth and quoted Hamlet, "There is more in heaven and earth, dear Horatio, than is dreamt of in your philosophy."

Were the Soviets thinking similar thoughts? How would they respond to being in the United States? We would know tomorrow.

Looking out of Donna Love's tent toward Soviet tents, in a mid-western camp-site.

CHAPTER 34

Sweat and Tears

Mid-morning on June 16, big silver buses pulled into the parking lot of Georgetown University and people spilled out the doors. People of all sizes, shapes, ages and colors—eager, dazed, gazing about in anticipation and curiosity. Their Aeroflot plane had landed only a couple of hours ago at Dulles. They were standing, most for the first time, in our nation's capital. I was making my way up the grassy slope toward them when someone came running, shouting, "Donna! Donna! He's here! Peter's asking for you!"

When we saw each other, it was like a mother-son reunion after a year's absence. He loped toward me, his large frame taller than most, his dark hair flopping, his dark eyes bright. He stopped in front of me and extended his hand formally, then accepted my hug. "Aaaaah, Dawn-ná," he picked me up and returned my hug. "It is good to see you again. My family send their greetings, too." He told me how much his daughter loved the Barbie doll. He gave me a bracelet from his wife. I gave him some math puzzles that my son John had sent. Peter, a teacher in small, disrupted Moldavia, and I, a suburban California woman of 60, had forged a friendship. During a time when our governments didn't trust each other, he and I did. I was overjoyed that Peter was there. I felt proud of our country, of being American, of the honest and open friendliness Peter and I felt for each other. I even felt proud of the weather. The sun shone on us all. An auspicious day to begin the USA-USSR Peace Walk.

Together Peter and I walked over to chairs clustered beneath a canvas shelter for an all-inclusive meeting. After introductory speeches and the orientation session, lunch was served at tables in the shade of the dining pavilions. That afternoon, tents were arranged, leaders explained plans and procedures. Sosyedstvases (neighborhoods) had their first meetings. Vitaly, a doctor from Moscow, and I were co-leaders of Sosyedstvase 6. He was formal, almost clicked his heels when giving a small bow and firm handshake. He was no taller than I, so I looked directly into his bright iceberg blue eyes. We were polite and careful in our initial conversation, but agreed to call each other by first names. Our group sat in a circle on the grass to introduce and explain something about ourselves.

I didn't speak Russian, and although all the Soviets seemed to speak English, some had less fluency. But with the help of those who spoke both English and Russian, we managed and laughed in our efforts to be understood. I asked what each of them thought of being in the United States, their first impressions.

"It is very clean," one said.

"In the airport I saw many stores. Do you all shop in airports? There were many things to buy."

"I think many Americans look like many Russians. We may not be so different as we thought."

"I am happy to be here among friends I met last year. Both from USSR and from America. I wish to see some schools. Will that be possible?"

"The first thing that happened for me when I got off the bus, an American woman gave me a big bouquet of flowers. Just as we at home do. I think Americans are very friendly."

"Now that we are here, when will we start walking?"

I reviewed the schedule. Tomorrow would be filled with tours and events around Washington, DC. I was sure our Soviet guests would enjoy the Smithsonian Institution collections and the dignity of our capital's architecture.

The following day, Sunday, June 19, the 10-mile walk would begin at nearby Georgetown University, cross the Potomac River, and end on the grounds of Takoma Park Intermediate School in Maryland. The woman who wanted to see schools nodded and smiled at me.

We paraded out of Washington. At the head the line, three women, two Soviets and an American, carried the long horizontal banner proclaiming AMERICAN-SOVIET WALK. Immediately behind the banner, a Soviet carried the American flag, an American, the red Soviet flag. I was the American woman carrying one end of the banner. Having moved from the middle of the pack to step forward to the head, I was certain that my son Sam would understand that I no longer needed to be safe in the center, as I had in Las Vegas over two years ago during The Great Peace March. I felt tall and strong, confident, a woman not afraid to be seen and heard.

Over the next 12 days, we walked 75 miles and bused 65 miles to six campsites in Takoma Park, Columbia, and Baltimore, Maryland; Wilmington, Delaware; Swarthmore and Philadelphia in Pennsylvania. At each stop townspeople came to our campsite to mingle with Americans and Soviets committed to walking for peace. Classroom children, clubs, civic and church groups came. They bought caps and T-shirts with our crossed flags printed on the front.

At the Wilmington campsite, the morning had dawned with Philadelphia grade school teacher Gret Gentile playing her flute as the wake-up call. An adolescent Soviet boy accompanied her on guitar. Arms and legs stretched through the openings of the dome tents, yawns and calls floated across circular neighborhoods. I waved to Vasylia. He bowed, then raised his hand. Within an hour we had collapsed the tents. As duffle bags were being loaded onto the gear truck, walkers heard an announcement over the bullhorn.

Walk leader Joe Kinczel called, "Everyone, please join in a circle in the hayfield." Three women walkers strolled around and offered us flowers. Joe announced, "Today we are walking for Jamie. We are walking for the 16-year-old son of Martie and Byron Olson of Iowa City, Iowa. Jamie died this week in a car accident." I heard the swift sucking in of breath. "The memorial service in Iowa City will be held today as we walk from Wilmington to Swarthmore, which happens to be an early home of the Olson family."

Martie and Byron were the coordinators of the Midwest region of the American-Soviet Peace Walk. A family active in education and in peace promotion, they had made all the arrangements for the Iowa portion of the journey. In the hayfield, Soviet and American walkers stood at 8 o'clock in 100-degree sunshine, with heat rash on our arms and legs, sunscreen thick on our faces, flowers in our hands and tears in our eyes. Sweat ran down and dripped off chins, mixing with the tears. Loss tasted salty. Episcopal deacon Judith Ain of Menlo Park, California, suggested we bow our heads in a moment of silence. A Russian Orthodox priest led us in prayer.

In that moment of silence, I thought of my own sons and wept, gratitude mingled with grief. In the silence, I heard bird calls and sniffles. I stood with bowed head in the stubble of the recently mowed hay and could see feet belonging to Soviets and to Americans. They looked pretty similar in Nikes and Adidas. We stood and mourned together the loss of a boy's life.

The members of the Soviet Peace Committee who were with us sent red and white roses to Jamie's family. A Soviet artist from Moscow told me, "I want to contribute to the memorial. What will it be?" He donated money to the Track Fund at Jamie's high school. Grown Soviet men wiped their eyes and blew their noses when told, "Jamie was an athlete."

The telegram sent from The Walk said, "Flower grown entwines our hearts. We walk with you. We hold your hand."

Tatayana hugged me to her amplitude and choked, "It is as Jamie is my son, too. Do you think it would acceptable if I tell Mrs Olson so?"

Peter—not my friend Peter Ganea but the English professor from the Language Institute in Kiev—stood quietly to avoid interrupting. He placed his hand on my shoulder and said, "Donna, I know this day is difficult for you and many of the Americans. I am at your disposal in any way that will be of help." His bow almost courtly, his brown eyes glistened with compassion. I was touched by his sincerity and thanked him. Our hands stayed tightly interlocked for several moments.

The shared sadness may have hastened the solidification of friendship we walkers were trying to establish. The Soviets had been complaining, "Not enough meat. We need it every meal. Not enough soup. We need soup twice a day." Their complaints reminded me of the previous year, when we walked and bused from Leningrad to Moscow, and the Californians wanted more fruit. The following morning, entire stalks of bananas had appeared on the breakfast tables. I hoped we'd see good soups on the buffets.

Americans bickered about differences in style. They took for granted that Soviets comprehended the system of meetings. Excited speakers forgot to allow time for translation. Soviets seemed to talk all at once among themselves. From Americans, they asked for further clarification and always the Americans responded, "Listen, just listen." Shoulders shrugged, mouths turned down, eyebrows rose, hands turned palms upward toward heaven in frustration.

In a meeting of Neighborhood Facilitators, held before the morning circle in the hayfield, our differences in styles pushed smack up against our peevishness. The chairwoman waved her 24-year-old hands about and cried, "Whoa! Wait a minute!" The Soviets waited. The Americans waited. The drone of the meeting began again. My Russian co-facilitator of Grupa Chaste (Group 6) and I exchanged glances and silently agreed that meetings were a drag.

The meeting dissolved. Even as Eileen was waving her hands and pleading for attention, Soviets poured away only to congregate by themselves, all talking at once, finally to disperse, nodding and repeating, "Da, da, da, da. Okay." Vasily and I agreed we'd work out things together and communicate among our Grupa members information that needed to be transmitted. We decided to each write messages and news reports and clothespin them to my tent. It became a bulletin board. Our neighborhood meetings were spontaneous when members of our Grupa asked for them. Sometimes our meetings were serious exchanges of cultural information; most of the time we laughed a lot and shared snacks.

Rules were few: no liquor, quiet after 10:30 at night. The logistics of moving 340 walkers each day, of coordinating the events and exchanges with the communities through which we passed, and of keeping all walkers healthy and mostly happy could have been overwhelming. But thanks to the lessons of the 1986 Great Peace March, our staff members were experienced and skilled. If those of us on this Walk, with our deeply entrenched cultural differences, could learn to function cooperatively and respectfully, we would set a model of hope for the world. Maybe Jamie's death would put into perspective our goals and give us patience with each other.

I witnessed small examples of compromise. The day before, retreating to the air-conditioned bus for one leg of the 14-mile walk from Wilmington to Swarthmore, I sat near 11-year-old Timur from Kazakhstan, and Johanna, 67, of Swarthmore, Pennsylvania. Johanna asked, "Do you have any brothers and sisters?"

"Yes," answered Timur, "I have two brothers and three sisters." He diagrammed a family tree, indicating that his mother's sister is the mother of the other children.

"Oh, no, Timur," Johanna instructed. "Those are your cousins."

After 15 minutes of debate, Timur nodded. "Yes, I now understand. I have two cousin brothers and three cousin sisters."

At an outdoor performance in the amphitheater in Bellevue State Park that evening, I knelt down on the grass to greet a graying American woman fanning herself. She clutched my arm intensely and wiped her eyes. "I never thought I'd live long enough to see those two flags flying on the same stage. Isn't it beautiful?" I asked if she would like to talk with a Soviet woman.

"Oh," she exclaimed, "could I really?" I asked Ada, a Russian mother of three and professor of economics at Kalinin University, to join us, and when I left them, the two women were deep in conversation with their heads cocked toward each other.

Bezhad, a biochemist, stood planted in front of me. "Donna!" he called me, pronouncing my name a drawn-out Dawnná, "I want to thank you for arranging my stay last night in a home. I cannot express the feeling of a full heart. Yes, the dinner was excellent, but my heart is even fuller than my stomach." He placed a handcrafted metal bracelet on my wrist. "From my people," he gratefully intoned.

Some of the young American women protested the Soviet men's "supreme chauvinistic attitude." I personally loved having my bags hauled to the tenting area. Sometimes I got so dissolved by the heat that I didn't know if I was perspiring or crying. One late afternoon I stood over my tent. Rain threatened. I should have hurried. I had put up that tent, or one like it, hundreds of times. I could do it alone in less than 10 minutes.

But that afternoon I could not get it together. I stood immobilized by the challenge. Blinking through the steam, I saw two Soviet men approaching. "Oh, no," I sighed. "Please don't ask me a question or ask me to do something for you."

One took my shoulders and moved me over into the shade of a tree. Then he joined the other to set up my tent, brought my bags from the luggage stack, and told me, "Now, Dawnná, you be sure to drink some water." Others who were clustered beneath the tree offered to share water with each other. I laughed and recalled that a friend at home, not knowing the Soviets, viewed them "all, just like sheep." I wished she could have seen us—Americans and Soviets—huddled there in the shade, surely looking just like sheep on a hot day.

Sister Margarella of Neumann College in Aston, Pennsylvania, addressed the walkers one day as we sat in their large lunch room. "Life is a walk," she said. "I am reminded of the words spoken from man's first walk on the moon, 'One giant step for humankind.' I am reminded of the Crusades, the walk up Calvary. Statesmen may blunder, but I predict that you will be successful. You will recognize the other, who is in fact our brother. You are, indeed, pilgrims for peace." She not only stood at the door to shake each of our hands, she actually held the door open for us.

I wished she could have been in Washington, DC, when we officially began this walk. True, The Peace Walk was enthusiastically greeted by members of the Foundry Methodist Church at 16th and P streets, but otherwise, people near the Capitol steps and along our route to Lincoln Memorial were less than enthusiastic. They seemed only mildly curious. We could have used Sister Margarella's support. One Washington woman did bolt out through her screen door when her neighbor called out, "Americans walking. They're walking for peace with Soviets!" The screen door slammed behind her as the woman dashed out to the sidewalk exclaiming, "Soviets! I gotta see me some Soviets!"

That's what we were there for. We wanted Americans and Soviets to see each other. To wipe away fear created by a blinding ignorance that threatened us with extinction.

Jamie was gone. Too soon, too young. We'd remember him as we struggled toward saving his world for children everywhere.

On June 24, we walked 15 miles into Philadelphia.

Walking into Philadelphia.

CHAPTER 35

Beyond the City of Brotherly Love

I wish I could remember all that we did in Philadelphia. We probably paraded down South Street, likely accompanied by at least one high school band. People along the curbs would have cheered as we trooped into a park or city square. Maybe near the Liberty Bell. We'd have been welcomed by local politicians and peace activists and sung to by choruses and choirs. School children would have asked for our autographs. We'd have eaten pies and watermelon after a sumptuous lunch prepared and served by church ladies. Many speeches. Many smiles and handshakes and repeating of *Mir y Drushba*, Peace and Friendship. On an outdoor stage, popular local musicians might have joined the various walker-musicians—Soviet as well as American—for a program at New Market Square.

All of this surely must have taken place, but I have no clear memory of that day, June 25.

Except the basketball game. In contrast to serious conversations, we had a literal free-wheeling game in Schenley Park in Philadelphia.

Jim McGowan, 57, Assistant Director of Disabled Students Services at Temple University and coach of The Rolling Owls, rolled into camp in his wheelchair. He was there to invite walkers to play a game of wheelchair basketball with members of his team. Both Soviets and Americans joined in a game with more crashes and spills than scored points. And later, over juice and "Soviet Dissident" cookies, the players exchanged life stories.

Jim McGowan had been, at age 19, a semi-pro football player. After he was stabbed in the stomach while walking down a street in Brooklyn, he entered the hospital for surgery. The spinal anesthesia caused paralysis of his lower body. Today, he is a sky diver and in 1987 attempted to swim the English Channel. With a good humored shrug, he commented, "Hey, it's life. Maybe my only one. It's mine to live. These guys are great. They might be labeled disabled, but they're not inabled. Like you walkers, we just gotta do our best and see what comes of it."

Chris Horner, 23, a handsome business administration major, had not a trace of self-pity as he told me, "Yep, broke both legs, both arms, and my back in a motorcycle accident in 1984." His legs remained paralyzed; he held them in his wheelchair with bungee cords. He was proud to have been playing basketball for two years. Chris told me, "This team is rated No. 1 in the nation." He continued, "I'm glad to see the USSR and USA beginning to talk. I've been scared. Not so afraid of the superpowers now that Reagan and Gorbachev are talking and now that I've talked with Soviets here. Now I'm afraid of the smaller countries that have the bomb and no control. The large nations must get together and agree to take control."

The following day, we bused to Pittsburgh, 300 miles, stopping along the way for a lunch and program so more locals could meet us. There were exchanges of little gifts; pins and buttons, postcards and baseball cards. Sometimes addresses so pen pals could correspond. The days were hot, the undiluted sun beating straight down on our heads, so the air-conditioned bus was a blessing.

We arrived at the banks of the Mississippi River and were credited with having brought desperately needed rain to the parched farmland area. After blistering heat in Maryland and Delaware, the cooling rainstorm in western Illinois and eastern Iowa was welcome. In the breakfast line at drizzly dawn, I turned to a young Soviet to ask him, "Do you like the rain?"

"Oh, yes," he replied. "It is very beautiful."

Pressed to tell me why he liked it, he continued, "Look at the grass. Already it seems to be getting a bit greener. And for the farmers, their corn will grow better. There will be enough. Their prices will not be so high, and we can buy it from you for lower costs." He grinned as though to lighten the seriousness of his comments. Or was it pleasure at the thought of lower prices? I didn't pursue that.

During the sun-drenched 10-mile walks, I could hear participants learning each other's languages. Sometimes in songs, most often in repetition of phrases. During the bus rides, Peter-of-the-Kiev-Language-Institute had been teaching Russian to everyone interested. The walk monitors, hurrying us through an intersection, cried, "*Posh-lee!*"—which means, "Come on, let's go!"—"Posh-LEE!"

Greeting local citizens along the way, Americans extended a hand and called, "*Dobre utra!*" Soviets held out their hands exchanging the same greeting, "Good morning, how are you?" People on the curbs looked intently at us and commented, "Hard to tell 'em apart. Which are the Russians?" We smiled, walked on, and exchanged glances. We had a private game, an inside joke, and I felt a member of an intimate group.

In the mornings before breakfast, Soviet and American women gathered for "woman talk," as we had last year. In Russia we had gathered in the buses before breakfast to stay warm and dry on rainy days. Now we climbed into the buses to stay cool. We discussed the roles of women in the family, jobs and pay, birth control and sex education, and the subject of respect for women.

"How much does your husband help in the home?"

"Have you had an abortion?" or "How many abortions have you had?"

"How can we women on this Walk use our common experiences and skills to promote peace for our children?" Children were my passion. I stood up to call out, "We *must* buy time to create peace. We owe our children the world!"

Conversations during the bus rides were deepening. The standard introductory questions were, "Where is your home?" "Do you have children?" but we were able to cut through the small talk to matters of more importance. I personally found the three days of busing from Philadelphia to Sunset Park in Rock Island, Illinois, a time for leisurely dialogues. I sat on the bus one day with Andrew Bochkorev, 34, a history teacher at the Technological School in Moscow. Our talks rambled across the subjects of housing, family, religion, pride, slavery and industrial conversion. Andrew would have liked to live in a detached house with a garden. He was "raised up" in such a home in the Moscow suburbs. As an adult he now lived in a flat in Moscow with his wife and four-year-old daughter. He was impressed with the number of private homes he was seeing in America.

Andrew had, as had all the Soviets during The Walk, been in American homes to dinner, to take showers and do laundry, to meet the neighbors, and to sleep. I asked what he liked about visiting homes. Andrew looked almost shy as he told me, "I like the way in which American families express their appreciation for the food they eat." I thought he meant that the family thanked the mother for her preparation of the meal.

No!" he looked closely at me. "I mean the way everyone bows their heads to thank God for their food."

Andrew continued thoughtfully, his clear dark eyes searching for words, "I like going to church with the believers. Well, you know, one can tell the difference in churches between the believers and the tourists, the ones who just come to hear the music or look at the beautiful windows. You can see the look in the eyes of the believers. And in their families. They are knitted together with their families. That makes for strength and durability."

I asked Andrew if he would write a statement in my notebook. Something he would like to say to Americans he might not have the opportunity to meet. He complied.

> *I think that American people have a great history. We can borrow many positive features of this system, but at the same time, such kinds of negative features as jobless and homeless people create a sad mood in the hearts of foreign visitors.*
>
> *I like the strong roots of American beliefs in democracy and in the Untied States Constitution. American trust in God creates a strong spiritual unity of American families and American society as a whole. In our country, we are*

trying to establish a normal relationship with different kinds of religions, which were not stable in the previous time.

We all are human beings. We (USSR) should come to a compromise with Americans with the purpose to avoid nuclear war. I am meeting with many Americans who express the strong will to establish a friendly relationship with the USSR, but at the same time I have met with persons who suspect the Soviets. Maybe because of stereotypes and misunderstandings created by the press. We had a lot of stereotypes about Americans and this Walk has helped us to get rid of them.

After writing these paragraphs, Andrew looked apologetic and asked permission to take a nap. We stopped our exchange of ideas and both dozed off as the bus headed west across Ohio. In a while, I wakened, but didn't move. Next to me, Andrew was asleep. On my shoulder rested the head of the "enemy" from the country President Reagan had labeled the evil empire. I wondered how Ronald Reagan, the man, would have felt if Andrew were asleep on his shoulder. I found myself immensely fond of Andrew, his age the same as my son Sam's, and wished I could take him home with me to introduce him to my family.

Later, Andrew's views were reflected by Alexander Murashov, mayor of Gurzuf, a small town on the Black Sea, 10 miles east of Yalta, sister-city to Santa Barbara, California. He wrote,

I think we need not ready-made opinions, but thorough informations about each other. Our time demands insistently that we make our best effort to know each other. Our peoples are very much alike and can easily become soul mates, however disgusting it seems to some false "patriots." Together we must fight against our common enemies, the forces of evil, which are hostility and alienation, ignorance, and national haughtiness, greed, and prejudice. It looks like mankind shall be developing a new World Morality. It is time to begin now.

Not all exchanges were so serious. At a pastoral campsite at St. Maur Seminary in Indianapolis, I heard veteran walker Billy Lieb of Santa Monica, the same Billy with whom I had visited the fourth-grade classroom in Salt Lake City in 1986, state, "That's a pretty big lake. I walked all around it early this morning."

Alex Shaskolsky of Leningrad smiled, "I think it is a cozy pond. It's warm and full of fish." Just another instance of differing points of view or language.

Alex agreed to write something in my notebook. At age 37, he was a sophisticated teacher of political science in a college in Leningrad. He wrote:

> *Stereotypes are dangerous because they serve as an excuse and basis for fright, for the arms race, and for hatred. It is a dead end. The more arms you have the more your opponents get, the more fright you are sharing. We don't have to love each other, but we have to respect each other. After all, our differences make us special. If all the seeds were the same, it would be boring. So we need empathy which can save our civilization, life on Earth, and which can serve as an inexhaustible source of creative development and efforts toward human perfection.*

Alex had brought, wrapped in his sleeping bag, an ancient samovar. He occasionally collected cones and twigs to build the fire to make and serve tea in a respectful and ceremonious manner, pouring from a porcelain teapot decorated with bright flowers.

As the American-Soviet Peace Walk began its second phase by entering Iowa, we began a second phase of understanding among ourselves. The constant conversation, the unending dialogue, the day-to-day experiences of camping together, brushing our teeth together outdoors in all kinds of weather, sharing bag lunches and avoiding bottom-line conclusions had elevated and deepened our appreciation of each other.

Just as the young Soviet in the rainy breakfast line empathized with the farmers, perhaps the farmers of Iowa would open to the Soviets who would be walking across their state. After all, some had already said, "Thanks. You've brought the rain. What else will you bring?"

A Soviet child carries the American flag while an American child carries the Soviet flag in a July 4th parade.

CHAPTER 36

Independence Day on the Prairie

The Fourth of July in Iowa City, Iowa, dawned as other days—hot. I emerged from my tent, and Vitaly, the co-leader of our neighborhood, stood waiting. "Congratulations on your Day of Independence. I hope it will be a happy one for you." His was the first of similar greetings throughout the day.

Sergei, 27, who offered daily to carry my luggage when we set up camp in the late afternoons, stood with me a moment, and with English too limited to convey his feelings, put his hand over his heart. Then he took off his shirt and placed his hand on his bare chest.

"Are you too warm, Sergei?" I asked.

"It is the people. I was not prepared. They are… they make… they love. How can I say it? My heart is hot! I have a hot heart. Is that correct?"

Seth Bixby Daughtery, an American food service worker from Lake George, NY, beamed, "All the Soviets I've made friends with come up and keep telling me what a special day it is and congratulating me on our country's independence. One thanked me for inviting him to celebrate our independence. It's something we don't think so much about because we've had our independence for so long. But the Soviets haven't."

"This is the first time it's meant anything to me," agreed Marie Connor, 27, of Baltimore. "This whole trip has made me more patriotic, understanding what this country means and what it means to be an American, especially in Iowa." She added, "The focus of this trip has been to develop mutual understanding of two cultures that have largely been kept separate. We Americans have a more carefree spirit. We appreciate nature and each other. The Soviets appreciate the arts and their families more. It's not a negative difference, it's just a difference."

I told her, "I think I'm ready to burst with patriotic pride. More than I've ever felt. I want to wear red, white and blue. If I were younger, I might dye my hair those colors. We are so fortunate to have the freedoms, and we take them for granted. I need to celebrate my gratitude."

Bill Mueller, 41, of Shueyville, Iowa, joined in. He was writing a freelance article about The Walk for Harper's Magazine. "This Fourth of July will mean more to me than in the past 10 or 15 years. We've definitely been taking it for granted." He continued, "These people (the Soviets) really remind me of what's important in this country."

The Soviet Revolution dates from November 7, 1917, and is a much closer memory for many people than the American Revolution 212 years ago. Bill Mueller explained, "Their national holidays are sacred days for them. At times during the day, I've felt embarrassed that I hadn't given a lot of forethought about this holiday."

Debora Wiley, reporter from *The Des Moines Register*, wrote:

> *"It (the Fourth of July) is important because it's an American tradition," said Donna Love, 60, a writer and former teacher from San Mateo, Calif. "People who celebrate tradition tend to have a continuity to their lives that is wholesome and reassuring.*
>
> *"We can learn from the Soviets about the thoughtful respect they give to us and our holiday," said Love. "So we can give the same respect to them and to other Americans."*
>
> *Love noticed during a group discussion on human rights that Soviets tend to start from a general context and work toward specifics. "Americans take an individual point of view and make it general," she said. "Recognizing the different ways we communicate is crucial to getting along."*

Seva, the paunchy leader of the Soviet Peace Committee, had ridden with an American political candidate in the Fourth of July parade. He grinned broadly as he flashed the two-fingered peace sign. The parade had been full of candidates, pretty girls, children on decorated tricycles, clowns, and a marching band that didn't march but rode on a huge festooned flatbed truck. We peace walkers had been honored to walk in the first part of the parade, and then we were given bleachers in the shade to watch the rest move past us.

Local people who had been planning the picnic for six months, showed their culinary skills with casseroles, fruit salads and barbecued pork. We sat in Hancher Green enjoying Soviet and American musical and dance performances. As I stood at the side, a woman took my hand and pulled me down, "This couldn't have happened even five years ago. Changes are happening. Peace has a real chance now."

A banner in Russian on the Coralville Fire Department welcomed the Soviets. Coralville firemen especially greeted Stalislav Yuzishin, 25, a fireman in Boyarka, 93 miles from Chernobyl. In late April, 1986, a nuclear reactor in Chernobyl had exploded, killing 21 and injuring thousands within an 18-mile radius. Two hours after the explosion, Stalislav and 89 other firemen arrived at the scene. He told Coralville firemen, "You know how it is. We had no time to think if we must go or not. We simply performed our duty. It is very difficult for me to describe what happened. And remember, it is because a good friend with me died, and five people more died after, and all of them were my friends."

Stalislav told us he received good medical treatment for three weeks after the explosion. He was involved with track and field exercises, and the sports helped him through the treatments and trauma. As he spoke of his experiences, I watched the Coralville firemen who stood solemnly listening. One big young man turned away and blew his nose. Stalishav then said, "My feelings in the United States are well, and my heart is well too." I wanted to hug him, but he seemed too reserved for that. As he held his hand over his heart, I did too.

The city fireworks display was cancelled because the fields were so dry that everyone worried about the danger of fire. Local families who wished to host peace walkers had attended several hours of orientation and Russian language sessions. Usually, two walkers, an American and a Soviet, sometimes three, if a translator was needed, went together to dinner, the treasured shower and laundry, to meet the neighbors, and to sleep overnight.

I was invited by Collette Pogue, whom I had met when she conducted a van full of walkers through four private gardens as part of the welcome offered by Iowa City. She was a member of Project Green, an organization of garden lovers who enhanced the beauty of the city. Collette had guided us through private hosta gardens where university botany students studied. Seeing how much I enjoyed these gardens, Collette invited me to her home to view hers. When I arrived, she and her husband, Tom, answered the door, and she hesitantly asked, "I don't know if you would enjoy a cocktail. I do have some white wine chilling, and I think Tom put a glass in the freezer."

"Oh," I sighed, "would you marry me?"

With glasses in hand, we wandered through their extensive gardens. I had never seen such a variety of hosta plants. After dinner, friends came over, and we talked about peace and friendship with the Soviets, among ourselves, within each of us.

The day ended with a profound appreciation for our freedoms, for being clean, for sleeping in a home, for the trust people have in one another. Iowa was a good place to be on July 4, a day redefined by one of the speakers as Interdependence Day.

We still had 14 days to go.

Rural tent site east of Des Moines, Iowa.

CHAPTER 37

I've Been Here Before

Two days later, on July 6, I wrote, "I've been here before. Right now, I am perched on a milk can in a breezy screened porch of a brick farm house near Mitchellville, east of Des Moines in central Iowa." With my word processor on a rough old pine table, I wrote another feature article for the *San Mateo Times*. Where to start? Lost in thought, I gazed out toward the horizon—emerald green all the way. Corn and soybeans to the edge of the earth. Even with the serious drought, the corn, although not "as high as an elephant's eye," was green and growing. Rose bushes rustled along the side of the house. I could hear children off somewhere running and shouting, playing a game.

And I could see a field of hundreds of dome tents. Mary and Joseph Fitzgerald, who owned this farm, were again sharing it with American peace walkers. The Great Peace March had camped here in 1986, two years ago, and this time we were Americans and Soviets. We had streamed into this relatively ethnically homogenous rural area full of white churches and on out to the Fitzgerald farm.

On the evening of July 6, Allan Alfeldt, International Peace Walk leader, addressed locals who sat on blankets in the mowed field in front of the house. "How many of you have been afraid of the Soviets?" he asked. Many hands shot up. "Well, look around you, they are here!" He went on to point out, "Our government has spent billions of dollars to keep the Soviets from invading. For today, that didn't work!" Folks chuckled and nodded to each other. Soviets stood up, wandered among the Americans, sat down next to them and began conversing, practicing their English, using gestures.

A woman sitting near me, turned around and asked, "Are you a Soviet?"

When I answered, "I'm from near San Francisco," she looked disappointed. It was the first time I had ever been shunned because I lived near one of the most exciting cities in the world. I got a tiny glimpse of what prejudice must feel like and knew the hurt, if only fleeting and fragmentary. I asked the Iowan to sit right there, told her that I'd be back, and found Irina from Novgorod. "Come, talk with a local Midwestern woman."

Professor of physics Bekhzad Yldashev, 43, of Tashkent, and I sat on the grass and chatted. He gave me a copy of his article recently published in a science magazine, which I scanned. In part, it said:

> In accordance with the modern theory of the evolution of the universe, an appearance of life on the earth was an accidental case. This happened only because of the fact that the density of matter in one moment of time after the Big Bang was the appropriate value. Nobody knows how it happened that our system was lucky enough to produce us.
>
> Unfortunately, we are alone in the visible part of the universe and, probably, there are not any forms of intelligent life similar to our own. From this point of view, I think the only way to have human beings in the universe is to preserve the life on the earth.

He leaned forward as he tapped the article in my hand and said.

"This is a sufficient reason to work for peace."

The next morning, as I sat on the milk can in the screened porch, protected from insects, I watched the Soviets and Americans taking down their tents and loading them into a U-Haul truck. As I wrote, I could see local Boy Scouts moving around, each pair carrying a small keg of water, a third Scout holding out plastic cups. They offered water much as young women in regional costumes had offered the round loaf of bread centered by a dish of salt, the Soviet symbol of hospitality, to American and Soviet walkers in 1987. I also could see the five grandchildren of Mary and Joseph Fitzgerald running and shouting, carefree and healthy. They all seemed to be preschoolers. They were sufficient reason to work for peace.

As I watched the children playing, I remembered a story an American friend, Alex, had told me of his mother, about my age, who was born in Kiev. Nazis had systematically murdered 200,000 people, beginning with the barbaric massacre of 50,000 Jews in a ravine on the outskirts of Kiev known as Babis Yar. His mother and others were forced to watch as "they lined up women, children, men and shot them."

At age 17, his mother was sitting in a movie theater during the middle of the day. All of a sudden there was a loud commotion, screaming and yelling as Ukranian Polizei and German Gestapo rushed in to herd everyone outside. Everyone in the theater was taken to a train, loaded in cattle cars, and shipped as forced labor to Berlin. She was a prisoner, not allowed to speak with or contact anyone. For a year, her frantic parents searched for her, not knowing if their daughter was dead or one of the disappeared from Kiev.

Then the family received the news that their daughter was in Germany and that they could all reunite. But only if her father (Alex's grandfather) who was an engineer, took his family and went to work for the Germans. Desperate to reclaim their daughter, they reluctantly accepted the Nazis' abominable offer. They lived in Poland until the war ended when they retreated with the Germans from the Russian Army, which was executing anyone who worked for the German war effort. It was chaos, with people starving and dying everywhere. Alex's grandfather fell, was hurt and couldn't walk, so Alex's mother, her sister and their mother pushed a cart with "grandfather in it. They were going west," Alex said. "They didn't know how or even *if* they would live to the next day."

I sat transfixed, tears spilling onto my T-shirt, trying to imagine the terror Alex's mother and her family must have endured. I prayed that those children, the Fitzgerald grandchildren out frolicking in the fields, would never experience such horror as Alex had described to me.

By July 7, we were camped in Living History Farms outside of Des Moines, right across the highway from the Hilton Hotel with the indoor pool, precisely as we had two years ago. Judith Rayne, 55-year-old computer programmer from Taos, New Mexico, and I grabbed our towels and suits and walked again through the lobby, just as my friend Shelah and I had back then. I jumped into the pool. Half a dozen bulky leaders of the Soviet Peace Committee splashed and wallowed in the deep end. I realized that in former years, when I had gone swimming in similar pools in St. Moritz, the thought of foreigners swimming together had been exciting. It had made me feel so international, a part of the jet set. Now in the pool at the Hilton just west of Des Moines, I had to remind myself that Judith and I were swimming with people from a country and culture very different from ours. Spitting out a mouthful of water, I laughed and shouted, "We really are all in this together! There are no artificial or political boundaries in a swimming pool."

The Russian nearest me laughed too and swam back to tell his friends what I'd said. Our laughter echoed against the walls and the arched ceiling. Two hotel maids passed by, noted the boisterous people in the pool and smiled indulgently. I wondered if they realized how far we'd come since our first tentative greetings three weeks ago.

I floated on my back and thought about the days still ahead of us. After a flight to Los Angeles, we'd bus north. On July 11, we'd walk through Santa Barbara en route to Monterey and Santa Cruz. Another bus ride to Marin Headlands, and on July 14, we'd be entering San Francisco on foot from Marin County, traveling south across the Golden Gate Bridge. We'd have a picnic on the Marina Green and proceed down Van Ness Avenue to City Hall for a welcome ceremony.

The Peace Walk ends in San Francisco.

CHAPTER 38

California, Here We Come!

From Des Moines, we flew to Los Angeles. I seemed to do my best musing on a plane. In my BPW (Before Peace Walks) life, I'd done my best thinking in a shower, but that was when I'd taken showers for granted, as ordinary. These last three years, I'd stood in showers and either shivered and hurried through the cold ones or stood and breathed in the joy of warm water and sweet soap and not thought of anything else.

I had been on planes mostly across the United States, twice across the Atlantic to and from Russia, and with the anonymity of a passenger, I'd had time to think about the importance of what I'd been doing. On the flight from Des Moines to Los Angeles, so near the end of the third walk, I recalled Joseph Campbell's discussion of the Hero's Journey. I felt that the Peace Walks were, for me, exactly that—a hero's journey.

I had left the comforts and familiarity of home to venture out into the darkness of the unknown, where there was no clear route, into the forest, the interior realm of the psyche. Once there, I had to fight my own monsters of judging others by appearance, of ignorance, prejudice and fear. I joined The Peace March with little more than curiosity. In my quiet, low-profile way, I wanted to walk across the United States just to see it. I did that, but also explored my own labyrinth, endured my own personal ordeal before I could find what was missing in my life.

The difficulties on The Walks had proven to be good guides. I had reordered my values about the importance of my appearance. Before The March, I would never have attended the Pittsburgh Symphony in hiking boots. I'd have missed that splendid evening for lack of proper attire. Having loosened those rules, I became less judgmental about the appearance of others. That was a big change that still sometimes wags its forefinger at me.

My clothing needs changed. About a year after The Peace March, I gave away most of my dresses, saving just two. One was a Mother of the Groom dress and the other a bright red wool to wear at Christmastime, the season of brotherly love. I learned to shop in thrift stores. Today I rarely buy new clothing and think of it as recycling wardrobes. The exception is shoes for my flexible, narrow, pronated feet, which, incidentally, grew by two sizes during my years of long walks.

I learned there was no shame in not knowing, that it is alright to say, "I don't know, but I'd like to find out."

My thoughts were interrupted by the stewardess who was passing out drinks and peanuts, but I quickly returned to my memories. Some of the changes in me were so subtle or had come about so gently, I barely recognized them. I recalled the people in the Midwest who had closed their minds and doors to us, and how, with a little explanation from Shelah and me, their fears had been erased and their hearts and minds opened. In my former life, I'd have said, "Oh, let them be. What do they know?" Before The March, if the lady at the hotel in Moscow had told me not to go somewhere, I'd have given up. When I didn't, she helped me, and I recognized both her concern for my well-being and her respect for my wishes, and I hugged her. The resistance, the indifference we marchers felt from the businessmen in downtown Chicago didn't anger me. It saddened me. I'd think of them later when Dale gave me an article, "How to Make Millionaires Safe from the Bomb."

The gates that a hero on his journey must go through are sometimes literal gates. I thought of the security gate at the airport near Leningrad, where the guards trusted us enough to refrain from opening our luggage. And in Dulles airport in Washington, DC, on our return from Russia while waiting for the carousel to disgorge our bags, we took pictures of each other. Over the loudspeaker, we heard, "There will be no photographs taken in this airport." One marcher bowed deeply and snarled, "Welcome Home! Peace!" I thought, "How pathetic that we don't get respect from our own authorities. They must live with massive fear."

I had learned that I wasn't nearly as fearful if I took action. Being idle, beaten down by fear, staying stuck in an unhappy marriage or in a punishing job, afraid of the unknown, was an untenable existence. I had developed a strong faith that, as my young fellow marcher Oliver had said, "Things usually work out." But, first, we have to step out.

Having found new self-confidence, a passion for peace as well as distance walking, I would, at the end of The Peace March, return to my homeland. And, I'd offer my gifts.

I must have dozed off because I was surprised to hear the attendant asking everyone to fasten our seatbelts and return our tray tables to the upright position.

The next day, in Los Angeles, after the city events and a rest, we bused 80 miles and walked 10. The California State Peace March was walking from the south and joined us at Manning Park in Montecito near Santa Barbara. Since each group had its beginning in The Great Peace March for Global Nuclear Disarmament, we greeted old friends as well as new. Together we walked into Santa Barbara, had lunch at the Andree Clark Bird Refuge and paraded down State Street to Leadbetter Beach for welcoming ceremonies of speeches, music and food. At a public potluck barbecue, we discussed peace issues—what can we each do?—with bystanders and temporary marchers.

Many of us slept overnight in local homes. I did—with Dale. He came to the barbecue, gave me big hugs, joined the circle dance on the sand, and took me up to his cabin in the hills. "Come walk with me," I pleaded. "We'd have such a time." Like so many of the original peace marchers, he had work to do at home. "You'll go for me," he said and slipped Snickers candy bars into all my pockets.

The next morning, we bused to Monterey. Along highway 101, we stopped at noon for a picnic in San Ardo, a scorched little crossroads south of the Salinas Valley. My seatmate was Carl Hagelberg, who had come from Pacific Palisades to visit his son Gus during The Peace March. Gus had wanted his parents to meet me to reassure them that the marchers were normal. Now Carl himself was on the American-Soviet Walk. He called San Ardo, "Valley of the Smokes" for the oil refineries humming there.

Some tough looking men were parked under the trees, drinking beer and tinkering with their customized motorcycles. They wore black T-shirts and tattoos and looked mean. Several of us watched as Alexei Shaskolski and Alexander Raskin, both from Leningrad, together with their friends, Ron and Pat Herson of Los Angeles, stopped dead in their tracks, riveted by the scene.

Pat, about 5'2", was all sunny smiles, friendly greetings and talk of peace, as she moved among the bikers, the rest of her entourage trailing close behind. The riders eyed the T-shirt Alexi wore with the flags of both countries as its motif. I held my breath because it looked like trouble, but within moments, one of the bikers was explaining the workings of his vehicle. Then he tore off down the street with Alexander as a passenger.

Pat took a picture with the American standing good-naturedly between Alexander and Alexi. They all shook hands in farewell, and the biker said, "Anytime we can have peace instead of a war, I'm all for that."

And our Soviet friends came away richer for having experienced a unique slice of American life.

Everyone was happy to be walking along the West Coast, away from the oppressive humidity of the East and the heat of the Midwest. In Monterey and in Santa Cruz, we drank in the fresh vistas of the beaches as we trooped along behind our flags. We raised our two-finger peace sign to onlookers, handed out our printed material, and welcomed those who walked with us a while.

Eventually we would reach San Francisco, the final destination of the American-Soviet Peace Walk. "The City That Knows How" had seen many parades of people walking to make a statement. I wondered if we, walking for global nuclear disarmament, for peace and friendship, would look any different to San Franciscans than all the other groups walking for a cause.

I thought of this as 217 of our Soviets friends, joined by over 1,000 Americans, coursed into San Francisco from Vista Point at the north end of the Golden Gate Bridge. On the bridge itself, we did not carry banners or wear the San Francisco Giants baseball caps the team had donated as a welcoming gift. Allan and Joe, the organizers of International Peace Walks had agreed with California Highway Patrol that we'd walk on the sidewalk as individuals and do nothing to distract motorists. We were excited tourists striding across the bridge. All during the hot, humid days of the Eastern and Midwestern portions of this trek, I had told walkers, "Just wait. When we get to San Francisco, it'll be cool." I was wrong. It was warm and clear weather on the bridge. The buildings of downtown San Francisco shimmered and glistened in the distance. I took 72 pictures.

At the southern end, at the request of city officials, we boarded buses for the short distance to Marina Green, where we wore our San Francisco Giants hats and ate our bag lunches. We talked with local marchers who had joined us for the day and wandered around looking for old friends.

An attractive young man called out, loped across the grass, and gave me a hug. He was tall and reminded me of someone I knew, but I couldn't place him. "Donna! You don't remember me! I'm Oliver!"

"Of course! I didn't recognize you." I had walked with Oliver in eastern Colorado when he had dreadlocks. "You're all cleaned up. You have shoes! I like your haircut. How are you? What are you doing now?"

He grinned down at me. "I'm the bookkeeper for Seeds of Peace." Suddenly the wind came up, and we shivered and zipped up our jackets as Walk Monitor Mike Brown announced, "We're moving!" The column was formed in record time. "Let's get out of here," Mike called. "Too windy. Too cold. *Poshlee!*" I lost Oliver in the crowd, but not in my heart.

On the way to Fort Mason, a Russian friend asked me if there were a place to buy toothpaste.

"Yes, there is. The Marina Safeway Store is right over there. I'll go with you," and we crossed the street. Once inside, I led Nicolai to the proper aisle. He stopped, bug-eyed, and murmured, "All these? So many choices! You have so many choices. We have one kind. How do you decide? What shall I choose?"

I grabbed a popular brand and said, "Here. This is good. Let's pay over there and catch up with The Walk."

As we headed back outside, Nicolai still talked about all the choices.

"Yes," I said, "you have made me realize how many we have. We are so lucky to have so many. So much. I hope with glasnost, your country will have more choices. And not just with toothpaste." We chuckled together, and I thought how often on this Walk I'd had opportunities to learn. I felt so rich.

I had planned to carry the Soviet flag down Van Ness Avenue to the Civic Center. Josh Stanley of Orinda, across the Bay, was our flag man. A normally mild-mannered retired Army officer, he was grumpy. "Can't find the flags, that's what's the matter. Someone locked them into Bus 3." Even Joe Kinzcel, a walk director, resourceful as he was, could not find a way into the bus, and none of us could find the bus driver. We trooped the length of Van Ness behind the Soviet and American flags owned and carried by a private citizen who had joined our Walk on the bridge. I missed our high-waving American, Soviet, United Nations and California flags. I had set my heart on carrying the Soviet flag in San Francisco. After our long trek, I wanted to stand tall in my home city. I felt disappointed, but trooped along greeting onlookers and asking them, "Come along with us for a few blocks. Walk for peace with Russians."

Our mile-long river of humanity was silent, respectful and powerful. No chanting, no shouting, softly singing, peaceful people walking for our lives. Shopkeepers and car dealers stood in their doorways, accepting the brochures that Jolene De Lisa, Gene Gordon and others distributed. There were no crowds of cheering onlookers such as we'd enjoyed in Iowa. No groups of school children with colorful posters such as had touched our hearts in Maryland and Delaware. Just inconvenienced pedestrians. A few, curious enough to ask, were surprised that there had been no advance publicity in San Francisco papers.

They asked, "Where's your media?" I wished I knew.

I thought the reception on the steps of City Hall was perfunctory. The pleasant Russian Choir of San Francisco sang. Mayor Art Agnos greeted us, smiled, shook hands, posed for pictures, proclaimed the day one of Soviet-American Cooperation and gave the framed proclamation to the chairman of the Soviet Peace Committee delegation. I hoped I was not just jaded by the repetitious rallies held on City Hall steps. At least some officials gave us recognition. I thought we might have had more attention if we had received more publicity. We walkers were convinced of the value of the peace walks, if even only among ourselves. Joe Kinczel spoke of the importance of our continued dedication. He was heckled by an inebriated man in the audience at the foot of the City Hall steps. What had we really achieved?

Only Tankred Golenpolsky, a 57-year-old journalist from Moscow, stirred sustained applause as he stood with his 12-year-old daughter and spoke with passion and eloquence of peace between our nations. "I wanted her to see your way of life, so I brought her," he said. "No one will now be able to impose stereotypes onto her. She will not grow up to think all Americans are bad because she knows many Americans who are good."

When the welcoming ceremony was over, three of us Northern Californians: Shirley Iverson, Josh Stanley and I, took our Illinois pals Sallie and Alan Gratch to the nearby Opera Plaza to debrief over a consoling glass of wine. In our casual walking garb, we apparently did not offend San Francisco's more glamorously dressed patrons. Some asked us if we were part of The Peace Walk and listened eagerly to us as we explained our goals. Outreach in the Opera Plaza. We felt better, lifted from our Plodding for Peace outlook. Sallie and Allan suggested that our neighborhood meetings would be good places to discuss options for future walks and how they could be improved.

"Keep track of the flags!" Josh slapped the table.

"Okay. *Poshlee*, let's go set up the tents and see what's going on at the campsite," Sallie stood up.

"Josh, where's your car?" Allan asked.

"Good question," he answered. "It's parked around here somewhere." The classic nightmare. We'd lost the car. Split into two teams, we scoured the streets bordering The Civic Center for almost an hour until Allan found it on McAllister Street.

We headed back across the Golden Gate Bridge and through the tunnel. Josh said no when I asked him to honk the horn in the tunnel.

"Why not? Our father did it when we were kids."

"Yeah, our dad did, too, but then he told us that the honking would make the tunnel collapse."

"Yes," I chuckled, "Ours did too. He said exactly that."

"It's true," Alan added. "Don't honk in the tunnel. We don't want our world falling in on us now."

Turning west toward Point Bonita, we found our campsite, nestled on a level spot between the high rounded hills of the Marin Headlands and barely sheltered from the whipping wind. We were camping, paradoxically enough, on the Rifle Range. Peter, of the Kiev Language Institute grumbled, "I think this godforsaken place is a reservation for Russians."

At least it was a quiet place, away from traffic noise. When I wakened to a new day and sat at a picnic table to write, the paper curled with dampness, and I had to stop. Drowsy walkers drifted by, and we all asked ourselves, "How can we make these Walks better?" Others offered opinions and asked when we'd have a meeting about the improvements that could be made. "Later," Allan Affeldt answered. "We'll talk about it later."

Gret Gentile, with her flute, wandered among the tents with her gentle wake-up call. Seventy-year-old Mim Broderick flourished her toothbrush and exclaimed, "Did you see those Great Peace Marchers who came to join us yesterday? And they brought their children! I am thrilled to see them again, still devoting so much of their time to working for peace."

Mim barely paused for breath. "Did you notice how dear and content their children are? Those families will inspire others. Our seeds of peace are being planted. Seeds of peace are falling on fertile ground." She waved her arms in the air, "Let's not be discouraged. We must keep right on with our efforts. Just look at how many people wore Peace Walk T-shirts yesterday!"

I remembered how cheerful Mim had been on The Great Peace March in 1986. One dispirited day in Ohio, she had suggested, "Let's just stop in here, in this thrift store, for a minute." She quickly selected a floppy hat, a cotton scarf, a child's umbrella, and a visor cap, paid at the register, and gave each of us women something new to wear. "Here, nothing like a new hat to make a woman feel chipper," as she plopped the floppy hat on my head. Now she encouraged us again with her enthusiasm.

She was probably right. We were sowing seeds and needed to be patient for the results. Did we have time to be patient? Well, as Jim McGowan of the Rolling Owls, had said from his wheelchair, we do our best and see what happens. As is said in Twelve-Step Programs, "Do the work and let go of the results." Not so easy in our goal-oriented culture of business and industry, where the bottom line is important.

Speaking of business, the day before departure was for shopping. Our Soviet friends wanted to buy some of the goods they had seen during the past few weeks. We Americans took them to appliance stores, discount marts and outlets. I bought dozens of tubes of toothpaste for them. They went home with TVs, boom-boxes, cameras, juicers, irons, cosmetics, books and American-style clothes. I wondered how they would get it all on the plane. Peter showed me gifts he'd found for his wife and children. I particularly remember the pretty sweater he had selected for his wife. Mostly what Peter took home was a dream. He wanted his daughter to attend school in the United States and, for a moment, I considered asking her to come live with me. But at age 61, I didn't think I was the right choice, so encouraged Peter to find a young family. Ultimately, through a church in Mississippi, she attended high school and college, even earning her MBA at an American University.

In our neighborhood, Grupa Chaste 6, meeting, Vasily and I listened to questions and comments about improving future walks. "The energy expended in setting up and taking down the tents almost daily could be put to better use. Perhaps we should set up camp on a college campus and stay there for a week, holding seminars, joining in community groups," one said.

Another offered, "We all devote individual time to giving slide shows, videos and lectures or discussions. That interest could be developed and expanded to be used collectively in a community, leaving behind us, as we move on, enthusiastic and well-trained peace leaders."

Tankred Golenpolsky's daughter sat near him as he talked about the changes taking place across the Soviet Union under Premier Gorbachev's program of perestroika. "One of the main topics is upraising the value of humanitarian things that are common to everyone, and those humanitarian values should be regarded by all means as more important than all kinds of class differences," he explained earnestly.

"These changes represent the last chance for a better society for my children. It gives me a chance to play out my dreams for a new democratic society," he said. "When you make new plans for the next Peace Walks, remember how fine this one has been."

"Wait a minute," I heard from someone in the back, "I think we must clarify the ideology, the marketable package. The leaders of IPW [International Peace Walks] are young. They have peace walk experience and actually perform miracles. Life on these walks is a series of miracles. But how marketable are miracles?"

My own faith in the "friendliness of the Universe" had increased a thousand times over, and my son Matt had long ago already described me as a Pollyanna. On the peace walks, we had answered the problem of conflicting wills and resolved the frustrations caused by the clash of differing opinions. No one held back; everyone was heard, every suggestion given respect. We had learned to made decisions by consensus. During our first American-Soviet Peace Walk, we each had learned to trust the other, and we had an opportunity to demonstrate our care and concern for each other. We had stood respectfully for each other's national anthems. But how could we appeal to elected representatives who knew how to affect political change? I wrote down all these questions so our leaders could address them at the end of The Walk.

As I was stuffing my notes into a plastic bag, I paused and thought, "I have conducted a meeting of Soviets and Americans, many of whom know much more than I do about politics and social movement, and I have done it without clutching a clipboard to my chest in fear and self-doubt as I did years ago in Junior Museum Auxiliary meetings. Is that a miracle or what!"

In 10 days in the Western region, we had five campsites among four days of walking a total of 40 miles, interspersed with four days of busing another 340 miles, and five stationary days.

For our entire trip, we camped in 23 sites over 35 days. Our 18 days of walking totaled 205 miles while 10 days of busing totaled 1,445 miles. We had 13 stationary days.

On our final morning, I looked around and realized that as people everywhere miss their families, I would miss these people. These young, old, optimistic, pessimistic, idealistic, pragmatic, Asian, European, and American people with their soft voices, thundering voices, willingness, eagerness and tears. I would see their faces in a crowd, recognize them across the street. And knew I would be living with them in my imagination. These 400 or so ambassadors for peace would be back in their other walks of life, sorting through souvenirs and memories and deciding what to do next. The Soviets said they were going home with the dust of America on their shoes and the love of Americans in their hearts.

I got a ride home to San Mateo and a week later was invited to a "welcome back" dinner party. At the table, I answered questions about my experiences on The Walks that I'd taken during the last three years. As I described the Soviets I had met, one friend blurted out, "You sound to me just like a commie sympathizer."

I took a breath and said, "Well, if you mean do I admire and respect the Soviets I have met, do I love and enjoy many of them, plan to correspond with some, want to see some of their children come to the United States to college? If you mean, do I appreciate all the material wealth and freedoms we have, and sympathize with them over their horrendous wartime losses and the daily struggles they endure, then, yes, you are right, I am a sympathizer."

There was silence for a moment. Then all at once, the hostess held up her silver coffee server, "Who'd like more coffee?" Someone asked, "Who's going to the Giants opening game?" One woman excused herself to head for the bathroom.

I could see how different I had become. Before my experiences on The Peace Walks, I used to be uncomfortable when the conversation turned to controversial subjects. I thought in stereotypes and generalizations. I used to be apathetic about nuclear armament threats, feeling too scared and too helpless to take personal responsibility. I used to be a quiet, acquiescent woman, a "nice girl." Now, instead of sitting at the foot of our family dinner table, I stood before audiences to expose the threat of nuclear annihilation and encourage individual action. Now I needed to learn how to express myself without offending these gracious friends. I felt a bit disoriented, as though someone had come in and moved all the furniture around. I still had a lot to learn.

I recalled President Dwight D. Eisenhower's statement, "Someday the Russian and the American people are going to want peace so much their governments are just going to have to get out of the way." Yes, that, and we needed to change our way of thinking. My Soviet friend Peter Ganea had been right when he said, "With American ingenuity and Soviet discipline, we can do anything!"

During these past three years, these years of walking and talking, busting out of my former box, eating rain-soaked salad, dancing with the KGB, admiring the adaptability of the cottonwood trees, and feeling happy in a fertilizer factory, I had learned that anything is possible.

EPILOGUE

Let there be peace and let it begin with me.

The peace walks left tracks on my soul. I felt spiritually deeper and broader, more sensitive to the needs of others, more accepting of differences among lifestyles, less judgmental. I felt privileged to live in a house with lights, walls of art, warm water, clean clothes, wonderful food.

But much of my life after the peace walks mirrored my former life. I still loved and took pleasure in my family and friends. I enjoyed opera, symphony, dramatic performances—even more than before. In reality, I enjoyed and appreciated *everything* more than I had prior to the walks. I continued to live, at least some of the time, back in San Mateo in the Mouse House. Other times I was with Dale in his cabin in Santa Barbara or we lived in his Palapamobile (converted bread truck sheathed in palm fronds) in San Carlos, Sonora, Mexico.

After the Peace Walks, I felt I'd returned from a hero's journey. An important aspect of the hero's journey is to return with gifts, some knowledge or wisdom, to share. Dale and I joined forces to create "Pretty Good Pictures for Peace." He was formulating a film about his thoughts on peace; I mailed postcards which advertised my eagerness to give slide show presentations to schools, civic and church groups—anyone who would listen for an hour.

In a Santa Rosa elementary school, my grandson Derek's teacher invited me to speak to the second grade. I was just beginning when she stopped me, "Wait a minute, I want the other students to hear this." She left the room and in a few minutes came back and said, "We're moving." At that moment, we heard over the loudspeaker, "All classes will meet in the auditorium. Right now. We have a special treat for you." Derek's eyes got big, and with a grin as wide as his face, he looked up at me and said, "Gran, I'll help you." I handed him the big inflated globe of the world, the one I tossed out to the audiences when I announced, "Our earth is in your hands," and we walked down the hall together.

To adult audiences, I explained that walking was a metaphor for what peace marchers believed needed to happen. That metaphor involved us spiritually and physically, emotionally and intellectually. On the walks we had time to understand each other; we grew to respect our differences. We recognized that steps in the right direction, however small, would bring us to our destination. I explained that walking was a slowing down, a process, and a grounding, the very act of which gave time to reach the resolutions and understanding we sought—still seek.

Some of the slides showed faces of the peace walkers, and people asked, "Is that one American or Russian?" When I challenged them to guess, they'd say, "She must be American, she has a big wristwatch."

"No," someone else said, "She must be Russian, she is smiling with her mouth closed. Remember some are self-conscious about their metal front teeth."

A third voice piped up, "She has to be American because she has good-looking glasses." These comments gave me the opportunity to point out that we tend to judge by appearances, and that we have better ways to make a determination, but in a slide show, all we have is appearance. We need to look deeper to find the person. The girl was a Russian college student.

After one of my talks, a woman handed me a bumper sticker and said, "If you promise to put this on your car, I'll give it to you." I promised, took it home and lost track of it for several years. By 2003, when I bought a red Ford Escape, I had found the sticker and put it on the back of the car. It is the only bumper sticker I have ever had. In an effort to establish a cabinet-level department equivalent to the Defense Department, blue letters on a white background say DEPARTMENT OF PEACE, in red letters, www.DOPcampaign.org. It is perfect on a red car! I always feel optimistic when I see someone in a parking lot, standing behind my car and copying the website.

Surprising honors came to me. The California Legislature Assembly awarded me a "Certificate of Recognition as an outstanding woman in international good will for her continuing efforts to secure world peace." The San Mateo County Board of Supervisors commended me on "being named woman of distinction in international goodwill and understanding." The Soroptimist Club presented me with a certificate "in recognition of her voluntary accomplishments in the area of International Goodwill and Understanding."

The Giraffe Project, an organization on Whidbey Island in the state of Washington that recognized those willing to "stick their necks out for the common good," published an article about me and asked for permission to produce a film about my personal changes on The Great Peace March. They were considering Joanne Woodward to play my part. Of course, I was thrilled, but didn't count on its happening, which was good, because nothing came of the idea.

The University of Oregon Alumni and my college sorority magazines printed pieces about me. I was the commencement speaker at Charles Armstrong School in Belmont, California, and felt like a celebrity, a hero returned home.

The recognition gave me opportunities to speak to groups about the importance of each citizen becoming personally involved in creating peace. I repeated my conviction that as we become involved, we ourselves are changed; we become less fearful, more optimistic and peaceful. I remembered again the boy in second grade whose teacher asked, "How many are afraid of the The Bomb?" Every child but the one boy raised a hand. When the teacher asked him why he was unafraid, he replied, "I feel safe because all the time my parents go to meetings to improve peace in the world."

I continued to do slide show presentations. Dale worked on his art projects and film ideas. After a few years, we gently drifted apart. Even though we loved each other, our day-to-day lifestyles differed too much.

I returned to San Mateo and renewed my friendship with a tall, charming man I'd admired for a long time. At 63 I fell so in love with him that I didn't see the red flags.

On our very first dinner date, the hostess in the restaurant, asked, "Two?"

I was nearer her, so answered, "Yes, and may we have the table in the corner by the windows?"

After we were seated, Mike leaned toward me and sarcastically asked, "And would you like to order the wine also?"

"Oh, no," I, not recognizing his injured masculine ego, blithely answered, "I don't know as much about wine as you do."

I had forgotten the rule that the man always talked to the wait staff in restaurants. I might have saved us disappointment if I'd recognized Mike's traditional values. In spite of his frequent rage at me, I was sure that "anything is possible," and we planned our wedding.

After 11 years, Mike said, "You're not the woman you used to be." He was right. I was no longer able to be an obedient housewife. Forgetting to have dinner on the table at 6 o'clock was only one of my many omissions.

Since our divorce in 2002, I have lived in a cottage in Capitola, California, above Monterey Bay. Santa Cruz County is home to creative, inventive, non-conformists. Here, with my independent streak and liberal point of view, I fit right in. However, there *are* rules.

The city of Capitola requires off-street parking for two cars, and I resented having to devote that much space in my tiny garden to cars. What else could I do with that slab of concrete? In the shower, where—now that I have returned to the luxuries of privacy and warm water—I once again do my best thinking, I recalled that I had for a long time wanted a labyrinth. With my hair still dripping, I opened the computer, Googled "labyrinth designers" and found Richard Feather Anderson, a geo-mathematician. Now, curbside, as though it were a decorated double-parking space, is smooth concrete with a Cretan pattern of imbedded 3-inch cubes of Mexican stone that delineates the path to the center. Hanging on the white picket fence is a framed explanation and invitation to walk the labyrinth, sometimes called a temple of peace.

One Christmas when my family was visiting, my son Marty said, "Mom, someone's coming. They're walking in your garden."

I peered out the window and said, "Oh, good, they're walking the labyrinth."

He exclaimed, "You let strangers walk in your yard?"

"They're searching for peace," I said, and returned to laying out chips and salsa.

Since my 80th year, I have written three memoirs and have found such healing through writing that I encourage others to write their stories. In memoir-writing workshops, I point out that when we write about our painful times, we gain understanding and can grow to forgive those who have hurt or disappointed us. That forgiveness sprouts peace.

I invite you, no matter what your age or circumstances, to push your boundaries and take up something that is meaningful and exciting to you. You might just find, as I did, that you not only help make the world a better place, you transform yourself in the process.

One day her desire for peace became so great... that she became PEACE

Imagine all the people living life in peace. You may say I'm a dreamer, But I'm not the only one. I hope someday you'll join us, And the world will be as one.

--John Lennon

Where Are They Now? 2011

As I was chronicling the Peace Walks, I began wondering what the past 25 years had brought to the marchers; or, what had the marchers brought to their years? So I asked. I didn't find them all, but here are the questions:

> Your age during The Great Peace March (or USSR-USA,
>
> USA-USSR Peace Walks). Your age now.
>
> Where, generally, do you live now?
>
> An incident you particularly recall while on The March/ Walks?
>
> How did the GPM impact your life?
>
> What job (s) did you have on the GPM?
>
> How do you now pursue the goal of global nuclear disarmament
> or world peace? Local peace? Personal peace?
>
> Any advice?

And some of the answers:

When Ida Unger, Los Angeles, signed her questionnaire, she added a heart. She writes, "I was 33 then and 58 now. I particularly recall singing with Pete Seeger and Pat Schroeder all night in the rain in Red Rocks, Colorado." Her jobs on the GPM were fund raising and supporting the school classes in the buses. She presently teaches yoga, "Peace, soul by soul." She advises, "We need another march to re-awaken the world."

Jonnie Zheitlin, of Ashland, Oregon, walked in The Great Peace March when she was 60 years old and looks today as she did then. She is 85 now and says, "The funny thing is I was a "senior" then. She remembers, "My partner, Billy Lieb, and I liked the hard rain because we could make love in the tent as noisily as we wanted and nobody could overhear."

How did the GPM impact Jonnie's life? "The GPM was one of those incredible experiences that validate some of my basic beliefs and values: Follow your passion. Do something outrageous that you believe in. You can leave your home/work and come back and start up again. We're all transients walking through. And we're all one—regardless of age, gender, or socio-economic background.

On The March, Jonnie was a mediator, "a child-care person," and once was on the Peace City Council. She says, "I was and am a psycho-therapist. One of my goals in working with people is to help them achieve inner peace. I used to be on the board of Peace House in our town and I sometimes attend vigils. As I get older, and time passes, I do less. Actually, my personal inner peace level is pretty high. I don't have a big bucket list.

"I don't believe in advice. I believe that people can/will figure it out. I do believe that compassionate listening is very helpful."

JD (John Dewey) Stillwater was 22 when I first met him in 1986 on The Great Peace March. He was a tall, pale, lanky, ambling young man with a direct look and wide grin. Today he is 47 and his appearance hasn't changed a bit. At the recent 25th Reunion, I recognized him immediately. He and his wife Ann and their children live in Harrisburg, Pennsylvania. JD's job on The March until Chicago, was on the kitchen crew. His favorite moments were those spent making state-shaped cakes for the highway patrols when we crossed state lines, and early chilly mornings in the warm kitchen truck making pancakes, hundreds of pancakes. From Chicago to Washington, DC, he played percussion in (GPM musical group) Collective Vision. His most memorable event was our staying in the fertilizer factory where we talked out "the town mode/country mode of walking" controversy and came to a compromise.

JD also walked in 1987 from Leningrad (St Petersburg) to Moscow and recalls Novgorod, when 250,000 people came out to meet us. His "most memorable moment was the afternoon before the big rock concert at Ismailovo Stadium in Moscow. "A stage hand had a seizure and fell onto me. I kept him from falling off the stage, but others there tried to force a piece of wood into his mouth and the language barrier prevented me from explaining that this was no longer proper first aid for seizures. They broke off all his front teeth. It was horrible."

When asked how the Peace March impacted his life, JD answered,

"With only one semester remaining, I took a leave of absence from Cornell University, to go on The March. I expected to finish school in Spring, but instead toured with Collective Vision and I met Ann and her son. Our marriage and daughter followed. Aside from my parents and siblings, there is very little in my life today that didn't come about as a result of The Great Peace March, from family to vocation to location."

JD says, "I currently work for The Circle School, a democratic K-12 school, a pioneering institution promoting free and responsible childhood." When he taught in a public neighborhood high school, JD felt the students were not being encouraged to think independently, and that bothered him. He believes that The Circle School standard of ethics makes them "the future of education."

His advice is, "Don't believe people who urge you to 'play it safe' with life. Do the bold things; you can <u>always</u> go back to being normal later, if you want."

Frank Sahlem of Inglewood, California, near Los Angeles, is tall and rugged looking in his broad-brimmed hat and beard. He resembles a Western frontiersman, even in being soft-spoken. He had his 31st birthday on the Peace March and recently turned 56. He particularly recalls "the high point, literally and figuratively, was the day crossing Loveland Pass. We all had been rightly concerned about weather in the Rockies, but it was a beautiful clear day and we celebrated at the summit with a great release of tension. It was all downhill from there; that was the day we all knew we would make it to Washington, DC."

The impact of The March on his life? "I have the ongoing good feeling that the world is still somewhat viable; I gained an enormous extended family and The March made my future wife want to know me." Frank's jobs were poetry coordinator, garbage collector, as-needed volunteer, and he walked every chance he had. To pursue peace, he votes a Democratic ticket, supports peace and justice organizations and demonstrates against war. He says, "I don't carry a gun, even in Inglewood, and I'm happily married for 22 years. His advice is, "Don't give advice."

I look beyond his beard and broad-brimmed hat to see a quiet, peace-loving, gentle man who is involved and responsible for making his world a better place.

Diane Clark is remembered as Peace City mayor. She was 44 years old. Now she lives near Fredonia, New York, in the very western part of the state, near the Pennsylvania line. She is director of Greystone Nature Preserve, 77 acres on the Lake Erie escarpment dedicated to wild life preservation and environmental education.

Diane recalls "an outstanding evening for me was holding Jackson Browne's hand and going tent to tent waking up marchers and asking if they wanted to hear a concert. It was way past midnight and he had offered to play for us after his big concert in, I think, Grand Rapids. His big motor van came bumping over the hills to the cornfield where we were camped. He got out with a small electric piano and we set up candles, chairs, etc. We decided as a group not to wake up everyone with a loud announcement, so the handful of marchers who were present at the time spread out and went tent to tent asking. It was delightful to hear his gentle voice asking marchers if they wanted to hear a concert. Some of the responses were, 'Don't be kidding me, man,' 'No, I got to sleep,' 'Right on,' and 'No, I have to lead the march tomorrow. Thanks.'

How did the GPM impact Diane's life? "I was asked to speak at anti-nuclear/peace conferences in the USSR, Poland, and Japan where I spoke for nuclear disarmament. I learned to trust the universe and experienced what a utopian colony could achieve."

And her jobs? "I joined The March in the earliest days. I asked to handle the litter pick-up. Soon I was also doing the recycling and then took over the garbage as no one had been doing it. We cleaned up the hills in Griffith Park (in Los Angeles), pulling out an accumulation of junk that had developed over the years. The county was amazed at what we put by the roadside; everything from old washing machines to recent dirty diapers. They hauled truck-loads away and declared us good citizens for cleaning the park so thoroughly. Peace City Council asked me to take on the role as mayor after we had passed Las Vegas. In all, I met 221 mayors, planted peace trees and exchanged city keys, and talked about global nuclear disarmament."

When asked how she pursues peace today, Diane says, "I founded Greystone Nature Preserve in 1998 as a way of promoting peace locally. Peace and appreciation of wildlife, flora and fauna are what we teach at Greystone Nature Preserve. Peace as an environmental education program that stresses our union with nature more than names or properties of plants and animals. My personal peace is in tending the organic gardens which bring forth a bounty of food and amazement at the vital life force."

Her advice? "I like Pete Seeger's motto, "Just keep keeping on." I am doing that in not using any extra energy or stuff, and in pursuing peaceful solutions to all conflicts that enter my life. My husband and I share one car and on average have one "car-less" day a week. We still pick up litter as part of the Adopt a Highway Program and the Great Lakes Beach Sweep, and on a daily basis. When we realized that we could not stop the huge industrial windmills from being erected on the Niagra escarpment where we live, we set aside our property as a not-for-profit nature center so at least a portion of the hill can not be invaded by them. I still correspond with peace-minded folks and organizations in Europe and Asia."

Gus Hagelberg was 19 on The March. It was he who asked if he could introduce me to his concerned parents when they visited. He did and we became friends, his father even joined the Peace Walk in the United States with 200 Soviets. Gus and his family live in Tubingen, Germany. He is still reeling from the death of their son Julian, aged 19, just the age of Gus in 1986.

He says his job on The March was mostly dishwashing. An incident Gus recalls, "We were bathing at the pool of the Moulin Rouge Motel in Las Vegas. It was such a contrast of cultures because we marchers were all white and all the other guests were black. There was some music playing in the background and a kid of about five started dancing with confidence just radiating from his face. I was a terrible dancer and watching him made me feel totally inferior. I learned a lot those days about being modest and humble." Gus also learned to appreciate nature. "It taught me the value of community and commitment. It helped me continue working for peace and justice to this day. Right now, I have no advice to give."

Sue Guist of Morgan Hill, California, is 80 now, but when I first met her in 1985, she was 54. She says that just as I first heard of The Great Peace March from Connie Fledderjohann, Sue heard about The March from me. Her jobs? Sue worked in the small, but important info trailer where she provided maps each day so we could find the next campsite. She also was secretary to Mayor Diane, handled computer and data entries, contributed to the blue-ribbon of letters, staffed the bookmobile, and during the last month of The March, worked in the GPM office in Washington, DC.

Sue likes to recall meeting the Soviets in Davenport, Iowa, on their Peace Cruise down the Mississippi River. "Two of them, a cosmonaut and an opera singer, signed my Peace Like a River banner. Then, I loved meeting and walking with the Soviets across the Golden Gate Bridge in the summer of 1988. That was a great joy."

How did The March impact Sue's life? She says, "It's who I am. It's in my dreams, still. Ask anybody who ever talks to me, about any subject at all, and I refer to The March." Sue volunteers at the San Jose Peace Center, joins Silent Walks for Peace, contributes her skills as a writer. In 1991, her book, *Peace Like a River*, was released. Even though she is "slowing down a tad," in June of 2011, she rode a Peace Train to Santa Barbara to participate in a demonstration at Vandenberg Air Force Base.

Jeff Share was 24 when he was working as a photojournalist for the *Los Angeles Times* and realized that The Great Peace March was a very important event and he wanted to document it. "I never joined The March. As a freelance photojournalist, I tried to maintain my separation in order to document the event and get newspapers and magazines to publish my work." Jeff says, "My photographs of The March catapulted my photography career. I won several international photojournalism awards. My next project that I photographed was about street children living and working around the world."

Asked to recall a particular incident, Jeff answers, "Before taking the aerial photograph in Nebraska, I had been photographing the marchers from on the ground and since Nebraska is so flat, there were no opportunities to show the expansiveness of The March. I decided to charter a crop-duster to get some height in order to see the perspective of fields and distance through which the marchers walked. However, since there was no media documenting the marchers in the middle of Nebraska, the march column was getting very spread out and it was not common for them to walk together in a tight line. This was a problem because just a couple of people now and then walking would not show visually the number of people who really were walking every day. So the day before I rented the plane, I spread a rumor in the camp in which I told marchers that *Life* magazine was sending a photographer in an airplane the next day to photograph The March and I urged people to walk together. This worked and the next morning, enough marchers grouped together behind the flags for me to get a photograph that was actually good enough for *Life* magazine to publish months later."

Twenty-five years later, Jeff gave me permission to use that photograph as the cover for *Walking For Our Lives*.

What is Jeff doing now? "After working for 10 years as a photojournalist, I became frustrated with the business side of journalism and media. I moved into education and taught elementary school in downtown Los Angeles for half a dozen years. After seeing the great potential to integrate media with education, I studied for my PhD at UCLA about how to bring a critical engagement with the mass media into public schools. I now teach in the Teacher Education Program at UCLA. Through working with new teachers, I lead them in how to educate K–12 students to think critically about media and how to create their own alternative representations. I have published a book about this, *Media Literacy is Elementary: Teaching Youth to Critically Read and Create Media* (2009). I also present at many educational conferences about the importance of engaging critically with media in the classroom."

Jeff continues, "I think the most important thing we can do to create change in the world is to teach our young how to think critically about everything, especially the media. Once kids start to question and think critically about the media that engulfs them, it loses its power over them. Commercial media can be very powerful, but when people recognize their own abilities to question and challenge those representations, citizens and democracy gain a new opportunity to struggle against the enormous corporate machinery. Technology and media today provide countless opportunities for people to push back and challenge injustice."

Bill O'Neill, who had studied at Harvard, celebrated his 26th birthday while on the Peace March in Nebraska. Now 51, he and his family live in Hyannis, Massachusetts. He often tells people about the debate over how we should walk and the compromise over city mode and country mode. "It's an example of how community debate can drag on, but can lead to creative and effective solutions."

Bill says, "The Great Peace March taught me not to judge other people by their appearance. I also learned that people working together can overcome chaos and countless obstacles."

On The March, Bill was co-director of media relations. From 1987 to 1999, he was on the board of directors of a local peace and justice coalition. "Today I work for a regional nonprofit that provides affordable housing. I also try to be an example of patience and tolerance, with more success some days than others."

I remember Carole Schmidt (Davis) as an energetic blond young woman with a bright smile and a bouncy step. She was 25 then and currently recalls two events, "strangely equal in their effect on me. In one, I was standing, poised to step over the line at the Nuclear Weapon Test Site outside of Las Vegas, and as I stepped forward, promptly was arrested. I was so afraid at first, taking on the government in a small way, being hauled off on the long trip to jail in Tonopah. But despite that, felt stronger, more empowered than ever to 'walk-the-walk,' to question authority, to know 'the power of the people.' To be proud to be an American.

"The second was coming over the hill in the Pennsylvania Allegheny mountains, in the fall when the leaf color was at peak beauty. Somehow the rich golden and copper hues, the smell of leaves, the heavy setting sun all reinvigorated me after walking 2,000+ miles. I felt so full of vigor and energy and, on a longer term basis, determined to protect this beautiful planet from the threat of nuclear terror and other disasters. I really became more sensitized, more appreciative of the natural wonders along our trek and headed into New York and Washington with a renewed strength."

Carole originally was a recruiter for PRO-Peace, the doomed precursor to the wonders of the GPM. "On The March, I was in finance and banking for the phoenix-from-the-ashes newly formed GPM. Oh, that was a doozer! I remember sitting on the back of Alan Affeldt's motorcycle with $37,000 in cash and check donations on my back. With no helmets, we zipped down the highway to deposit our lifeline money in the next town's bank branch. Yikes, when I think back! We were a scrappy bunch, weren't we!

"Later I worked on the advance team for the Chicago portion. Oh, and I gave haircuts.

"The March impacted my life in endless ways. It still does impact me. First, it taught me to take chances on myself, to trust myself, to take risks. I am forever grateful for that! It taught me the power of people standing together. It taught me to open my brain to alternate thoughts. It taught me that I'm a survivor! It taught me to stop and smell the roses, and that there are incredible people in this world and I had the privilege of knowing many of them."

I asked if she were continuing toward the goal of peace? Carole answered, "Yes, in how we practice and teach our children to be non-violent, to be tolerant of people's beliefs, to give people the benefit of the doubt, that they are good. On a more organized level, we are still active members of peace-related issues, e.g., Million Mom's March against guns and violence, supporting various Portland community-based peace and justice-related causes, in developing a 'What is peace?' program for our daughters' schools, in keeping the GPM spirit alive through the network of marchers. That spirit lives on today. We are teaching our kids to take chances in life, to do what is right and just, to stand up for those treated unfairly or unjustly. We, as a family, are traveling when we can afford to, to continue to be good world neighbors, to celebrate the wonderful cultures around us. I tell people that despite being an active, voting American, I am a humanist before being a nationalist."

Advice? "Some life-altering event should be required learning in everyone's young years, something that forces people out of their comfort zone, to embrace more of what life has to offer. I think, and support, that more women should govern as women are truly the peacemakers."

Joe Kinczel met Lori Graff on The March and is glad she ultimately accepted his proposal of marriage. At 52, living in Nederland, Colorado, feeling blessed with his family, he looks back on his March experiences. "I worked for PRO-Peace, starting in October, 1985, and dealt with information technology or simply computers for The Walk. We kept all sorts of information such as marcher records, kitchen menus, route maps, accounting information, and mailing lists. I kept that same job for the duration of The Walk, but the focus was on using the mailing list to send out fund-raising letters. I believe I raised $20,000 for the GPM by doing this. At the end of The Walk, I gave our mailing list of about 15,000 names to Greenpeace in Washington, DC. For a week or two, I also was on the board of directors that transitioned between PRO-Peace and the GPM while we were in Barstow and I also worked as city manager for a week or two.

"On the IPW (International Peace Walks), I was the walk director with responsibilities for negotiating with the Soviets for walks in the USSR and for logistics on The Walk in the USA.

When asked to recall an incident on the Peace March, Joe answered, "There are so many. Here is a poem that I wrote Lori for Valentine's Day."

What began in February 1986 continues 25 years later in February 2011.
Twenty-five years have changed many things and yet, many things are still much the same.

In February 1986, I saw you sitting on the ramp of the luggage truck,
With your stuff haphazardly spread out all over the place like a yard sale
Completely blocking my way. And I thought there sits trouble.

But trouble never looked so good and since I could not pass, we sat together and became friends.
Now we have two children, a dog, many friends, many houses, many cars, and 20 years together.

February 2011 I see you sitting in the middle of our bedroom,
With your stuff haphazardly spread out all over the place like a yard sale
Completely blocking my way. And I think there sits trouble.

But trouble never looks this good and since I cannot pass, we sit together and become friends.
After 25 years, you are still becoming my friend.

Joe continues, "I'll also describe an incident that involved you,

Donna. During the 1988 Soviet walk in the United States, we ended our last day at San Francisco City Hall for speeches. We all were exhausted and burned out. An intoxicated Native American guy from the crowd grabbed the microphone out of my hand and started to give a rambling speech. While trying to take the microphone back, I pushed him, then stopped and let him give his speech. Afterward I was feeling really crummy about pushing him and a guy from the crowd was yelling at me, calling me a liar and hypocrite and who knows what else. You were standing next to me witnessing all this and simply put your arm around me while the guy was yelling at me. At that moment, I so needed that support. Ever since, I have always had a special place in my heart for you. Thank you."

The March impacted Joe's subsequent life: "My spiritual practice started as the result of an invitation from a fellow marcher to attend a Buddhist retreat immediately following the GPM. You already know I met my wife Lori on The March. Many of my dearest friends around the country and the planet are from the various peace marches. My business came directly out of the IPW walks. My first business after the International Peace Walks was American-Soviet Homestays and that became American International Homestays and that became AIH Destination Management, Inc. We used to send Americans over to the USSR and have them live with families and then bring the Soviet families here to the US. It was sort of an exchange program. My current website is www.aihtravel.com. In short, the marches formed my subsequent life. They are the seminal events of all that followed."

In current practice of peace, Joe meditates and practices mindfulness daily, holds fast unto joy and happiness in daily life and lets go of anxiety before it transforms into anger or fear. "I try to treat my wife, kids, family, and friends with loving kindness. I eat consciously and exercise regularly. I disentangle our family as much as possible from corporations associated with Wall Street, the military-industrial complex, large oil companies and factory food production. Our investments are primarily real estate. Our cars are biodiesel and we eat organic as much as possible."

Advice? "This is the advice I give myself. I want to be the very best that I can be every minute of my life and to try with a sense of humility to make every place I encounter better than when I found it. I want to do the right thing by everyone in my life. Everyone and everything is a part of me and I am part of everything."

Jonnie Zheutlin's daughter, Cathy Zheutlin, was 35-years-old on The March, and created her own job by becoming the video documentarian; she joined because she wanted to film it.

How did The March impact her life? "The Great Peace March led to the Soviet March where I met my future husband. We are married still, 21 years later. So many changes have ensued."

Cathy recalls an incident of The March. "Ram Dass sat down in front of a bright white truck to talk to us and I didn't like that background for the video, so I took off my pink summer dress, and put it behind him, and did the taping in my underwear."

Currently, Cathy is promoting world peace by showing her GPM documentary film, Just One Step, and contributing to the Peace Alliance. She participates in local anti-war protests in Portland, Oregon, is a member of the social action committee of her Jewish Renewal Congregation, is a member of the Oregon New Sanctuary Movement, does healing body work, makes films about inter-spirituality to bring peace through the recognition of mystery and silence in the common heart of all religions. (See www.holyrascals.com)

Her advice: "Follow your heart."

I met Bea Novobilski when we were camped near the California-Nevada border. She carried a bright rainbow flag and had a vibrancy about her that led me to mutter, "I'm going to meet that woman and walk with her." We became friends.

She had her 57th birthday in June in Iowa and fortunately it fell on a Saturday, not a Wednesday, which she spent as a member of the dishwashing crew. The March impacted her life by making her "more aware of current events pertaining to war and its disastrous circumstances for humanity." Now, Bea, living in Carpinteria, California, attends any current gatherings about peace in Santa Barbara County. For a while she planted a tree whenever she heard of the death of a peace marcher. Her memorial grove was decimated when the Army Corp of Engineers built a levy for flood control.

I wrote to Lynn Andrews, author of *Medicine Woman,* which Connie and I had read prior to The March. We spoke with Lynn and she advised us to "get a totem." She now conducts retreats, courses, a sacred forum and local International Councils of the Whistling Elk at The Lynn Andrews Center for Sacred Arts and Training in Arizona.

Lynn wrote, "Thank you so much for the update of your journey and your book. Most of all, thank you for the Walk to create awareness for us all about the threat of nuclear disaster. Totems are a must; they are faithful and will always guide your path. My thoughts on peace? Peace began with you and me. Let's walk. (Signed), hope and light, Lynn Andrews."

I met Petru (Peter) Ganea of Moldova, a republic of the former USSR, in 1987 on the Soviet-American walk between Leningrad and Moscow and he came to the Peace Walk in the United States in 1988. He was 42 when he and I sat together on Bus 6 in Russia and became friends. He is now 66 and is semi-retired, "on pension," from teaching.

He has emailed his answers. "You asked what specific incident I recall. Actually, it is hard to remember some separate incident. Nevertheless, I'd like to mention the special atmosphere that accompanied us during both Walks. We really were like a big family, and if in the first days of the 1987 Walk from Leningrad to Moscow, between the American and Soviet participants there was some psychological gap that somehow distanced us from each other, very soon we managed to build bridges of friendship and mutual understanding because we had a common goal: to call people's attention to the need of building a world free of war danger, a world in which people will live, work, raise their children in conditions of peace and mutual respect. The big question is, did we succeed in our aspirations? When I look back at those times (and when I analyze today's events on our planet), I have the impression that we were full of romanticism, even pretty naive. We see now that it is the politicians who make decisions affecting the lives of millions. However, we were sincere in our actions and aspirations and that is already something worth living for."

How did the Walks impact Peter's life? "They were a great and very important experience for me. After those Walks, I felt that something changed in my life. I began to be more careful toward the people and the environment. In fact, I try to do my best to live in harmony with the surrounding world with peace in my conscience, which is not so simple here. Here in Moldova, we have a very peculiar situation. Because of many reasons -- economical, political, social, etc, -- our society is practically divided into two hostile parts. As a citizen and as a teacher, I try to occupy a neutral position and to make some peace between them and though it seems almost impossible, I keep trying. The thing is that having become an independent state, many people changed their mentality dramatically and we have had several severe conflicts that makes it very difficult to establish peace on this land."

And Peter's advice? "When we were involved in those peaceful projects, there were two superpowers in the world, the USA and the USSR. Now there is only one superpower, the USA, and you have put a very heavy burden on your shoulders. We'll see how you'll manage this burden. But you shouldn't forget that another superpower is about to appear. I mean China. I think that you might have to organize similar Walks in that country, so, my advice would be not to neglect this perspective."

Jolene De Lisa, 58 on The March, and I, 58 on The March, were sometimes mistaken for each other. We both had tan skin, salt and pepper hair, were slender, and had big smiles. She has answered that she did many jobs on The March, ranging from kitchen to media. The impact of The March was important to Jolene until September 11, 1991, when her son Kirk was killed in an accident. She has written, "My world turned upside down and obviously, in many ways, a person just can't move on as if it never happened. I have written three books and *The Children's Peace Book* has given me the most joy. Peace IS the answer and that is what I practice every day in some form or other,.eg, calls, letters, and meditation on world peace."

Although they were not on the Peace Walks, I asked my four sons how my participation affected them. Sam was 33 when I left home for The Great Peace March. Now 57, he wrote this:

"I grew up in an upper middle class home in the Bay Area. My father wore a suit and tie. He rose in the dark so he could ride the commuter train into San Francisco. He arrived home when most families were already eating dinner. He was usually tired and looking forward to a drink. My mother was a stay-at-home mom. She took care of me and my three brothers. She was positive and supportive. We had a nice home, two cars and were without any problems. On the weekends my parents would, occasionally, go out to social events dressed in formal attire. They always seemed excited to go to whatever gala event they would be attending. I think we were Republicans.

"Later in life I was living in Sonoma county working as a building contractor. I had left the Bay Area after high school and relocated to Eugene, Oregon. There I worked in a lumber mill, eventually graduated from the University of Oregon, got married, had children and, after being there for 10 years, decided to move closer to my birth family. Our new home was Santa Rosa. We were definitely Democrats.

"After my parents split up, Mom did some changing. She sold the big house, got her teaching credential, started a tutoring service and I'm pretty sure she stopped going to the gala events requiring formal attire and a permanent smile. Anyway, I had always been proud of Mom. She was beautiful, energetic, in an authentic way, and had a small town sense about her. I understood, on some level, that she was planning to walk across the country in support of nuclear disarmament.

"I was working as a building contractor in Santa Rosa, and one day I needed to make a run to the lumberyard. There were usually guys in the yard to help me load material I needed onto my truck. One of the yard men had a very engaging way about him and after my going to that yard for so many years, he and I had a certain kind of friendship. He was bright, had long hair, a beard, and I knew he was biding his time working there.

"On this particular day, as we were shooting the breeze while loading my truck, he mentioned that he would not be working there any more. I asked him why. And without hesitation, he said that he was going to walk across the country to raise awareness about nuclear disarmament.

I said, 'You're going on The Great Peace March.' He was shocked that I even knew about it. I said, 'Guess what? My mom is going on it, too!'

Our friendship changed at that point. As we stood there smiling at each other, I was aware that Mom was doing something big. I was aware that she was doing something important. I was also aware that she was doing something real and that other people would be doing it with her. One of those people was standing right in front of me. And as I stood there, in the lumber yard, I thought back on all those years that I had know this woman. I thought about all the changes that she had made during her and my life. And I knew that this was going to be a big moment in her life. And, at that moment, it was a big moment in my life, too. The underlying feeling that I had just then was that I was really proud to know this woman."

Sam's recall of his conversation with Casey Kraft is surely more accurate than mine as quoted in Chapter 6. But I'll say again, memoir is as dependable as the writer's memory. The facts may be muddled, but the essence is true.

Holly and John Love celebrated their 25th wedding anniversary this year, 2011. She was 31 when, a few weeks before I left for the Great Peace March, I gave a tea party for friends to meet my lovely future daughter-in-law.

An incident Holly recalls is, appropriately enough, related to their wedding week-end. "Donna left The Great Peace March to fly from Denver to Rhode Island for her son John's and my wedding, May 24, 1986. A sister-in-law had carried Donna's clothes on the plane from San Jose so she could change from marcher to Mother of the Groom. We all were so happy to see her!"

How did The March impact Holly's life? She says, "It opened my eyes to an issue that was not a part of our daily lives as newlyweds and then parents of young children. It made us very proud that our mother/ mother-in-law walked to bring attention to this very important issue."

An occupational therapist with a specialty in young students, Holly is a gentle professional who lives peace well. She believes, "Peace begins with me" and aims to be at peace with herself and "through this, spread peace close to home. I'm studying yoga which helps me to be peaceful and share a peaceful tone."

Her advice: breathe deep and try to stay in the moment.

Dale Clark joined The March on a soggy night in Delaware. He was 63, an artist from Santa Barbara, a friend of my tent-mate Shelah's. Today he lives near Tombstone, Arizona, and continues to have creative ideas.

One of his recent projects involves brightly colored inflatable Friendship Balls. His instructions read, "Send your greeting to the children of Iraq and Afghanistan. Use sharpies to draw or write your message of Peace and Hope on a ball. The balls will be deflated, shipped to these troubled lands, re-inflated and then given to children." (www.stupidwise.com)

The incident on The March that Dale recalls is "being called a commie rat." The March intensified his concern about nuclear war. "Nukes are still the major concern; 200 nukes and we could join the dinosaurs. I hope my art work of awareness makes a difference. We must remember that we need each other."

When I flew to Los Angeles two weeks before The March would actually leave, I met a group who walked 10 miles every day in preparation for the long walking days ahead. Ann and Dick Edelman were part of that group. Dick was a psychiatrist and Ann was a writer who also played the cello. As a friend since those pre-walks in Los Angeles, Ann was the first to reply to the questionnaire.

"I was 62 on the Peace March and am now 87. We have lived in the same house in LA for more than 50 years. Hard to imagine!"

She continues, "Peace activism was a vitally important part of my life long before the Peace March, starting during the days of the Vietnam War. I attended more peace demonstrations than I can begin to remember, and phoned, wrote letters, tried to activate other people. Just before the Peace March, I was a speaker for Beyond War, a wonderful effective group, and was on my way to perhaps becoming part of the state organization. When I heard about The Peace March, I knew that was what I had to do. I thought how great and what fun to walk across the country; to be the peace activist that was so important to me and to have a wonderful adventure at the same time.

"My main job on The March was speaking, training speakers, especially in the terrific Beyond War BB demonstration. I gathered and printed materials to be distributed, attended and encouraged others to attend the wonderful speakers who visited The March. I also liked to help out when needed at other tasks, such as washing dishes or cleaning the camp site, but these were not my regular jobs. I was in the Education bus."

What impact did the GPM have on Ann's life? "It had an enormous impact on my life. I think there were times when I was as happy as I've ever been. I felt that was exactly where I belonged and what I should be doing. I loved the walking, being outdoors, feeling the connection to the earth and the sky that I had never felt before. I loved getting to know a variety of people whom I never would have encountered in my middle-class LA life. I learned to accept, enjoy, respect, and listen to people who thought differently than I, and whose life experiences were different from mine; the anarchists, for instance.

"One seminal moment I recall. On my day off, I was telling Mary Jane how she should do my job, organizing the materials we distributed. I was going on at great length when suddenly it occurred to me that Mary Jane was every bit as smart and capable as I was, which I said to her, and told her to do it however she wanted to. On The Peace March, it was sometimes easy to think that I was a Very Important Indispensable Person. That day I shed that notion and it has never really returned.

"After The Peace March, I continued most of my peace activities, speaking, attending rallies and demonstrations, writing letters. The local peace marchers also kept in good touch with each other in various events, and Dick and I always went to the yearly reunions. I will always have a special feeling for the peace marchers because we shared this incredible experience. It enriched my life enormously, and I gained a confidence that I had never had before.

"Lately, because of age and illness, we have definitely slowed down. I continue to be politically aware and to influence events in what ways I can; responding to email requests to sign petitions, writing letters to the editor and to our representatives in Congress. I worked for Obama's election.

"But now it is time for the young people to take over!"

I can see Ann shrugging her shoulders and lifting her hands, palms upward as she relinquishes some of her involvement in her lifetime of peace activities. It's part of her wisdom.

This summer of 2011, The Great Peace March for Global Nuclear Disarmament held its 25th Reunion in Ventura, California, at Emma Woods State Park from August 1 to 7. I arrived on Thursday, August 4, and checked into a nearby Best Western Motel. About a dozen other marchers were already there. Ann and Dick Edelman and I drove out to the campsite in time to line up for dinner.

And it was just as though 25 years had been erased. All of the 150 people in line were almost the same as they had been the evening that Jackie Smith had found me in the dinner line in the Mojave Desert at Stoddard Wells Road 25 years ago. Same quiet, happy faces. Same consideration and grace. No shoving, no clutching attitude about "my place" in line.

There was, however, lots of searching for recall of names, some salt and pepper in the hair of those who were 20-somethings on The March. Many brought their spouses and children. Their children were bright, serene, confident, and talented. As I talked with one, I asked her age and she held up four fingers. I told her, "Can you believe that I am almost 80 years older than you are? Isn't it amazing that someone that old can still walk and talk?" Her eyes were big and so was her smile as she exclaimed. "You belong in the Guinness Book of Records!" We shared a delightful laugh.

Jackie Smith arrived on Friday and we roomed together. She'd brought her musical slide show that ended with John Lennon's "Imagine," bringing tears to many wistful eyes. While she was setting up her projector, I read excerpts from *Walking For Our Lives* to listeners who are the heroes of the stories. Dan Coogan showed his slides of marcher faces, each one looking beautiful.

For days we March graduates milled around, sat around, sang a round, hugged each other, and laughed. We roared at the mock-wedding in which several brides, both feminine and masculine, in thrift store dresses married several grooms, both masculine and feminine. Others caught the bouquet of stiff plastic purple tulips and demanded to be married with all the rest. It was a silly, spontaneous performance that reminded us of the humor we all shared. The no-talent talent show was no less entertaining with many of the children winning applause and whistles of appreciation.

I had a shoe box of Peace March photos to give away so was often surrounded by marchers reminiscing about our adventures together. I asked the questions for the survey and was given answers, some of which I have relayed. I chose 18 marchers because 18 is a magic number to the Great Peace March. Remember, in Hebrew, the characters 18 mean new life. The marchers at the reunion related over and over the ways in which they continue to live and work toward new life in peace around the world.

In transcribing these written interviews, I have come to realize that this chapter is full of guidance. No one is saying, "do it my way," but I feel that these maturing marchers have lifted lights—candles, if you will—in showing a way, many ways, to create peace in our world.

As we have stood in circles and sung to each other over the years,

Dear friends, dear friends,
Let me tell you how I feel.
You have given me such treasure.
I love you so.

Donna Rankin Love. August 2011

What Can We Do?

We Can Contact:

Local peace organizations

Nuclear Age Peace Foundation
1187 Coast Village Road
Suite 1, PMB 121
Santa Barbara, CA 93108
Tel 805 965 3443

United States Institute of Peace
2301 Constitution Av, NW
Washington, DC 20037

WILPF
Women's International League of Peace and Freedom

Watch these YouTube videos:
World Peace and Other Fourth Grade Achievements
Peace One Day

Books by Donna Rankin Love

Walking for Our Lives
Driving for Walking for Our Lives
To Make the House Complete
Tell Me A Story

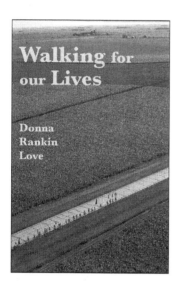

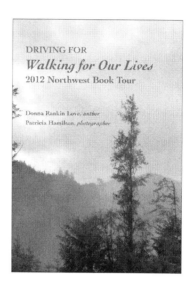

BOOK ORDER FORM

✔ **TO ORDER AUTOGRAPHED BOOKS:**

Walking For Our Lives   #_____ x $25 per book = $_____

An autobiographical perspective of the Great Peace March for Global Nuclear Disarmament and two other peace marches in the US and Soviet Union. The memoir follows the journey of Donna Rankin Love from her life of comfortable conformity to becoming comfortable with herself. Through her tales, we discover how Donna's experiences walking in the Great Peace March for Global Nuclear Disarmament transformed her opinions of what is important and what is worth fighting for from the easy choices to the meaningful ones.

Driving for Walking For Our Lives #_____ x $15 per book = $_____

An account of the author's book tour of the Pacific Northwest in May 2012. Photos by Patricia Hamilton. Insights and tips into the planning and executing of a successful book tour.

To Make the House Complete   #_____ x $20 per book = $_____

A chronicle of experiences as author Donna Rankin Love moves into two houses in Mexico, a farm in Oregon, a beach cottage in California, and a marriage - all of them needing work. She is keeping the beach cottage.

Tell Me a Story   #_____ x $20 per book = $_____

A book of 42 short stories that comprise a memoir. Topics range from her parents' wedding day through her small town childhood in southwestern Oregon, her family life on the San Francisco Peninsula, and walking across America.

                    TOTAL BOOK ORDER: $_____

✔ **PLEASE SHIP BOOKS TO:**

Name:_____

Address:_____

City, State, Zip:_____

Send check or money order and this order form to:
Donna Rankin Love, P.O. Box 1213, Capitola, CA 95010.

✔ PLEASE contact me about your Memoir Writing Workshops
My e-mail is: _____

    • •   On-site, telephone, and online sessions available   • •
TO ORDER BOOKS ON-LINE:
www.donnarankinlove.vpweb.com
www.amazon.com